HOLDING ON
OR
LETTING GO

HOLDING ON

OR

LETTING GO

Men and Career Change at Midlife

SAMUEL D. OSHERSON

THE FREE PRESS
A Division of Macmillan Publishing Co., Inc.
NEW YORK

Collier Macmillan Publishers
LONDON

The Free Press
A Division of Macmillan Publishing Co., Inc.
866 Third Avenue, New York, N.Y. 10022

Collier Macmillan Canada, Ltd.

Library of Congress Catalog Card Number: 79-7849

Printed in the United States of America

printing number
1 2 3 4 5 6 7 8 9 10

Library of Congress Cataloging in Publication Data

Osherson, Samuel D. date
    Holding on or letting go.

    Bibliography: p.
    Includes index.
    1. Vocational guidance—Case studies.   2. Age and
employment—Case studies.   3. Middle age—Psychological
aspects—Case studies.   4. Personality and occupation
—Case studies.   I. Title.
HF5381.089   650'.14'0240564   79-7849
ISBN 0-02-923480-8

To J. S. Bach

Contents

Preface

In a seminar on psychotherapeutic technique I once attended, the instructor (an analyst) was explaining his manner of working with people in the analytic situation. While describing how he saw himself interacting with the other person to facilitate personality change and growth, he focused on the role of the analyst as a source of interpretation and feedback for the patient about his experience. The analyst mentioned, however, in an offhand manner that in filling this role one must always take into consideration how much the person can "hear about" himself at that point in time. I was struck by this comment, with its sense that people differ in what they can learn about themselves when opportunities for such learning are presented. In considering the adult experiences of the men in this study, I realized that we have the opportunity to "hear about" ourselves all the time, in many of our daily experiences. As we act in the world we have the opportunity to reflect on who we are in our behavior—in comparison to who we think we are—and to contemplate the way in which what happened to us today or yesterday relates to what we expected for ourselves. People differ, probably characteristically, certainly from one situation to another, in the extent to which they can hear about themselves from their experiences. Some people can learn lessons easily, hearing much about themselves from small and large events in their lives; others have more difficulty learning about themselves and listen less carefully to what their experiences have to say.

The men in this book, like all of us, had experiences that said things about them, and each differed in the degree to which he listened to these experiences. In discussing the course of adult development through midlife I have tried to trace what these individuals heard about themselves at different points in their lives, how they went about listening, and how they made use of what they heard.

Acknowledgments

THIS BOOK could not have been written without the cooperation of the subjects themselves, and I am grateful to all for their openness and willingness to discuss their lives with me. In a sense the extended interviews required in this study meant, for both subject and interviewer, forming a relationship with each other—albeit a temporary one—and I am indebted to the subjects for their willingness to do so. Beyond this, I feel privileged for the opportunity to have come to know each of the participants. Their names and lives have been disguised within the text for the sake of confidentiality but this does not detract from the debt I think the study owes them for allowing us to learn from their experiences.

Before this research project was conceived I found the original concept of the Department of Social Relations at Harvard, as it existed during my graduate training, to be a model for the study of lives. This was exemplified for me in particular through the teaching and research of Robert White, David McClelland, Erik Erikson, and Robert Bales. For their encouragement and support at various stages of the research I also wish to thank George Goethals, Thomas Cottle, Milton Kotelchuck, Joan Liem, Daniel Osherson, Donald Warwick, Norman Watt, Lane Conn, Allen Adinolfi, Gregory Hinrichsen, and Julie Snow.

Throughout the entire project the support and guidance of Dr. Elliot Mishler, director of the Laboratory of Social Psychiatry, has been invaluable. Dr. Mishler's rare combination of methodological sophistication, breadth of knowledge, interest in the social sciences and arts, and understanding of the complexity of human behavior has been an inspiration to me. I am deeply appreciative of his willingness to give of his time in discussions and reading manuscripts. Indeed, Dr. Mishler's intellectual and personal support is most directly responsible for the completion of both the research and this book. In addition, I am very appreciative of the encouragement and support over the last four years of Dr. Miles Shore, superintendent of the Massachusetts Mental Health Center and professor of psychiatry at the Harvard Medical School. I am grateful as well to other members of the Laboratory of Social Psychiatry for their helpful questions and comments, in particular Dr. Stuart Hauser.

I also wish to express my gratitude to Dr. Daniel Levinson of Yale University and Dr. Herbert Hendin of Columbia University. Both offered extremely valuable encouragement and guidance in the early phases of this research. I also wish to acknowledge the important help of Dr. M. Robert Gardner of Boston.

For their encouragement and help to me in learning more about the life of modern artists and craftsmen I would like to thank Mr. Richard Linzer of the Massachusetts Arts and Humanities Foundation, Ms. Lois Moran of the American Crafts Council, and Mr. Paul Soldner.

In addition, several of the staff at the Laboratory have been more helpful than they know in reducing the anxiety of a somewhat compulsive writer through their efficiency and grace as secretaries and typists, in particular Suzanne Sullentrup.

Finally, I want to note that the research reported in this volume was completed when I was a Postdoctoral Fellow in the Research Training Program in Social-Behavioral Science, Laboratory of Social Psychiatry, Harvard Medical School. Support was also provided in part by grants from the U.S. Department of Labor, the National Institute of Education, and from the Whiting Foundation.

HOLDING ON
OR
LETTING GO

1

Focus

"Around 35, everything started to come
apart in my life."

I had a profound philosophical crisis, when I was 35 or 40. In
terms of a way of looking at the world and at myself. I realized that the key I had been using was a key that didn't unlock anything really.

—Mr. Markowitz

The poignant words above describe an experience of personal crisis often
reported during the midlife years, for our purposes the years from 35
to 50.

This book is an exploration of the experience of such crisis—one characterized by confusion, uncertainty, doubt, and depression, and a reexamination of the direction one's life is taking at work, as a husband, or as
a father. For some individuals at midlife, both the earlier work or marital
choices and the fundamental assumptions about who one is no longer
seem as sturdy or satisfying. The keys of one's life open less important
doors, while dimly perceived doors—new alternatives, possibilities for the
self, solutions to old problems—remain locked and resistant.

Our specific focus centers on the results of an intensive interview
study of a group experiencing such turmoil and difficulty: men who made
a dramatic midlife career change, voluntarily leaving established professional positions to successfully pursue careers in the creative arts or crafts.
The issues that these men struggled with before, during, and after the
midlife career change are similar to those reported for many people at
midlife who do not evidence such overt changes in their lives. We often

1

study cases of overt difficulty to understand problems and challenges ordinarily mastered more silently. So, too, I plan to use this group to shed
light on the origins and quieter resolutions of the commonly reported crises experienced by many other men and women, at work and in the home.

One important finding is that the movement from a first to a radically different second career at midlife cannot be validly isolated from its
roots in the broader life histories of these individuals. These men are of
particular interest because the career changes reflected not just work
problems or "career crises" but were rooted in much broader issues at
midlife. Problems at work and the resulting career change were integrally
involved with conflicts around who one was as a professional in a career,
as a son, as a husband, as a father. Events at work and at home cannot be
separated from experiences earlier in the life cycle, particularly the decisions about career and marriage characteristic of young adulthood. This
group offers a clear picture of how events and problems at work become
intertwined with fundamental human problems and dilemmas in other
domains of a person's life, both at midlife and earlier.

A second important finding is that a career change can have very different meanings, depending on whether it proceeds from adaptive growth
or from more defensive processes. We find very different ways of coping
with the experienced crisis at midlife in this group, from which a career
change emerges. Different patterns of midlife passage give rise to these su-
perfically similar career changes.

My particular focus in this book is on the changing nature of self-definition during midlife, and the manner in which individuals cope with the
choices, anxieties, and ambiguities that arise from the reassertion at this
time of the questions "Who am I?" and "Where am I going?" I examine
how and why these questions reasserted themselves at midlife for these
people and delineate a model of adaptive and maladaptive patterns of
midlife passage through the crisis of self-definition, from which the career
change emerges.

I will argue that the central crisis in this group at midlife is one of
loss. The loss is of the self as expressed and defined by the career and marital choices of adolescence and young adulthood. Who one is at midlife can
be profoundly and disturbingly different from the expectations and fantasies of young adulthood, when one usually makes the first choice of a wife
or career. Coming to terms with the lost self implicit in this discrepancy
forms a central task of the midlife years. We find in this group that work
was a key element in the unconscious attempt in young adulthood to define oneself in the image of idealized parents as role models of what it
meant to be an adult. This difficulty with the task of self-definition and
identity formation and the attempt to define oneself in terms of values ap-
propriated from parents represent one kind of problem in separating psychologically from these key figures. The difficulties and inconsistencies by

midlife with these attempts at self-definition meant the opportunity for a fuller, richer, more confident definition of self. For some, the career change represents such a fuller definition of self; for others it represents a retreat from the sometimes painful and frightening process of acknowledging and making real new possibilities for the self. A third important finding, then, is that the process of separation from parents and the autonomous definition of self can extend into midlife. Career and marital choices through the life cycle can become the arena for such struggles around self-definition and separation from parents.

Understanding the specific career changes of the individuals in this group, then, becomes part of understanding the larger process of how individuals change and grow during adulthood, and why some people confidently confront definite changes in their lives while others seem less able to evolve and learn through experiences of transition. How do people come to terms with the reality of their achievements and situation at midlife in the face of wishes, dreams, and fantasies of young adulthood? How do work and career choices in young adulthood and midlife become involved in the process of self-definition? What are some of the other meanings and functions of work and careers—particularly professional careers—beyond just providing a livelihood? How do we as adults hold onto our parents at the same time as trying to separate from them? How do adults continue to evolve and grow at midlife? When does a career change, or a divorce, reflect continued personal growth and development and when does it mean a turning away from such opportunities? Of what value is a turn inward at midlife, and the acknowledgment of painful or confusing feelings and interests? How do people integrate and express new potentialities of self as they mature in adulthood? These are the questions this book is concerned with.

My intent is to place the crises at work reported by these individuals, and their subsequent dramatic career changes, in the context of their general life situation and adult developmental experiences. I will utilize a developmental, life-history perspective, and I plan to introduce dimensions of analysis not ordinarily included in the study of the evolution of careers and career changes: how key tasks and challenges were dealt with earlier in the life cycle; the impact of developmental conflicts brought forward to midlife; the role of events at midlife in other life domains besides work; and the importance of the subjective meaning of work for the individual in shaping his career. The purpose is to better understand an emergent area of research in human development: the complex maturation of work, personality, and social situation through the life cycle.

In the next section, I describe this specific study of career change at midlife, then turn to consideration of the larger, general issues of adult development to which the research is directed, and finally present a summary of the chapters to follow.

The Group of Career Changers

Twenty men were interviewed for our study, using a free-associative interview procedure described briefly below and in more detail in the Methodological Appendix. All participants in the study were white males between the ages of 35 and 50 and were interviewed within three to ten years of the career change. The men were drawn from a number of different initial professional positions: research scientists, business managers or executives, engineers, lawyers, and university faculty. Eighteen of them went on to graduate schools of one kind or another soon after college. As a result, the career changes of this sample meant that an average of 2.1 years of postgraduate education was left behind, as were eight of thirteen marriages.

There are three second career groups: visual artists, actors, and potters. Participants were selected on the basis of the following criteria: Three or more years were spent in the initial professional career; at the time of the study, between three and nine years had been spent full-time in the arts or crafts since the career change; during that time the art or craft had been completely or nearly completely self-supporting and had resulted in some evidence of creative achievement (juried exhibitions, membership in professional repertory company, awards or fellowships). All participants were volunteers, located through advertisements in arts and crafts journals and by direct mailings to members of professional arts and crafts organizations.

In each case the career change came out of the individual's desire or choice to leave his first career. All resigned; none were fired. Most of these men were in senior positions—tenured faculty, partners in a law firm, senior scientists, or administrators and executives. To understand the maturation of work, family, and self in adulthood it seemed most important to study voluntary, dramatic changes in order to observe clearly the many complex psychological factors involved in such a redirection of one's work life. In choosing the sample I was particulary interested in obtaining a group of men who had apparent freedom of choice; that is, they had made their choices relatively unconstrained by immediate economic pressures or severe financial considerations so as to better reveal some of the psychosocial considerations involved in such work choices in adulthood.

Professionals were chosen for study because this group is relatively underrepresented in the still skimpy literature on work and adult development. There is, of course, a substantial literature on work dissatisfaction and, to a lesser degree, patterns of coping with problems at work among blue- and white-collar workers. We have, however, much less knowledge about patterns of career evolution and personality development among highly educated professional people despite indications from fiction and the media of difficulty and stress among these individuals at midlife (Bellow 1964; Sheehy 1975; Trausch 1974). Indeed, because of the great internal investment in the career, high expectations as to what one will accomplish at work, and prolonged educational experience of professionals, some observers feel this is a group particularly vulnerable to difficulty at midlife (Sarason 1975; Tartakoff 1966; Figler 1978). One of our purposes in selecting a group of career changers from among professionals was to allow further understanding of the meaning of initial professional career choice, its role in adult personality development, and some of the life history sources of midlife dissatisfaction and stress.

The Free-Associative Interview Situation

The interview procedure with each person consisted of a five-session sequence completed within a two-week period. Each session lasted one and a half hours and was conducted in the participant's home or studio.

The aim of the free-associative interview method is to elicit the participant's own organization of his life history and subjective frame of reference on his experience, past, present, and future. To do this, little restriction is set on what to discuss, and the interviewer refrains from overly directive questions or instructions. The technique takes the person's spontaneous associations, memories, dreams, and fantasies—as well as responses to structured questions—as essential sources of data. An extended discussion of the interview procedure, patterns of question asking, and method of data analysis can be found in the Methodological Appendix.

Contact began before the interviews were started. Initial direct contact was usually made by the participant, who wrote or called me as a result of our advertisements and mailings. Many of those who replied had fascinating stories to tell but did not exactly fit our selection criteria. If a person did fit our criteria a preliminary meeting was arranged at which we informally discussed the purposes and procedures of the research and signed an assurance of confidentiality. After the person expressed a willingness to participate in the project we arranged a schedule and setting—usually the person's home or studio—within which he would feel comfortable in discussing his life and where we could be assured of privacy and little interruption. During the sessions the participant and I were seated face to face and our conversations were taperecorded.

The interview procedure was standardized in that all five sessions with a participant were completed within a two-week period. This particular grouping of sessions was extended long enough to allow development of a relationship or "working alliance" yet spaced closely enough together to allow continuity between sessions. I was impressed by how much richer information results from an interview procedure in which there is prolonged contact between interviewer and participant. The relaxed atmosphere resulting from five meetings meant that each of us could repeatedly digest material from previous sessions and return to material overlooked or only partly discussed earlier.

As a result of this procedure we have almost eight hours of interviews for each person, resulting for each case in over two hundred pages of tape transcription, in addition to my own notes and observations made immediately after each session. Just after leaving I would often make notes about key themes and issues discussed, as well as observations about the person's behavior and affect during the sessions. Meeting where the person lived or worked also allowed me to gain a picture of the person's life apart from our discussions in the interviews. Thus I was often able to meet the participant's wife, children, or friends. In many cases a participant would offer to show me current work—sculpture, paintings, a show script, or pottery—and many an interview session was preceded or followed by a brief discussion of that work.

The free-associative interview material, when transcribed, produced impressively rich, detailed information on life history. As I hope to show, the model of midlife that is discussed in the chapters to follow—the key issues, tasks, and resolutions—emerged directly from these men's own descriptions. The men were, of course unaware of any particular theory or model that informed the research,* yet their accounts and descriptions of their lives present clear illustrations of the theoretical material I will discuss. I was impressed by the articulateness of these men, and their willingness and ability to reflect on their lives. Psychodynamic observers are often accused of "overinferring" from, or reading into, people's descriptions, yet it seems to me that a natural order and consistency emerge that should be readily apparent when people are allowed to talk freely about their lives and concerns. In presenting the results of this research, I have tried to retain the richness of these men's accounts and to illustrate the interview methodology by presenting detailed excerpts at key points in the narrative. At times in later chapters we also return to excerpts discussed earlier so as to cull deeper meaning and more information from this material.

Let me now introduce the men who play an important role in the book, and indicate how the frame of analysis applied in the chapters to follow emerged from recurrent themes and consistencies in the interview material.

---

*More precisely, the theoretical model presented in the book did not begin to emerge until the study was approximately half completed; that is, ten of the men had been interviewed before detailed analysis of the transcripts was begun in earnest.

Six Men

While I draw on material from all twenty participants at different points in the discussion, much of the book is organized around intensive case studies of six illustrative individuals.*

MR. MARKOWITZ is a 50-year-old** former scientist with a Ph.D. who spent most of his initial career working for the U.S. government in the Southwest. Eight years ago he left his position to pursue a career as an actor in New York City. He married at the age of 20 and remains married. He has several children, now grown up. Mr. Markowitz is from a lower-class Jewish family, raised in Boston.

MR. O'HARA is a 45-year-old potter who six years ago left his position as a college professor of history (Ph.D). He was born into a middle-class Irish family in upstate New York and now lives in New England. He was divorced from a fifteen-year marriage at the time of career change and has three children.

MR. GOODSON is 36 years old. He was an assistant professor of physics (Ph.D.) until five years ago, when he left his position to pursue a career as an artist in the Northeast. He has never married. Born and raised on the West Coast, he comes from a middle-class Protestant family.

MR. ANDERSON is a wood sculptor. He is 44 years old and left his career as a lawyer nine years ago. He was divorced from a long marriage around that time and has one child. He was raised in the South, coming from an upper-class family.

MR. PREZINSKI is a 42-year-old painter. His initial career was an engineer in private industry (Ph.D). His career change occurred seven years ago. He has been divorced from his wife for five years and has one child. He was raised in a suburb of Chicago, in an immigrant Catholic family from Poland.

MR. LONZETTI was a business executive (MBA) in the Midwest until five years ago. He is 42 and a portrait photographer. He is married and has four children. He comes from a large Italian family in Philadelphia.

These six cases were selected for intensive analysis and presentation because they reflect a range of different initial occupations and second careers and illustrate varying patterns of development at midlife. Despite the variations in initial career choice in young adulthood, and subsequent type of change into the arts and crafts at midlife, there are major similari-

*To protect the anonymity of participants I have changed background characteristics that might identify them. Except for minor changes or deletions to insure confidentiality, however, quoted material from participants throughout the book is as it appears in the interview transcripts.

**All ages and dates refer to the time of the interview.

ties and continuities in these men's descriptions of their life histories. This in itself is important. We find recurrent themes in midlife development occuring across people with very different professional backgrounds, initial occupational and family settings, second careers, and educational backgrounds. This similarity of key reported experiences and the reports of recurring presses and concerns were quite unexpected.

The dramatic career change is the most obviously interesting feature of this group, yet the career change itself is only a piece—the tip of an iceberg—of much more extensive life changes and developments at midlife.* Understanding these changes and the overt, striking career changes that resulted involves an exploration of these men's life histories. Let me describe and illustrate the midlife experiences of the men in this group.

A "Crisis" before the Career Change

When I first began this research the time of the career change itself appeared to be the period of greatest interest. It seemed to me that the transition from an established, secure, professional position into the creative arts or crafts would be the time of greatest turmoil and difficulty in these individuals' adult lives. Certainly one might expect this from the challenges inherent in such transitions. Such challenges include the separation from the concrete attachments and friendships of the initial workplace, alterations in the everyday routines of one's life (for example, the structure of time and pacing of activities during the day), profound changes in social position and status (from relatively high-status professions to the lower-status arts or crafts, with the concomitant financial consequences that ensue), and the development and testing of new skills and abilities as artists or craftsmen.

*The fact that the career change at midlife was a shift into the creative arts or crafts, rather than some other career or work setting, is thus not the central focus of the book. This book is not about the experience of the arts at midlife, although Chapter 4 does provide discussion relevant to this question. A finding worth noting is that whatever special talents as artists or craftsmen these men possessed seems less relevant to understanding the career change that occurred than do the more general conflicts and life history experiences with which these men struggled. The focus of the book is, then, on these key developmental conflicts and people's ways of adapting to them, and how career and family choices through adulthood reflect this process of adaptation. The meaning of the arts at midlife assumes a secondary role to these key questions, as does a more social analysis of the economic or social forces that have given rise to the phenomenon of midlife career changes. Those particularly interested in the former topic might start with Eliot Porter's discussion of his career change from medicine to nature photography (1965) or a fascinating interview with a former NASA engineer who has become a highly successful and skilled woodcarver of birds (Montgomery, 1979); those interested in what career change implies about the nature of work and careers in our society might see Sarason (1977), Krantz (1978), or Lefkowitz (1979).

However, it soon became apparent that the years preceding the career change were also a time of considerable interest, since this was the period during which members of the group report the greatest difficulty and turmoil in their lives. The career change in this group thus occurred toward the end of a period of overt confusion and uncertainty. This can be seen in several reports of the midlife years immediately preceding the career change. I first return below to the quote that begins this chapter; descriptions from two other participants follow it.

MR. MARKOWITZ: I had a profound philosophical crisis when I was 35 or 40 in terms of a way of looking at the world and at myself. I realized that the key I had been using was a key that didn't unlock anything really. I remember there was a whole period where I became very interested in people's lives. I suddenly was reading biographies of famous people, especially scientists like myself.

MR. ANDERSON: I needed a vent for all this energy. I got more and more antsy and my wife said, "You really ought to do something about it. There's something wrong." I was very nervous, anxious. We talked a lot about it and it was not a little from the result of her pushing and insisting that I asked the questions that maybe I hadn't asked before. I cast about and went through various kinds of machinations to figure out what was going on.

MR. O'HARA: Then began a whole period of trying to compartmentalize my life and keep things going—to be a teacher, an artist, a lover, a husband, and father, and they were all kind of separate worlds. But when all the truths were out—and it did come out—I was faced with trying to bring it all together or simplify it by throwing some of them out. I got scared because I was really out of control. . . . My life exploded in a number of directions, a number of fragments, all of them contending for equal status. It was very confusing and I had a number of feelings.

Note the broad terms in which Mr. Markowitz frames the description of his midlife years: he describes having "a profound. . . crisis." He was not just feeling dissatisfied with his work situation; the problem was more extensive, involving broader ties to different aspects of his life situation. His use of the word "key" is revealing in this context. Keys are centrally important tools; they let us in, they keep us out. In short, they mediate the relationship between ourselves and the outside world. Mr. Markowitz is using the word key as a metaphor for knowing or understanding the world, his "way of looking at he world." This particular way of understanding didn't work for him at midlife; it "didn't unlock anything." There is an element of the unexpected in his description, as if events occurred at midlife for which he was unprepared. This is implicit in his comment about the "key," as if earlier understandings and assumptions about himself had proved insufficient. We get a sense of the deeply personal impact of this period as he indicated self-questioning and a turn inward with a sudden interest in biographies. His description of his midlife years carries with it the sense of experiences occurring that are a challenge to his understanding of himself and the world.

This hint that the midlife career change has roots in important inner life experiences of the person can be seen as well in the second and third examples. Once again general difficulty and confusion are reported over an extended period of time. Mr. Anderson's report carries with it the sense of understandings called into questions, of earlier answers suddenly proven inadequate at midlife. He indicated this when he says that "I asked the kind of questions I hadn't asked before." Again thoughts and feelings are described in tones of the unexpected.

The career changes for these men thus seemed to emerge out of a prior period of confusion and turmoil. To summarize, the following are of particular interest in these men's accounts of the midlife years preceding their career changes: (1) a sense of difficulty with, or the overt failure of, earlier ways of understanding oneself and the world, leading to (2) problems of living that were beyond simple issues of work and employment and instead touched to the very center of "who I am" (3) over an extended period of time, and (4) involving overt confusion and inner turmoil, with (5) a conscious or unconscious turn inward to contemplate "who I am."

Clearly, something else besides dissatisfaction at work was taking place. The many issues which converged in the career change and the similarities of experience among the men in this group indicate that the career change was not a haphazard random event but rather an ordered consistent life development. Furthermore, the career change seems to be not just a transformation in relation to work but rather is part of a broad change in life structure.

Resolution and Stability in the Present

By the time of the interviews, the acute crisis at midlife had been dealt with and our participants had stabilized their lives. There is a sense of resolution, as we find members of the group having moved into new, stable roles and opportunities that are personally gratifying. Some of the men in the visual arts and crafts derive their income from teaching, others from sales, commissions, and fellowships; most from a combination of teaching and selling of their work. The actors support themselves primarily by performing. In each case these people report themselves as happy in their new careers and satisfied with the change.

We shall see in a later chapter that the same event—the midlife career change—emerges from very different resolutions at midlife between individuals, with different implications for our assessment of the person's current psychosocial functioning and adaptation. Nonetheless, the self-descriptions of their current life situation exhibit a general sense of calm and satisfaction.

We find a sense of overt optimism and confidence in facing the future and evaluating the past. As one person put it:

> I feel I have my strengths and my weaknesses as a person. There are some things I can do and other things I can't do. I've kind of accepted those and I feel good about that. And I feel that I have the potential [laughs] of being one of the major artists in this century, OK? That may sound bizarre sitting here in Boston, Mass., you know, but I believe that. I believe that I have a tremendous amount of talent and potential and I feel that I haven't really tapped my resources.

For several individuals the satisfaction in the present is linked to a sense of greater personal freedom and the absence of constraints experienced in the initial career. For example, Mr. Goodson describes his current life as a painter and teacher as "almost the perfect thing for me. I can test myself, and the thing that is happening is that I'm finding no boundaries." Mr. Goodson contrasts this to his feeling when a physicist of always "playing a role." He comments that outwardly he looked like a physicist, but inside he was "very confused and feeling that I'm not really the scientist. Now I don't feel that. I don't feel like I'm in a shell. I'm home. I feel like I'm approaching this with no holds barred."

Our participants' discussion of their work in the arts indicates that they have moved into new work roles with new challenges, possibilities, and demands. The new role-taking and establishment of a functional life structure in a new career are in part indicated by ability of members of the group to support themselves at their work. Beyond this, the successful transition into new roles is indicated by recurrent discussions of key role demands and their internal impact, indicating socialization into their second careers. Some key challenges for this group include the altered nature of the work itself (from the initial career to the arts or crafts), the transition to becoming a teacher of the arts or crafts, and the challenge of having to "sell" their products to an evaluative audience. As an example of the different mode of work, Mr. Anderson contrasts his work in the arts with his initial career in the law:

> [*How have things been for you since you became an artist?*] The joys and the excitements have been heady, more heady than before. Writing a good journal article in law, or a decent memorandum, or handl-

ing a case, well that's small potatoes to me. Some satisfaction, but no great deal. Making an image, where you are riding on something that has a lot of mystery and intuition — you can't understand it all as you go along. But being disciplined enough to persist and to hang loose at the same time and do all those things at once, and then to finish and not be able to see it because you've been too close and you have to wait, and finally deciding that the image is really good—[*laughs*] It's terrific!

A great part of the process of sculpting—at least half of it—is being a child. Being playful, being sad, friendly, happy, a child. Then at the same time the great thing always has to be to get away from it and reobject to it, to plug in an analytical perspective and be very tough on this child's image.

Several of the members of the group are teachers of the arts or crafts at present, and we find recurrent discussion of the role demands and internal experiences of teaching:

Teaching art in evening classes at first seemed very strange to me. I said, "Well, how could I do that?" Somehow I reached the students. And it came off very well, even though the class was constantly shifting and changing. People would only come for one or two times and they would never come again. There would be some that would stay on. But there were some regulars and it was very open. That really gave me some confidence at the time about teaching. For a couple of years it was pretty shaky. But every year I learned a little bit more about teaching, became a little more confident. I find it a great job. Most of the classes are a joy. I see the way my students react to me. They tell me they go away high. And I say, "You made me high." And it's that kind of a good relationship. It's funny, I never dreamed that I could be a teacher. It was such a surprise to me.

The challenge of "selling" the artistic product varies according to the specific career in the arts or crafts. For the visual artists and potters the challenge is the concrete one of selling their products—paintings, sculptures, pots—to stores or galleries, but the actors face the more intangible challenge of "selling" their performances. Mr. O'Hara remembers some of his early feelings of "being like a little kid looking at Willie Mays" when comparing his pottery to other work in crafts stores, and Mr. Markowitz reflected on the challenge for an actor of putting his "product" up for evaluation:

[*What kind of difficulties were there in becoming an actor?*] Well there was really a fear of being rejected. I mean it was foreign to me to offer myself to anyone. To say, "Here I am — accept me or reject me." I would always say that the essence of science is that if you don't believe me, do the experiment yourself. I didn't have to argue with you. The essence of acting is, "I'm going to make you believe me." There's no way I can force you to. But I'm on the line. If you don't, it may be some failure of my own. But you're out there and there's utterly no way of getting everybody in that house to see what you see, to feel what you feel. There's no way. I've had people fall asleep on my performances. I've had to walk out through the set, they were so enraged by what was going on. And I could swear that I was doing good.

The movement into new roles following the period of crisis at midlife is not limited to the area of work. Some men have divorced and some have remarried, others have recommitted themselves to their marriages after experiencing significant marital difficulties. New patterns of friendship have been formed as the sharp changes in work and family status have produced new patterns of social relationships. Since leaving careers meant leaving friends connected to the workplace, moving into new careers meant finding new networks of friends and relations. As the activities and interests of these men shifted, some describe themselves as growing closer to, and others apart from, their wives:

MR. PREZINSKI: I have different friends now. There weren't many people I wanted to be friendly with after I left engineering, and also I felt myself in such a period of transition in terms of what I was doing. It was difficult. I didn't have any friends when I first got into the arts, I was all by myself. I took classes, but even there I didn't make any friends really. It was very lonely. I feel that the Artists Cooperative has been very good for me. I'm sure it's been good for a lot of people. And it's not just the fact that you could exhibit your work there in the gallery and so on. It's a lot more that that — it's the social relationships with other people. That's really an important thing about it.

MR. LONZETTI: It's a big change for my wife. But my wife . . . she's what's enabled me to pursue what I'm doing—her belief in me. She believes in my talent. And she believes that I'm gonna do something with it.

MR. O'HARA: [*What was your wife's response to your growing interest in art?*] I think she was torn, but she didn't talk about it. I could cajole her into my life, but in other ways she didn't like it, especially once I got out of the university. She didn't like the art world. She felt lost in it.

Despite their general satisfaction with their midlife changes, participants often communicated the difficulty of their choices and a sadness over the loss of what was left behind at work or in the family. As well as a sense of the resolution of a crisis and the transition into new life situations, we find a sense of rupture and breakage in these men's perceptions of their life history. To varying degrees, there is, a demarcation between "the way I was then" and "the way I am now." Although participants differ in the degree to which the rupture seems healed, most communicated a distinct sense of having changed from "then" to "now," with the period of crisis interposed between the two states. In the first interview Mr. O'Hara began in this fashion:

> Well, where do you want to start? My life is such a vast space. It's 44 years. I feel I am at the midpoint of my life and that I've completed the first half. I've raised a family, more or less, and I've gotten a divorce, and so I have raising a family done. So what's ahead of me is kind of adventurous. It's a life which is less socially oriented. I think I have fulfilled all these debts to society. The future is something I haven't mapped out, and I'm not going to worry about that. I wanted to draw that line so I could talk about the first forty years at least. That kind of seems to me an encapsulated time.

Similar language indicating a distinction between past and present appears in a number of interviews with other men in the group, with the career change serving as a marker or watershed. One man commented near the end of the interviews that "there were those last years of depression, and then the decision to make a change. You've come to me at a time when I'm beginning a new phase." Another said, "I guess the general feeling is that everything I did for the first forty years of my life, although it's part of me, just seems like another life completely, very slightly connected to where I am now."

For these men the career change into the arts and crafts seems part of a reconstituted life situation. Their lives at present are not dissimilar to those of many other men in their age group. By the time of the interviews the experience of crisis was over, and we find these individuals in new, transformed work, personal, and social situations. From this perspective, rather than reflecting some idiosyncratic adult experiences unique to this group alone, the career change seems part of a process of coping and adaptation, as the turmoil of the earlier period of crisis seems to have lessened and become resolved.

Yet, given the type and degree of change this group has carried out, one might inquire as to its relevance for concerns of most other people. Why study a group having carried out a career change, and into the arts and crafts at that? Perhaps the nature of midlife observed in the study is unique to such individuals, or perhaps the findings are just an artifact of the free-associative interviewing technique. These are legitimate considerations, and in the section that follows I consider what we know of midlife from other social science research and from popular literature. We find that the midlife experiences that emerge from this special sample—with its rich data and unique methodology—are consistent with what we know of midlife from very different types of studies.

Midlife as a Distinct Stage in Adult Development: The View from Other Sources

The reports of crisis and change at midlife among our men overlap with and extend findings from other studies of adult development using diverse samples and methodologies.

We know in terms of demography that there is considerable change and innovation in life situations during the midlife years. Career changes are not uncommon in our society. Exact figures will vary with the specific definition of what constitutes a career change, yet, regardless of the definition, such change is substantial. Byrne (1974) cites five million people as changing occupation in a given year. Sommers and Eck (1977) report that 30 percent of the work force and 10 percent of professionals and technicians experienced a career change between 1965 and 1970. Similarly, Folger at al. (1970) reported that 10 percent of Ph.D.s can expect to be employed in a field other than that in which they obtained the doctorate within the first seven years of work, and that after eighteen years the figure may be as high as 40 percent (Freeman 1971). Holland et al. (1973) report from their longitudinal study of a group of 30-to-39-year-olds that less than a fifth of the sample remained in the same job over a five-year period. As Ginsburg comments, "Occupational choice is a process that remains open as long as one makes and expects to make decisions about . . . work and career. In many instances, it is coterminous with . . . working life" (Ginsburg 1972, p. 172).

Changes occur in the individual's relationship to work even in the absence of such overt shifts as career changes. Changes in the quantity, quality, and mode of working of scientists, businessmen, and artists at midlife have been noted by different observers (Lehman 1953; Pelz and Andrews 1966; Dalton 1977, and Jacques 1965).

Beyond this, a number of studies indicate a striking incidence and prevalence of a variety of signs of personal disorganization among middle-aged males: neurotic and psychotic disorder (Srole et al. 1962; Riley and Foner 1968); alcoholism (Moon and Palton 1963); marital dissatisfaction (Pineo 1968); career difficulty (Levinson 1964a, 1964b; Heistand 1971; Figler 1978); and psychosomatic and hypochondriacal complaints (Blumetal 1959).* The potential difficulties of the midlife years have become

*A recent review of this symptomatology can be found in Rosenberg and Farrell (1976, 1977).

an area of public concern reflected in the large number of newspaper and magazine articles and books reporting the possibilities of "creative divorce," midlife career change (Bayer 1970; Trausch 1974), and the "predictable crisis" (Sheehy 1975), the "dangerous years" (McMorrow 1974), or the "inner world" (Chew 1976) of midlife.

Certainly the image of midlife in popular literature presents a picture of difficulty and crisis: A number of recent novels have advanced portraits of despairing businessmen and professionals confronting a sense of "dead-endedness" in their careers, boredom in their marriages, anxieties about their children or their own parents, and angst at the recognition of their aging (Bellow 1964; Kazan 1967; Heller 1974). We often find imagery and metaphors of loss, disorganization, and mourning during the midlife years in these narratives. This theme of the intertwining of loss, separation, and growth is central to our analysis of midlife in our career change group and is a theme that has been present in literature through the centuries. Jacques (1965) traces the emergence of such "tragic and philosophical content" in the work of a number of great artists to their life experiences and development past midlife. Jacques reminds us that Dante's opening stanza of *The Divine Comedy*, often interpreted as an allegorical religious reference or social comment, can be understood as well to reflect the poet's own emotional crisis at midlife:

> In the middle of the journey of our life, I came to myself within a dark wood where the straight way was lost. Ah, how hard it is to tell of that wood, savage, and harsh, and dense, the thought of which renews my fear. So bitter is it that death is hardly more.

A central theme of more recent poetry and fiction is precisely the loss of "the straight way" as one matures as an adult, and the struggle to come to terms with experiences at midlife that somehow seem profoundly different than those anticipated when younger. Heller (1974) aptly titled his novel *Something Happened*, as his main character struggles at midlife to understand exactly what it was that led him to where he is in his life. In his poem "The Oven Bird" Robert Frost asks, "What does one make of a diminished thing?" as many men ask of their lives during their middle years. In his poem "Waving Adieu, Adieu, Adieu," Wallace Stevens (1972) invokes imagery of loss, commenting "that would be waving and that would be crying":

> To be one's singular self, to despise
> The being that yielded so little, acquired
> So little, too little to care . . .

Here too we find the necessity of confronting a loss ("that would be crying") in acknowledging the discrepancy between who one is ("one's singular self"), and who one had hoped to be ("the being that yielded so little, acquired so little").

So we find that loss, change, and innovation at midlife are present in demographic studies, in media representations of adult development and as a theme running throughout literature. We find, too, that research on adult development earlier and concurrent with this study indicates that adulthood is a time of considerable psychosocial change, growth, and innovation.

Evidence from a number of recent studies of the human life cycle indicates that the adult years may have a number of distinctive features, tasks, and regularities.* Adulthood was once conceived of as merely the playing out of themes and dynamics established in childhood and adolescence. The elaboration early in this century by diverse investigators of the enduring importance of early development led to a view of adulthood as the tablet for childhood and adolescence writ large. Significant interest in individual development during adulthood in America can be traced at least to the work of Erik Erikson (1963). Based on clinical observations, Erikson presented a conception of adulthood in a continuing series of publications beginning with *Childhood and Society* in 1950. Erikson argued convincingly that a sequence of developmental tasks characterized maturation past adolescence, and he described them in terms of polarities: intimacy versus isolation, generativity versus stagnation, integrity versus despair. Erikson is actually relatively silent about the midlife years, as the task of achieving intimacy generally characterizes the twenties, while the problem of generativity versus stagnation occurs in the late forties and fifties.

Further clinical studies by Jacques (1965), Shore (1972), Tartakoff (1966), and Wolfenstein (1966) have pointed to the importance of midlife as a time of reassessment and the attempt to come to terms with one's own accomplishments and achievements.

More empirical work has begun to support these clinical insights. Thus, Neugarten (1968) described midlife in terms of a shift in orientation to personal time: toward attention to the amount of time left in one's own life cycle rather than that which has passed. Gould (1972) and others (Stein et al. 1978; Rosenberg and Farrell 1976) note an increasing preoccupation with self through the midlife years, and a turn inward toward self-exploration.

The most detailed studies of psychosocial development through midlife yet available are the Grant Study of Adult Development (Vaillant 1978) and that of Daniel Levinson and his associates at Yale (1978). I shall review these studies in greater detail in Chapter 6, but it is worth noting at this point that these studies of samples different from that utilized in the present research also report findings of change and innovation at mid-

*This research is reviewed in greater detail in Chapter 6.

life. Levinson (1978) followed a group of forty men through the midlife years. He describes the "midlife transition" and middle years in terms of such tasks as reappraising the past, modifying the social structure of one's life, and integrating previously unrealized aspects of the self. In his sample of executives, factory workers, biologists, and novelists Levinson found turmoil and struggle similar to that reported by our group of career changers. Describing the adult life cycle, Levinson comments, "It consists of a series of alternating stable (structure-building) periods and transitional (structure-changing) periods"(Levinson 1978, p. 49).

The Grant study has studied over two hundred individuals as they matured from the college years through later adulthood. Reporting findings from questionnaires and interviews with ninety five of the men, Vaillant offers a view of midlife as a time of inner exploration and personal change:

> As adolescence is a period for acknowledging parental flaws and discovering the truth about childhood, so the forties are a time for reassessing and reordering the truth about adolsecence and young adulthood. (Vaillant 1978, p. 219)

We thus find a consistent picture of the importance of midlife emerging from recent social science research, and the findings of turmoil, difficulty, shifts in life situation such as divorce or career change, and growth are not unlike those reported for our group of career changers. It would be easy to assume that our understanding of midlife is quite advanced, yet in truth most research in this area has used special samples of one kind or another and methodologies that have their particular limitations.* We are only now filling in bits and pieces of our picture of midlife from a variety of divergent studies, recent and still ongoing, each with its particular strengths and weaknesses. Each provides new findings and thus a gradual deepening of our understanding of midlife.

The strategy in this research project is to study in a detailed manner a small, carefully focused sample. With our particular interview techniques I have tried to provide a situation where each man is allowed to talk about and organize his life history in his own way. This detailed, focused, and carefully analyzed talk of men about the ways they understand where they have been in their lives, where they are at present, and where they

---

*The view of midlife derived from findings of the Grant Study, for example, is based on a sample drawn from pre-World War II classes of an elite eastern university (Vaillant, 1978). How representative is this group for understanding the adult experiences of less privileged or advantaged individuals? And Levinson and his associates drew their sample from two business enterprises in eastern Connecticut. Careful, detailed studies of the complexities of human development often must pick special, narrowly defined samples.

are going is the data on which most of the findings of the book rest. In the report of the findings in the chapters that follow I strive to retain the richness and depth of this interview material whenever possible. So, too, when discussing these sections of interview data I try to refer as precisely as possible in the text to the specific words or phrases in the interview passage that provide the basis for the inferences or generalizations that are made.

Although the model that emerges from this particular sample and methodology is not inconsistent with what we know of midlife from other, very different studies, we find new results that broaden our understanding of the nature of midlife and its connection to other stages in the life cycle. Some important topics examined in this book are the relation of midlife to earlier developmental stages such as adolescence and young adulthood; how life choices and work experiences are tied to conflicts surrounding separation from parents; the relationship of the dynamics of the process of separation and loss to the midlife struggle to further wean oneself from parents and integrate previously unacknowledged aspects of self; and the specification of different types of midlife passage and the manner in which these crises are resolved.

A Personal Note

I am integrally involved in the picture that emerges from this book of career change and adult development, since I conducted the interviews, analyzed the data, and wrote this volume. So, it seems worthwhile for me to tell some about myself, to allow the reader to judge how my own interests, values, and conflicts have helped shape the book.

I am in my mid-thirties, recently married. I grew up in a middle-class suburb of New York City in Westchester County, N.Y. My father is a retail businessman; my mother is a psychotherapist who for many years was a writer of fiction. Education and professional training were seen as important goals in my family, and my decision to become a psychologist fit well into this view of the future. I was in graduate school during the height of the Vietnam War and took a position teaching at an inner-city university after receiving my Ph.D. The war left me with a deep residue of skepticism toward institutions and beliefs that were sacrosanct during my childhood. I have one brother, also a psychologist. When first beginning this study my interest in this particular group of career changers lay, most simply, in my own struggles with a similar issue in the early 1970's. At that time I experienced a painful conflict between my professional training and work as a teacher, researcher, and psychotherapist and my fascination with the classical guitar and the work of a musician. For me music seemed to express my true soul; my career, in contrast, seemed a dull plodding into the future. I wanted to know how other people had

struggled with similar issues: the feeling of a divided inner nature that demands resolution, of passion split off from one's work, and the painful uncertainty of how to express in the world who one "really is." As this study
proceeded and I heard these men talk of their lives, my focus shifted from
a fascination with the meaning of the arts and the belief that creativity
could only be expressed in the arts as traditionally defined, to a desire to
understand both the complexity of the work and family choices we make
as adults and the real meaning of creativity in one's life.

I still love music deeply, wish I could make music better, and believe
that there is more wisdom in the Brandenburg Concerti than in the collected psychological journals of the last decade. Nevertheless, I do believe
that art and science need not be sharply divided, that there is a deeper
truth that unites these activities; that analysis and metaphor, the right
and the left hand, can work together.

Summary: Key Questions about Midlife and the Organization of this Book

We find in our group of career changers evidence of conflict and difficulty at midlife, followed by a period of turmoil and change, with a sub-
sequently stable, reorganized life situation. The midlife experience of
these individuals can be summarized as follows:

Disruption of self (crisis)	⟶ Process of reorganization of self (adaptation to crisis)	⟶ Reconstituted self (new, stable roles and opportunities)

We have seen as well that a variety of studies have reported midlife as
a central time of turmoil and difficulty in adult development. The midlife
experience of these individuals raises some important questions about
adult development:

1. What was this crisis at midlife? How did it come about?

2. Given this crisis, how do people adapt to and cope with their
   confusion and disorganization at this time? What is the role of the
   career change in this process of adaptation? Are there different
   patterns of adaptation?

3. The process of reorganization seems to result in a reconstituted
   self. What is the relation of this state of the self to the self-organization with which these individuals entered midlife?

These are the questions that will guide the material to follow. I thus take these features of the midlife experience of these men as the central foci of the study: disorganization at midlife leads to a process of adaptation which leads to a new structuring of one's life.

These features of the midlife years will be examined from two complementary perspectives: The first focuses on inner experience and the person's own understanding of the events in his life. Here we are interested in how each of these men subjectively organizes and interprets his life history. The second perspective applies an analytic framework to conceptualize the subjective experiences reported by these individuals. We can label these as a subjective-phenomenal and an objective-analytic perspective.

In terms of these men's subjective experience, I will argue that midlife was a time in which the self itself was called into question. By this I mean that the central organizing definitions of "who I am" were lost or profoundly threatened. After this period of crisis comes a period of recovery or reconstitution of self, from which the career change emerges. This is consistent with the recurrent reports of deep confusion, intense inner turmoil, the tone of the unexpected surrounding particular life events and experiences in adulthood—as if these men were not prepared or could not easily explain such developments—and overt uncertainty about the past and future direction of one's life. These indicate that central ways of understanding the world, of interpreting experience, were proven inadequate at midlife. Further, the introspective turn inwards, the broad struggle in a number of areas of their lives, the recurrent concern with experiencing contradictory feelings and being out of control, the vague memory for details of the time (indicating possible diminution of ego function), and the emphasis in these individuals' reports of there actually being a pre-change "period" or "stage"—a defined "time" in their lives— leads me to conceive of this as a distinct period of crisis in self-organization, followed by a process of reconstitution of self from which the career change emerges. To account for this I will explore the adequacy and requirements of a loss and grieving paradigm as a guiding framework for our analysis of the psychosocial development at midlife of these individuals.

In Chapter 2, I will attempt to reconstruct the pattern of self-definition that underlies the key work and marital choices of young adulthood. I then attend, in Chapter 3, to the fate at midlife of the self-definition represented by these key life choices. From this I develop in Chapter 4 a perspective on career change that sees this decision as resulting from a larger experience of separation and loss. This will be done by expanding our concept of loss from its usual sense of concrete object loss to include situations in which abstract meanings, purposes, and values are called into question. After describing the "loss" encountered at midlife, I outline in Chapter 4 different patterns of midlife passage functionally similar to "grieving," from which the career change emerges.

Our second perspective is an objective one, in which the observed vicissitudes in self-definition during the midlife years are seen as reflective of a renewed crisis of separation-individuation from the idealized parents of childhood. A major theme in this analysis is the ambivalent nature of the process of separation-individuation, extending into adult development. From this perspective the key work and marital choices of young adulthood discussed in Chapter 2 express a dialectic between opposing motives: on the one hand, to define oneself autonomously with a sense of personal control and responsibility; on the other, to rely on idealized, grandiose images of parents as the basis for self-definition. As seen in Chapter 3, the midlife years reflect a continued dialectic between these polarities. As we shall see in Chapter 4, the "crisis" of midlife is one of separation-individuation in which the major challenge is to define oneself in a more individuated manner.

We can also ask why midlife took the particular course it did in this group; that is, what are the developmental roots of these observed midlife patterns? In Chapter 5 these patterns are related to particular types of adolescent separation issues, which are in turn traced to childhood ways in which these subjects came to experience their own subjectivity in coping with painfully ambivalent feelings toward their parents.

We begin our life history analysis in the next chapter with young adulthood, the time when a person is primarily concerned with defining and establishing himself for the first time as an adult. Choices relating to work and marriage played a key role in this process for the men in our group.

2

Young Adulthood

The Affirmation of Self in Career and Marriage

A Perspective on Young Adulthood

In order to understand midlife in our group of men we have to begin with young adulthood. During the young adulthood years most individuals make decisions about work and family, and these choices reflect a variety of meanings and purposes. Much of the descriptive and analytic work on the life cycle past adolescence defines as a major task for those in the 20-30 age range as finding a place or "niche" for oneself in the adult world. At this time a young person is engaged in the attempt to leave his childhood and adolescent status in his family of origin and to establish himself as a separate, autonomous adult in a larger social community. Levinson et al. (1975) see this period as one of "getting into the adult world." Erikson (1959) sees the predominant task at this time as that of "intimacy"—making and stabilizing satisfying marriage and work choices.

The young adult is engaged in a *project*, to define in the adult world the kind of person he is and thus to make real his post-adolescent identity. From this perspective, the work and marriage choices of the young adult affirm (Perry 1970) or implement (Super 1957) particular patterns of self-definition—expectations and assumptions about who one is and who one will be in a particular occupational role. Levinson et al. (1975) capture this early project of the young adult with their concept of an initial life structure, which we can see as an envelope of meaning and purpose organized primarily around the twin spheres of career and marriage.

These theoretical notions alone would direct our attention to the role played by initial career choices in our group's manner of "getting into the adult world," particularly since all the men made clear, overt career—and often marital—choices in their early twenties. Beyond this, these individuals' descriptions of the initial career choice in young adulthood also contain hints that some important dynamics were at work at this time. For example, we find the following descriptions of their perception in young adulthood of their careers: "Science seemed like an ideal life." "The possibility of a career. . . . This was going to be my life." "The university seemed like a glorious world . . . the only place to exist in American society." "I wanted to redeem myself by becoming a teacher." These quotes imply powerful expectations surrounding the initial career choices: science—a career—is equated with one's "life," a university with a "world," teaching will "redeem" the person. Despite the fact that these men at times will dismiss the initial career choices as misguided or meaningless (one person explained that his becoming a scientist was "brought about by a series of random events"), as they continue to discuss in the interviews their post-college entry into the adult world we find that a coherent picture emerges of the personal meaning and purpose expressed by these choices.

Let's take a working definition of "meaning and purpose," as the salient ego-syntonic cluster of goals, values, and assumptions about the nature of the world that underlies our life choices. These goals and assumptions represent the self affirmed, or made real, by career and marital choices. I believe it is possible to reconstruct from the interview data the pattern of self-definition with which these men first entered the "adult world." To do this I want to distinguish between the social and personal meanings of a person's occupational choice.

The choice of a particular career can be seen first in terms of its social meaning for the person; by this I mean the perceived role attributes that make a particular career attractive and desirable. For example, a lawyer might report the importance of verbal disputation, or the opportunity to defend others, as aspects of what it meant to him to be a lawyer at the time he decided to commit his time, energy, and money to law school. A reply framed in terms of the perceived social role attributes of an occupation is usually the answer we receive in response to the question, "Why did you become a _____?" These expectations of one's "public self" reflect the psychological representation of the role of lawyer, businessman, waiter, or doctor, as well as that of being a husband or wife. In addition, though, any career choice has personal meanings that underlie, or are reflected in, the social role attributes that are so attractive to the individual. Thus, crudely, a lawyer may value the verbal skill demanded of his role (social meaning) because it represents to him an invulnerability to attack from others (personal meaning) or because he finds this a means of captivating others and hopes to achieve wide recognition and adulation. Or a doctor may respond that he chose medicine as a career because of the opportunity to heal the sick and conquer illness (social meaning), yet underlying this role may be such personal meanings as proving himself to be an individual without harmful impulses, or—as Alfred Alder claimed in relation to himself—of defeating forever the frightful specter of death and finitude (Adler 1956). So we have in any career choice an incomplete-sentence test, the second part of which the individual usually cannot answer directly: "I will become an (*occupational choice*) with *perceived role attributes* (the social meaning), so that (*personal meaning*)." Both aspects of this choice must be reconstructed to understand the meaning and purposes represented by the initial life structure in young adulthood. Further, the particular role attributes of an initial career choice may express a number of different meanings. In particular we might expect that such choices embody a transition into the adult world rooted both in the movement out of one's family of origin as an autonomous adult as well as movement into one's adult family with childhood conflicts unresolved. Thus, a young doctor's desire to find a cure for cancer may have its roots in an amalgam of sibling rivalry and unresolved conflict within the family of origin for example, to finally establish his superiority over his brother, as well as the desire to make a positive contribution to the world, to utilize his productive or creative talents and interests, and to be an autonomous, valuable, independent adult in the larger world community.

In our group the dialectical interplay within the career and marital decisions of young adulthood is striking, as these choices represent a definition of self both in terms of unresolved childhood conflicts and as an independent adult separate from the problems of childhood. In our six case studies I will summarize a complex of data from the interviews by pointing to the major links between the person's key life decisions in young adulthood and the particular kinds of self-definition that were affirmed by them. To do this I will pay particular attention to the personal meanings of perceived social role attributes at the time of career choice. Each of these career choices in young adulthood was an attempt to bring into being a particular vision of the self. In terms of the goal-orientedness of the person's career and marital choices, what were the particular ways of being that the person was pointed toward in young adulthood? How did the perceived attributes of the specific career affirm this goal? What were the central assumptions and expectations about who one would be that underlay these work and marital choices? We shall see that an idealized or "wished-for" self was at the core of the life choices of young adulthood in this group.

Case Studies

Mr. Markowitz: "Science seemed like an ideal life."

Mr. Markowitz is a 50-year-old actor in New York who five years ago left his position as a microbiologist in Colorado. He entered graduate school in biology immediately after college, marrying at the same time. By his own description, the choice of science as a career was heavily invested, as he relates having seen science as an "ideal life" since his youth. When we examine the perceived contents of this ideal life we find emphasis on social responsibility, the life of the mind, and the safeguards of methodology.

Mr. Markowitz describes his early exposure to what Mitroff (1974) has called the "storybook image of science" through fictionalized biographies of Pasteur and others, as well as by his "reverence" for several relatives who were scholars. Mr. Markowitz recalls being attracted to the life of a scientist as a "socially responsible" person contributing to the benefit of mankind. The unambiguously positive contribution of the scientist to society—confirmations of the scientist's "good" inner nature—were important perceptions and assumptions for Mr. Markowitz.

> I was always concerned with the social benefits of science, right from the beginning. This was why I got into science. Because I felt it was *the* socially valuable activity. When I was young I read things like Paul DeKruif's *The Hunger Fighters*. Talk about what a great thing that is! Hunger fighters. Goldberger with his fight against pellagra. Or Sinclair Lewis's *Arrowsmith*. The life of Pasteur. These were all the greatest good to me.

Mr. Markowitz's descriptions of other scientists reflects his emphasis on their socially valuable work, the power of their minds, and their benevolent inner nature: A teacher while in graduate school was "really brilliant . . . I truly loved that man"; another such teacher was "godlike"; and a laboratory chief on his first job was "an absolute genius of a man." For Mr. Markowitz these men were idealized figures as well because of the perceived exclusion of affect and emotion from their personal lives. For Mr. Markowitz the true scientist was capable of great disinterest and dispassion, able to exclude the "bias" and "danger" of emotion. This emphasis can be seen in his discussion of "truth telling" and the structure of science:

> I grew up with the idea that science was a good life. There were things that I really admired about the world of science. One was, in

research anyway, the quality of being disinterested, of working on a problem and not being involved in what the answer was. To me that was very good. Even more important was the quality of truthfulness in science. And the truthfulness was forced on the investigator, because if he told a lie he could very easily be discovered. In science you have built in a truth-telling operation. If you don't tell the truth somebody's going to find out. You might last for a year or two. But somebody's going to run the experiment and find out that you weren't telling the truth. That was very important to me.

Central to Mr. Markowitz's perceptions at the time was the belief in the intellectual life of the scientist as providing ideals, sufficient guides to conduct and behavior. This is implied in his comment that "truthfulness was forced on the investigator." The demands for rigor and the controls of the methodology served to insure the dispassionate nature of this "ideal" life and were often emphasized in Mr. Markowitz's discussion of the scientist's work.

With the equal-arm balance, when you do your first analysis you count the swings, you count the number, OK? You go away after the first time, you come back, you cover up your first data on the swing; although it seems impossible that your first data could influence your second data, you still cover it up, because you have subconsciously a desire that that thing should weigh a certain amount. And knowing the deep dark recesses of the mind, you don't trust your mind, no matter. You've been given all kinds of training in how to be objective in picking up errors and all that, but you still don't trust yourself. . . . You want the thing to make sense. You have a real stake in having the thing make sense, in having your idea come out.

The self-definition of Mr. Markowitz as socially responsible and dispassionate extended into choices about marriage as well. He married after college because he "was in love" with the woman and the "proper" choice was marriage. Their first child was born within a year. Throughout the marriage Mr. Markowitz was very much concerned with his ability to make a living, with not being a failure financially, as well as maintaining a dispassionate, wise, unemotional stance as father and husband:

A person's a responsible husband, he goes to work in most places, he keeps his nose to the grindstone, he works and works so that his children can have clothing and food and shelter and all that. And that's one choice. If he is a person—married or not— who feels that the tremendous love that he had for the woman before he marries her should go on and on . . . then he can't take time off from that. In other words there's a division of energy and labor, so that either you cultivate the role of lover, or cultivate the role of provider, but it has to be one or the other. In my case I never knew I had a choice. I was brought up to be responsible. To be the provider.

I'd look at my kids not as somebody to be loved and cuddled and played with. I'd look at a kid as somebody to be examined to make sure the kid's not sick. To make sure the kid is not doing anything dangerous, make sure he's not sticking his finger into beer cans, make sure the kid is not running out in the street and getting run over. As opposed to just enjoying. The kids always tell me that there was an insurmountable wall. I was playing a parent role. I felt that they were first of all a responsibility. I had to take care of them.

We can summarize Mr. Markowitz's self-definition—implemented by the career choice of microbiology and the decision to marry—as one who is socially responsible and an unambiguously good person, omniscient (the power of pure thought to comprehend and guide his experience), and nonaffective and unbiased (uncorrupted by the "deep, dark recesses of the mind").

For all our men there are clear developmental roots to the patterns of self-definition in young adulthood. These roots extend back to early childhood and center on the experience of their subjectivity—the inner world of impulse and affect—in their particular family settings. I discuss these patterns in detail in Chapter 5, and will only summarize in this chapter the unresolved uncertainties for each person about their subjectivity woven into the pattern of young adulthood self-definition. The developmental origins of Mr. Markowitz's definition of self resides in unresolved anxieties about the meaning of his aggression and affect, and narcissistic injuries in relationship with his father dating back to early childhood. Mr. Markowitz's father is described as a quiet, remote, stern figure; his mother is perceived as a more colorful, seductive woman. The father was a small businessman in Boston "obsessed" about being a business failure, as he had difficulty providing for the family. For the young Mr. Markowitz there were questions about his father's masculinity and adequacy: "The implication I got from my mother somehow was that he was a homosexual. . . . He had been ruined for marriage." The mother-son alliance was important. Mr. Markowitz was the only child and formed a close relationship with his mother, with fantasies of having replaced his father: "It was almost as if I were her husband . . . a surrogate husband. I took care of her. She would come to me for advice and I'd give her advice. I supported her." In this context the inner world for the young Mr. Markowitz became a frightening, dangerous area that led to aggression, jealousy, and disturbing attractions. The passive, aloof father became internalized as a powerful, judgmental, godlike figure to whom one was accountable.

We find ample evidence in the interviews of Mr. Markowitz's profound discomfort with, and uncertainty about, his inner life. He is a person who does not feel at home with his impulse and affect. Indeed, he has
considerable anxiety about his "real nature," whether he is at heart an
evil, impulsive person or a good controlled one. His attitude toward impulse can be seen in his comments about two scientists, Ernst Haeckel and
H. G. Wells: "The only trouble [with Haeckel's theories] was that they
were inaccurate. . . . He was a little too enthusiastic." Wells "made terrible mistakes. He was a very enthusiastic man but not accurate at all." Mr.
Markowitz described himself at another point as "a little overpowerful
. . . when I became enthusiastic about something," with a tendency to
overwhelm other people. There is, throughout, a fear of being out of control that tinges Mr. Markowitz's account of affect and impulse: Being in
love is "like a disease . . . almost a derangement"; when he argues he becomes like a "fanatic" or a "shark"; and "when you get emotionally involved it gets distorted—your view of things." As he says, "We're taught
not to express anger because it's dangerous to express anger. You might actually not be able to control it." This inference regarding Mr. Markowitz's
anxiety over, and distrust of, impulse receives corroboration thematically
in the interviews, as repetitively such expression leads to trouble, usually
in terms of intrusion from, and accountability to, others.

A major personal meaning of the social role of the scientist is that it
provides a reassuring control of impulse, with (in Mr. Markowitz's eyes)
little necessity of looking inward to one's affective life. Thus the demand
for rigor and the controls of methodology built into his work were salient
because they reflected these personal meanings and purposes. The choice
of science as a profession represents part of Mr. Markowitz's movement
away from his inner world of aggression and emotion in adolescence and
young adulthood by finding situations and persons that would define him
in the idealized image of his father: responsible, affect-free, intellectual,
and a clearly good person.

In attempting to define himself as separate from his family of origin,
Mr. Markowitz built on abilities and interests, the desire to make a contribution, the love of the "touch and feel" of the laboratory, and the intellectual capacities needed for the rigorous research of the scientist. Yet much
of his childhood world is also represented in these choices.

[*How is it that you chose science as your field in college*?] Well, I had
good science teachers. I don't know, nobody in my family was interested in science. I'd be reaching now for it and it might particularly
interest you because your field is psychology. OK, my parents were
fairly opposite, that is, my father was reserved all the time, my
mother was emotional and affluent, and somehow I grew up with the
feeling that my father's way of living was the right way. That it was

good to be in control, to be analytical, to stand aside, to stand away and look at something. Because when you got emotionally involved it got distorted, your view of things . . . . I identified with him, I suppose.

With a parent especially it's difficult. Whether you've rebelled or not, there's still the huge weight of authority, because here's a person who has lived so much longer—in fact, has manufactured you. And I wasn't thinking so much from the standpoint of knowledge, but more of just a kind of emotional security.

I remember when I was doing graduate work. I just had a funny thought. [*laughs*] My father was tremendously well read. This was his favorite hobby, to read. He read everything and retained everything. It's like the old joke: A man whose wife was always saying, "I know, I know." One day his friend came up to the apartment and to his amazement he saw the man putting a horse in the bathtub. He said, "Hey, what are you doing?" He says, "I want my wife to come into the bathroom and come roaring out saying, "Hey, do you know there's a horse in the bathtub,' and I want to say, 'I know, I know.' " [*laughs*] Well with my father that's the way it was. He knew, he really did. Now here I was into graduate work in science and he didn't know anything at all about what I was doing. I'm not sure that's it but it just seems to me I recall, they visited me, my mother and father, and there was a kind of respect.

This excerpt seems to capture some of Mr. Markowitz's desire in adolescence to achieve his father's respect, and the difficulty he experienced in doing so. We find Mr. Markowitz in something of a childlike posture, trying to be a "good boy"—knowledgeable and respectable— so as to be respected by his father. His father is, further, perceived as very difficult to satisfy, as implied by the joke of being unable to tell him anything he doesn't already know.

Note that there is little room in Mr. Markowitz's world of young adulthood for the irresponsible, the ambiguous, the playful, and the ordinary delight of periodically removing one's nose from the grindstone. This is because deep down Mr. Markowitz does not trust himself as a responsible, socially contributory provider; he is afraid of being out of control, too "enthusiastic and overpowerful." Thus he needs to feel controlled and accountable, restrained by others as he felt by a "godlike" father as a child. Yet Mr. Markowitz does not forget his desires and wishes for playfulness and pleasure; rather, he feels resentful at the control he perceives all around him. Mr. Markowitz has moved into the adult world in the "role" of responsible husband, father, and scientist; yet in doing so he has attempted to let go of the conflictual playfulness, spontaneity, and passion he experienced when younger. As we shall see, he also holds onto these aspects of self: Mr. Markowitz locates those attributes outside of himself, in other people, particularly children and women. They are the ones with the opportunity for play, passion, and fun.

Mr. Anderson: "The competition was to become . . . an expert."

Mr. Anderson left his position in a successful southern law firm at the age of 35 to pursue a career as a sculptor. He married immediately after law school. An essential percieved attribute of law had to do with its professional "expert" status, achieved particularly through the mastery of verbal-analytic skills.

> I went to law school because I could think pretty well and analyze things. What the world of the law was actually like I really didn't have much of an idea at all. I thought I was pretty good with my head, I could be analytical and arrive at conclusions and I had a brain that liked to play around with problems—difficult-to-solve problems and ones that were really only approximate solutions. All I knew was I was pretty good with my head, with verbal things. I could write. . . .
>
> You know, there were certain things that had enough romance to them, plus enough practicality, plus were very difficult for me, and obscure enough, that it was worth my doing. Without really asking whether I wanted them. [*Can you explain what you mean by "obscure enough"?*] Well, in the sense that in terms of my family, in going after this it would have been very obscure. One of the main things you learn at law school is how to talk legalese, and how to think in those ways. . . . It becomes a special world that— Like, "I'm doing something special that you guys don't know about. I'm an expert." That's pretty blatant, but honest talk. I suppose there surely was an element of that.

As well as the clear importance of words and verbal skill we find in addition Mr. Anderson's emphasis on social poise. His guiding image of law before his training was that of the highly skilled barrister using his professional skills and training to benefit his clients. There was an emphasis on the "proper" and "decorous" demeanor of the lawyer, far removed from a world of turmoil and "unruly" behavior:

> I had a very strong sense of duty. That there was a certain pattern or path that I ought to follow . . . that some profession I was going into would lead to a certain social responsibility that I sought after graduation, after college. And there was a disassociation in me between what I really wanted and what I thought I ought to do. Law was one

of several professions that seemed suitable for me. I can't say what kind of social respect I wanted or class-consciousness I may have had. What seemed appropriate for me to do. . . .

This emphasis on being "proper" and "correct" extended into marriage. Mr. Anderson's description of his fiancée at the time of marriage and his manner of choice indicates emphasis on these attributes:

I don't know what kind of world I was living in. I really can't understand the kinds of questions I didn't ask. I think I was running a lot on the same thing I was talking about with law, like that's the thing to do. You get to a certain age you get married. I got married when I was about 27. And this girl looked pretty good. And I thought I liked her a lot. We seemed to share a lot of things. Interest in art, interest in music. I didn't see the things that could have been seen then. I still can be quite blind, I think. I have to be very careful if I get close to somebody how well I see them, as opposed to this image I have. And I think I was looking for security in marriage in the original, somehow. This would be someone to take care of, to get money for. . . . It pulls together in a package that felt good to me. And having a wife, oddly enough, that meant that I could then do my thing. Be a husband. A lawyer. Earn money. Support my wife. She'd do certain things in return. And we'd have ourselves a life.

Mr. Anderson's descriptions of his future wife is of someone filling a role: a person who seemed correct and had the right attributes for them to have a life together.

This young adulthood self-definition in terms of propriety, expert professional status, and verbal proficiency and poise was rooted in issues of competition and separation in Mr. Anderson's family of origin. Mr. Anderson comes from a wealthy southern family. His father was a respected owner of a real estate firm, and is described as very controlled and calm. Mr. Anderson's memories of his family emphasize poise and propriety: "formal dinners and a certain shaped pattern of things, the way people behave." There was considerable jealously and envy of an older brother, perceived as socially poised and verbally facile. A devaluation of self, with agression and impulse that "didn't fit the mold," occured as the brother was seen as the one truly loved by his parents, since he (like his father) was without the "strange curse" of unruly feelings. Out of this came an intensified sibling rivalry with a devaluating of his "useless feelings" and the unarticulated hope of making himself into a proper person, like his father and brother. The devaluation of self and idealization of verbal skills and social poise (represented by his brother) can be seen in Mr. Anderson's concern with "carving out my own space," so as to be appreci-

ated by his parents, separate from his brother. Such dynamics are powerfully expressed at two different points in the interview sequence. In the
first interview Mr. Anderson alluded to issues of competition:

> I recognized much more recently a very strong competitive streak. I
> don't sit on it anymore but watch myself very carefully. The competi-
> tion [*at the time of law school*] was to become an expert, you see.
> Now, competing with whom? That I couldn't say, without spending
> quite a bit of time on it.

By the fourth session Mr. Anderson had found the time, and in the
following excerpt he gives a picture of his relationship to his brother. Note
the sense of rivalry and envy of the older brother apparent in his description ("he would get a lot of praise in my presence," "I'd forget that he was
a lot older," "how well he expressed himself"). Much of this rivalry as described above centers around the use of words and self-presentations. Mr.
Anderson expresses powerfully as well the feeling of being overshadowed
by his brother, or undervalued in his parents' eyes. He says, for example,
"I had just been swallowed" by his brother and directly links the career
choice to his desire to "have a relationship with my parents."

> It seemed to me [my brother] would get a lot of praise in my pres-
> ence—in my family. [*What was the praise for?*] Letter writing . . . I
> can remember . . . he was in the army and I was home still. I'd read
> the letters and there was quite a bit of talk about how well he ex-
> pressed himself.
>   Oh, I forgot one real trauma in connection with him. It was real-
> ly one of the worst days in my life, I think. I don't know how I could
> forget it . . . it was my parents' wedding anniversary—I don't remem-
> ber what I was giving for presents, but my brother had bought and
> built a whaling boat model. At a younger age I wasn't making mod-
> els. I couldn't seem to do it as well as he. I'd just do things that he did
> a lot. And I wouldn't do them as well, and I'd forget that he was a lot
> older. For some reason I thought I was supposed to be an equal or
> something. So I'd try to make a model by myself and he'd be at school
> or something and it wouldn't come out very well. So, this model ar-
> rives . . . it was quite a beautiful thing. It was built out of a kit. It was
> a nicely scaled . . . all the details, you know. The sweeps and tubs and
> all that. And he presented it. That was their anniversary present.
> Mother and Dad. I don't know, I wish I could tell you, and even my-
> self the exact ambience, or what had happened. I can't do that. [*How
> old were you then?*] Maybe 13 or 14. The effusive response. My
> mother was in tears because it was so beautiful. And it just went on
> and on and on. I really went haywire. I was crying too. I was crying

because I hadn't done it. I had just been swallowed up. Any present that I might give in that situation would be. . . .

I think Tom got a lot of the—in any sort of equality at all he got more. I don't know. I have no rancor about that. Although I care about it, I only talk about it because we're talking about it. I just want to leave it alone. I just want to be free of it. If I was going to have anything of mine, and I want, by God, to have it, that would include the input and decision to go to law school. He didn't go to law school and I could talk about things that he didn't understand. And I would have a relationship with my parents. And one of the problems in every school was that he had already gone there. He had already gone through college. He had already gone through my prep school. He had also already gone through our elementary school.

In young adulthood Mr. Anderson was attempting to remake himself in a manner acceptable to his family. He hoped to be perceived as similar to his brother, to be as highly valued. The road to becoming a "worthy," "valued" person was law, in that through the legal profession he would finally come into his own, becoming like—and yet separate from—his idealized older brother, who had become a successful business consultant. As Mr. Anderson says, in becoming a lawyer, "the competition was to become . . . an expert. . . . I could talk about things he couldn't understand."

The image of the "expert" lawyer—separate and equal to his brother—is representative of so much of what Mr. Anderson in young adulthood wanted to be. Yet we also find evidence of Mr. Anderson's struggle to define himself separately from the conflicts of childhood. This can be seen particularly in his discussion of what he and his wife shared, an interest in the arts. Although in college Mr. Anderson had had an intense interest in the arts and humanities, he was unable to truly sort through his own interests and desires:

My father helped me find an advisor at college. It happened to have been a friend of his, which sounded good. I talked to the guy, he was OK, but we talked about schedules and what courses are you interested in. And it would have been almost impossible for me at that time to have said, "I don't know what I'm interested in. The way I feel now, I'm not interested in anything. Because I mean the arts are nice, and I'm sort of interested in that, and I like to write a little bit, and I've done pretty well in school in all these things." That didn't seem to mean anything. So what. I've done very well but I came out of a school where most of the courses you could take were either French, Spanish, or German, and you had to take math, and you had to take English Lit, either music or art, and so forth and so on. I didn't know how to choose anything, nor did I have the sense of myself that I had the power of choice. I was totally lost. I sort of treated it as a surface thing: "I'm pretty good in history and it's a good major in general and I like to read and . . . I don't think that's a unique situation. Retrospectively I regreted my incapacity to seek out people and admit my feelings. Starting down at that level. Saying, "I really don't know what I'm interested in and it feels like I'm not interested in anything. I know that isn't so but that's the way it feels."

Mr. Anderson was unable to affirm these aspects of self in his career choice. Yet with his wife he felt he had found such an affirmation—he married a woman intensely interested in the arts and the creative process:

We took a trip to Europe together once. We both went for the first time. It was then that I discovered that not all the world looks like the United States. In fact the visual arts were everywhere. I was astounded. I was floored. I couldn't believe that people could be that interested in painting. That it was really important. I then discovered that visual arts and plastic arts in the United States generally were just a whole different thing. Most people just don't think it's very important. And I thought it was. So, walking around Florence, or Rome, or Vienna, or any of the places . . . Paris, Ghent, or Antwerp, or Amsterdam, I saw a lot. I had just finished school. A real exciting time, my wife had just gotten a bachelor's degree in art teaching. She had a job in a public school. I knew very little about art history. But she did.

So one aspect of his marital choice was an attempt to hold on to attributes of self and interests that were important for him to affirm. This can also be seen as an underlying component of law, as perhaps unconsciously Mr. Anderson seemed to hope that it would afford the opportunity for "creativity" and giving shape to things in words.

Mr. Prezinski: "The Conquered Man"

Mr. Prezinski became an engineer for private industry, proceeding directly from graduate school to a position of some responsibility. His struggle to separate from his family of origin and truly define himself is represented by the conflict between his college major of engineering and the desire to develop his skills and interest as an artist and designer.

I guess I was always interested in the arts. From way back. Even while I was at college, I was interested in the arts and architecture. But somehow or other I had gotten started in engineering. I had a lot of friends in architecture. I knew them more than I knew the people in my engineering class. I did things like I made handmade posters while I was at school and they would say, "Wow, did you make that poster?" And I would say, "Yeah, I did that." "Wow, that's good, why don't you study architecture?" Well I was very interested in architecture but I was afraid to get into it. Because I didn't think I had any talent. I felt inferior, like absolutely worthless. I didn't think of myself as creative or imaginative. I didn't have faith in myself. I thought the others in the architecture courses were much more creative. [*What does it mean to be creative?*] To be imaginative, to think things up, original things. I didn't think I could do that. I really felt quite inferior in that sense. Nothing was very clear to me. It was all kind of muddled. But I felt nobody encouraged me into architecture.

I knew also I was weak on dealing with people. That would just be a hard thing for me. I might get all shaken up. I was always shy and afraid of people. Social engagements were difficult. I mean even cocktail parties were difficult things for me. I couldn't think of anything to say to anybody. Things like that. Basic things like that always made me fearful of how I would ever get a good job in architecture. How would I ever do it? Nobody would ever give me a job.

There is a clear sense of defeat and loss in Mr. Prezinski's description of the turn away fom the arts and into engineering, as if he were giving up important aspects of himself. In one of the interviews he said, "I actually lost touch with intuition and human things. . . . It replaced my feelings." The work involved in architecture was a source of anxiety to Mr. Prezinski for two reasons: the appeal to his inner life of impulse and affect—revealed in his comment that "I didn't think of myself as creative . . . or imaginative"—and the interpersonal nature of the work. These two aspects of architecture are intertwined for Mr. Prezinski, because when we look deeper at his perception of the social demands of architecture we see that his specific anxiety is about defending himself or his products in a hostile social world.

I was pretty insecure. My whole life then was like I felt like a cork in the ocean. I looked on the whole world as being threatening. I wasn't ready to cope with it at all. It seemed like anything I did could be destroyed so easily. I didn't think of myself as an artist or architect, or as having any imagination. Other people always seemed so much stronger.

I happened to know all the people in the architecture class. So I liked being with them and I liked what they were doing, though I was afraid of doing it myself. I was doing some kind of art work making

advertising posters for a lecture series in college. The guy who ran it
was really impressed with them. And they were pretty good. People
used to pick them up. They were too good. People were stealing them.
They would disappear. The ones that were good would go away over-
night. They'd all be gone.

And I thought my friends were all very talented, very superior.
Well they knew a lot more about architecture, for one thing. But my
feeling was that they were so advanced, so far ahead of me in every
way, that there was no sense in trying.

From this perspective, Mr. Prezinski's comment that his posters in
college were "too good" and "people were stealing them" stands for a
deeper anxiety about the debilitating responses of others, responses provoked by his own self-expression. Running throughout Mr. Prezinski's recollection of the choice between engineering and architecture is the sense
of being unable to stand up for his artistic productions or opinions against
the hostile or destructive reactions of others. Particularly revealing is his
comment at one point that "it's so easy to destroy someone with criticism,
especially when you're learning in the arts." Criticism from others for Mr.
Prezinski is particularly powerful—it destroys.

The appeal of engineering was that it freed Mr. Prezinski from attending to his own subjectivity and from the necessity of defending himself in a social world. Mr. Prezinski thus cites the appeal of the logic and
geometry of the field. In part the appeal of this was the elimination of
more imaginative, emotional "sticky" thoughts and feelings:

I was also good at mathematics. I guess that's probably part of it too.
And I did enjoy it. More applied mathematics than theoretical. I
don't think I was ever into the more abstract things in mathematics. I
liked mathematics for solving practical kinds of problems. But it did
fascinate me. The numbers fascinated me. The relationships. I was
fascinated by geometry. So that's part of why I didn't go directly into
the arts, because I actually did a lot of mathematics. I was sort of on
the fence, there were two sides to me. I liked the logic of engineering.
You know, all through my education it was very rigid. A lot of memo-
rization. There wasn't much creativity. It never got sticky. You were
asked questions and you had to respond in a certain way. There were
answers to every question; all you had to do was memorize it all.

Apart from his interest in mathematics and his talent at it, Mr. Prezinski hoped that engineering would rid him of his desires to be powerful,
big, strong, and sensual. The clarity of numbers and procedure would
eliminate the role of his affect or impulse and the "silent," intermediary

role of the engineer—juxtaposed between architect and audience (the public)—would provide the anonymity he desired. Thus, Mr. Prezinski remembers his "faith" that logic can solve problems:

> I guess all my education was so . . . intelligent. I actually lost touch with intuition and human things. I think that that represented to me the worst and most fatal part of my education. Because I was so convinced of rationalism. It was sick. *[By "intelligent" you mean what?]* Well, rational. It's a belief I guess. Rationalism. You know, like everything is rational. Whatever it is, you've got a science for it. I mean faith in intellect and logic. Logic can solve any problem. And that is actually as much of my religion as anything. It replaced my religion, and my feelings.
>
> After college I didn't really have any doubts about what I wanted to be. I was sure I wanted to be an engineer. It just sort of came to me. I did like the beauty of bridges. That's the aspect of engineering that I liked. I thought I would design those great suspension bridges. Those beautiful things. There was always the beauty of it. That also dragged me into it. I didn't just see it as calculations, but in terms of . . . forms and beautiful things. Bridges mostly. . . . But I was able to work by myself, I didn't have to go out and deal with people socially.

As this last section of interview indicates, Mr. Prezinski was safely hidden in the numbers and remote office of the engineer, sequestered from the intrusive, assaultive eyes of others. Unlike architects, who were constantly involved in social interaction and had to defend their aesthetic judgments, the civil engineer—in Mr. Prezinski's view—was not under such scrutiny, and had to depend less on the salient, public egocentrism of the aesthetic impulse in the world of bridge and tower construction. For Mr. Prezinski, the engineer's social role attributes of anonymity and mathematical orientation were in the service of an anonymous and non-egocentric self-definition. The former attribute meant he would avoid public, social self-expression or self-assertion; the latter attribute meant he had banished his aggression, appetites, desire and sensuality. He comments that "civil engineering was the only way to make a living" after leaving college. This reveals more than economic considerations; for this frightened young man the only way to get into the adult world seemed to be through a vehicle such as engineering, because it would eliminate unsatisfactory parts of himself:

> Things of the spirit weren't in my life in the fifties. I guess I was still operating under the idea that the rational mind and science could take care of everything. Everything was just a matter of science. You could take anything and pure thought could really do something. And

I don't feel that anymore. I feel that—for myself I feel that that was rather empty. I think the world is really much more mysterious than all of that. Rationalism was involved actually in my work in a way too. Like you become like your work, to a certain extent, too. . . . Everything seemed so abstract. My working life, but also my inner life too, I guess. Whatever there was of my inner life.

In adolescence and young adulthood Mr. Prezinski was moving away from his inner world of appetites and desires. It is as if he was saying, "I won't be threatened if I have no impulses or desires." His work would be a shield against his inner life.

Mr. Prezinski's uncertainty about the meaning of his subjectivity is prominent in the interviews, and many of his descriptions of himself alternate between a sense of potency and a sense of impotency. Sometimes he is "like a demon—very strong"; at other times, he says, "I felt like I had all my power taken away." In his descriptions "people are forceful," and "destructive," while he feels "impotent" and like a "cork on the ocean." He is alternately stifled, "threatened," "compromised," "destroyed," and "didn't feel strong enough" to accomplish anything, while at other times he describes himself as "really bold," "dominating," "stronger" than others, "more ambitious," "an autocrat," and "pretty high." We also find a characteristic sequence within the interviews with Mr. Prezinski, which we can summarize as follows: power or strength results in impotence, or the loss of strength. In several associational sequences the former leads to the latter. More specifically, in these sequences Mr. Prezinski starts out with the expression of his initiative, or curiosity, or perception of the world through production of a piece of art and—as a direct result of his subsequent salience—soon is made impotent by someone else's actions toward him. In other words, his power is taken away from him by someone else, and he is too weak to prevent this. Clearly the expression of his inner life—specifically his wishes, interests, and desires—seems both an attractive and a frightening possibility.

The struggle in adolescence and young adulthood to choose between the arts and engineering reflected this uncertainty and the consequences of self-assertion. On the one hand, attracted to the "egocentric," "strong," "sensual" life of the architect as artist, Mr. Prezinski also struggled with his anxiety over his own subjectivity and the possible consequences of asserting and expressing himself. In engineering, Mr. Prezinski found a vehicle for moving away from his subjectivity and defining himself as nonsensual and unselfish.

This pattern of young adulthood self-definition has its roots in Mr. Prezinski's experience of his strength and initiative as a young child. His parents were Polish immigrants, and his father is described as a "weak" man who did not assert himself with his wife. Mr. Prezinski's mother is perceived as "dominant" and "manipulative." From an early age a sense of his weakness and vulnerability seems to have been a major factor in Mr. Prezinski's self-image; this powerlessness is captured in his image of being "like a cork on the ocean." In particular there was a fear of people, and an inability to defend his interests and desires against others. His parents' perceived intrusiveness seems to have been the substrate for later difficulties with others. He comments about his parents at one point that "they were too much for me to cope with." There was, for the young Mr. Prezinski, the considerable anger and rage engendered by his "strong" mother and the disappointment of his "weak" father who offered little opportunity for an alliance with his son. In Mr. Prezinski's early memories we find strong anxiety about the destructive consequences of his rage and anger. In Mr. Prezinski's childhood feelings of being "a cork on the ocean" we see the transmutations of such intolerable anger and rage into feelings of weakness and inadequacy. There is aggression and hostility projected onto others, with a resulting fear of retribution for self-assertion and social expression. Interested in art from an early age, this sensitive child's experience of art became intertwined with the expression of his impulse life and all the frightening consequences of such self-assertion and interpersonal salience. By adolescence and young adulthood we find a sense of self organized around feelings of powerlessness and weakness. The career choice of young adulthood is part of a larger movement away from the subjective—a movement toward the rationality of science and away from the impulsiveness of art and architecture.

In this transmutation Mr. Prezinski is the conquered man, apparently conquered by others and in reality kept in chains by himself. Yet Mr. Prezinski's comments about his choice of engineering as a profession indicate a struggle to define himself separately from his family and his childhood conflicts at the same time that he was unable to do so.

> I liked the mathematical adventure, but then I found out later that it wasn't that much of an adventure. There was a great book I had read on inventors, by Mumford. Fascinating. That intrigued me, and I read about Huxley, Darwin, Pasteur, and others, and it was really thrilling. They really gripped me. That was one aspect that made me kind of excited about science.

In the belief in adventure and the enthusiasm over the lives of great scientists there is surely the underlying hope of integrating his own wishes and desires into an adult role as an engineer-scientist. At the same time, Mr. Prezinski recalls feeling "afraid" and "fearful" of other interests and comments. "My parents suggested I get interested in engineering. I had no basis for knowing that I wanted something else. It just struck me that the only thing that you could really make a living at would be engineering."

Mr. Prezinski was attempting to establish himself outside his family, in the larger world of responsible adults. Yet when he says that he "had no basis for knowing" what he wanted, we see his separation difficulties built into the initial career choice: feeling not informed enough is the essence of leaving home; in a sense we all feel unprepared to make it on our own. Mr. Prezinski, perhaps more than any other member of our group, laments all that he did not get from his parents and others in the way of encouragement, advice, and support to choose a career in the arts. In young adulthood he was struggling with the fact that his parents' wishes, values, and demands were truly not enough to be the sole guides to what his life should be. Engineering was very much tied to his childhood experiences of feeling alternately like "a cork on the ocean" and a "demon." His work was to be a means of being powerless and divesting himself of what he experienced as his demonic inner life, which he felt afraid to affirm in the world. In so doing, Mr. Prezinski was moving into adulthood unseparated from the comforting feeling of being a nonthreatening, "innocent" child among more powerful, controlling adults.

For Mr. Prezinski the definition of being an engineer and an adult were rooted in his childhood struggle with his parents. He let go of important parts of his affect life, represented by his interest in the arts, while moving into the adult world; yet he also found ways to hold onto these aspects of self. The intensity of his conflict in college, for example, indicates that Mr. Prezinski remembers his wishes, desires, interests, and appetites; on the other hand, he does not acknowledge these aspects of self as valid or develop means of expressing them in the world. Rather, he located his interests and desires in other, stronger people. His more "talented," "advanced," and "superior" friends, for example, were the ones who majored in the arts, while he remained on the periphery of this group. His intense interest in his friends' accomplishments and his reliance on them to experience the self-expression he himself desired indicate that Mr. Prezinski tried to affirm or hold onto his own interests and desires, separate from the conflicts within his family setting. Yet the career choice—built primarily around his childhood sense of powerlessness—reflects the difficulty Mr. Prezinski had in affirming his own desires, interests, and appetites in the world.

Mr. O'Hara: "A university was to me an incredible, glorious place."

After college, Mr. O'Hara continued on to graduate school for a Ph.D. in American history. The decision to become an academic was predicated on a particular perception of the university. As an undergraduate, Mr. O'Hara found the academy an "incredible, glorious place . . . rich," "the only place to exist in American society." The "glory" of the University had to do with the "freedom of expression" he experienced there.

[*What was it about the university that was attractive to you?*] It seemed to be at that time the only option in American society. Socially, well, freedom of expression . . . I very much accepted its values. Where I grew up, you see, it was the only cultural resource, of any kind of culture. Very important thing to me, as an introduction. Theater, music, history, literature, people, were experimental. There weren't really very many options elsewhere. It seemed to be the only place where anyone with any imagination could live. The diversified opportunities for experiences on all levels—sensory, music, seeing new things. A university was to me an incredible, glorious place. A place where everything was possible.

The perceived social role attributes of a member of the academy for Mr. O'Hara thus centered around the appeal to the life of the senses and emotion. This role attribute of freedom of expression meant as well a receptivity to dispassionate, free investigation of areas of interest with one's colleagues, and—perhaps most importantly—a commitment to honesty and fairness in one's dealings. The self-definition implicit in such perceptions can be summarized as one who is accepted both whole and as a hero. Both these dimensions of the self "affirmed" in young adulthood are expressed in the following passage:

I had so many expectations in graduate school. Part of that whole trip through the university was the need to justify my existence by being a hero of some sort. It was really spectacular. A terrific burden from my birth. To be recognized as someone very special. The hero assumption. . . . I think the hero is finally accepted, real, there he is, whole—weird, very weird. To be what you should have been when you were a kid, accepted whole. Long struggle to get to. [*Accepted whole means?*] To be accepted for who you are, and that you are a valuable person. That your feelings and emotions count.

I wanted to become a professor, which is an acceptable profession. But it was essential that I should reach such glorious heights. Once I decided I was going to be a scholar another part of me really got inflated by that role. I was going to be a great scholar. So I wanted to know everything. So part of me, my ego, got very invested in it. And when it came to writing the dissertation, it had to be a first-class dissertation. It had to be a major contribution.

For Mr. O'Hara, becoming an academic and joining the "rich," "glorious" world of the university meant being intellectually powerful and gaining validation of his inner life of affect and intuition from others, particularly males. Mr. O'Hara summarized this expectation about the life of an academic when he discussed the importance of being "accepted whole"—a man of intellect, yet with a rich inner life. Further, Mr. O'Hara's perception of the life of an academic was as a great, redeeming adventure, producing recognition and acceptance. This aspect of his young adulthood self-definition is summarized in his term, the "hero assumption."

His desire to do a grand piece of work, recognized by others, was expressed in an ambitious undertaking—a complex, difficult thesis spanning two disciplines:

> So much was involved in that thesis—my search for identity, security on an intellectual level. There was a six-year period of trying to write it. It became such a thing. I had a lot of fantasies about how important it was, the dissertation. It was my passport to security. The thing that established my intellect in the world had to be a major piece of work.

The acclaim and sense of acceptance and validation Mr. O'Hara sought from his career can be seen as well in his description of his relationship to the faculty during his graduate school days:

> I was involved in a very competitive world in graduate school—research, [concern with] who was a seminal thinker. . . . There were bets made on various graduate students. I was one of the golden-haired boys to come out of graduate school in 1956.

Mr. O'Hara's experiences in graduate school were consistent with this pattern of self-definition. He was the "golden-haired boy" of the faculty, and he was offered several prestigious teaching positions at different schools. He was "wined and dined" during job interviews, and he explained that he was "seduced" by the reception he received at the school at which he ultimately chose to begin his teaching career.

The desire to be "accepted whole" and the "hero assumption" were also woven into his decision to marry while still in graduate school. He picked as a wife a woman perceived as "very definite, unconfusing," a woman who "seemed simple" or without hidden motives. Mr. O'Hara's description of her emphasizes the acceptance and nurturance he experienced from her:

> My wife has a very musical voice. She was a good singer, perfect pitch. I think the thing is I really fell in love with this voice. She kind of really swept me off my feet. Really enchanting. . . . The voice and red hair, and there were a lot of things I didn't see about her, but I was really entranced by her.

Fantasies about being a hero can be seen in his description of his wife as his muse, as Mr. O'Hara hoped to engage in historical scholarship that would be well received. Although his wife retained a slight withering in her right leg as a result of polio, Mr. O'Hara remembers fantasizing that he would be able to cure her magically, as a gift to her. Mr. O'Hara's description of his relationship with his wife emphasizes his need to have her be strongly supportive and accepting:

> It was a very symbiotic relationship. There was a lot of identification, at least on my part. It was very symbiotic. . . . She's another part of me. I thought she was a good mother. She extended my sense of boundaries, who I was.
>
> What she did was part of me so that I identified with the things she did. . . . Her ability to love and to give brought out my ability to love and to give.
>
> One of the reasons I married this particular woman, I think, was that she seemed simple and I was complex, and that was a way of pulling a lot together. I was never confused because she was definite and clear. She seemed a very definite, unconfusing person. I knew where I stood, that she accepted me.
>
> There was always a struggle in our marriage between my fantasy and the actual experience. I had this ideal vision of the way in which she functioned as my woman and also my muse. She was pretty entranced by it too. The enchantment which I had to work hard to get. So I was always supportive in the relationship, but also trying to change her. The vision always being that she would transform. And in lovemaking she would. But after the lovemaking she would go back and it was always very frustrating. . . . It was a kind of magical thing that I think I wanted from her. [*What kind of magic did you want from her?*] It's very, very difficult to define, because it's so subjective. The Tinker Bell quality and Peter Pan and the very, very rich use of her voice. She would be my muse to whom I would write.

Mr. O'Hara's patterns of self-definition, affirmed by the career and marital choices of young adulthood, involve the image of the hero, who does important, "redeeming" work and is accepted whole, obtaining love and acceptance for his hard work. Most centrally, Mr. O'Hara would be praised for his work in the responsive, open, clear environment of the university.

In Mr. O'Hara's expectations and wishes about himself in young adulthood note the emphasis on validation, feeling "special," and the avoidance of divided or uncertain responses from those around him. In this, Mr. O'Hara is striving to find a situation where he will not experience the ambivalent pulls, painful rejections, and secretive, mysterious allegiances he knew as a child. Mr. O'Hara's memories of growing up are characterized by a sense of division. People and things are "fragmented," "divided up," "kept apart," "separate," "differentiated." People "throw away a part of themselves"; "boundaries" divide people. He remembers his family as dominated by secretive "plots" and "scenarios." Mr. O'Hara's parents separated soon after his birth; this, combined with the rural setting of the family's home in upstate New York, meant that Mr. O'Hara grew up isolated, the "property" of a perceived unstable, intrusive mother, cut off from the rest of the world by the boundaries of their home. Most importantly, Mr. O'Hara remembers blaming himself for his parents' divorce and their bitter lifelong feud. Mr. O'Hara felt tightly bound to his phobic, manipulative mother, who surrounded her son with demands for secretiveness and webs of verbal fantasy. His older brothers and his father "formed a little subgroup from which I was excluded." His father's rejection was a deep narcissistic wound for Mr. O'Hara. The hope for a father to provide support and a bulwark against his mother was continually dashed by this remote, rejecting figure. Thus, in addition to his father's rejection and his parents' separation, there was the pain, humiliation, and confusion of shifting loyalties and hidden motives throughout his childhood. Guilt over feelings of "collusion" with his mother against his father, and anxieties about his own sexual identity, led to a grandiose idealization of his father in childhood as a hero off on a great adventure. This was the explanation for his father's absence. We thus see disappointment turned to advantage as the rejecting father becomes a powerful heroic image of what it means to be a man. The great man was off on heroic adventures in business and finance (his father was a banker), which kept him away from his family. The divided feelings and conflicting, shifting loyalties to each parent a child would feel in such a situation were never truly integrated for Mr. O'Hara. Childhood was a time of "hidden plots" between the parents toward each other and their children, with "family skeletons" resting unacknowledged, and with injunctions against "spilling the beans" (openly inquiring about or discussing heavily loaded affective issues). For Mr. O'Hara, school became a refuge from the secretive, hidden life at home. From elementary school on, he describes being very invested in the school, with its clear, fair, and ordered rules. Most importantly, Mr. O'Hara's own interests and abilities were experienced in terms of the intuitive, "crazy," feminine world of the senses and fantasy of his mother and the intellectual, unemotional, masculine image of his father. Mr. O'Hara's own interests in self-expression and the world of imagination during adolescence represented "feminine" qualities, particularly frightening for an individual uncertain of his masculine identity. To breach the split Mr. O'Hara felt within himself between his "feminine" intuition and imagination and his "masculine" power, intellect, and strength, to make up for all that was wrong with him and that had resulted in so much pain, guilt, and defeat in childhood, and to avoid forever the agony of rejection became Mr. O'Hara's project in young adulthood. Through his hard work and effort he would make things right and be appreciated for it. The road to becoming a hero accepted by all was the rich, open, male world of the university. Running throughout Mr. O'Hara's experience of young adulthood is a sense of himself as giving gifts to the world and hoping deeply for love and acceptance in return: his dissertation would be a "major contribution," his teaching would be "spellbinding," he would cure his wife of a chronic disease as well as write great works for her.

In this we see the failure to separate from the pain, humiliation, and narcissistic injuries of childhood. For Mr. O'Hara, work was to be a means of making gifts to the world, for which he would receive love in return from surrogate parental figures. Thus, in his role as a university teacher and a husband-father, Mr. O'Hara was replicating the situation he experienced as a child. Yet in this career choice we also see movement separating him from the conflicts of childhood. For example, Mr. OHara says that "the university meant leaving home . . . and a kind of new beginning." This indeed captures the hope for a different future, becoming an adult separate from the mysteries and hidden life of his family. As well, his unarticulated hope was that his marriage—dominated by the need to redeem himself and be accepted—would also mean "a new beginning":

> I had met my wife in Europe, on an extended vacation after college. Then I returned home. After I was there for a month I called my girl-friend up in Stockholm and told her to come over and we got married. . . . I'd left her in Europe and she'd gone back to Sweden to live. [*What was it that you missed?*] Well, I'd become a different person in Europe and had grown and had a real relationship with her. I came home and there was no place for me to be. I didn't belong there. I was aware of my family's attempt to put me back where I was when I was a child. I didn't like this. So I told her to come over and told my parents. . . . They were very upset. And I got married to her much against their will, though they went along.

Further, movement out of his family is indicated by the fact that Mr. O'Hara was giving his gifts, making his contributions, in the larger adult world. He was attempting to be productive in the larger adult world of the university. And even as his giving gifts to the world repeated the conflicts of childhood, it also expressed the faith that he could make things right, that he could have an impact in the world that would "redeem" and "justify" him.

Mr. Goodson: "Doing work solely for the good of mankind"

Mr. Goodson was oriented toward a career in science from college, yet, like Mr. Prezinski, he struggled as well with his interest in the arts. Considerable talent in painting had led him to consider pursuing a career in the field. Yet this was never a really serious consideration because, as Mr. Goodson says, "I never really thought that a man could go into art as a career." Rather, science seemed "the responsible and respectable thing for me to do . . . it had a certain amount of integrity to it." The appeal of science for Mr. Goodson lay in particular, in its social productivity, the anonymity of the scientist's role, and the "storybook image" of the scientist as the independent explorer working in his laboratory. These themes are captured below, as Mr. Goodson recalls some of his initial perceptions and assumptions about science.

Remember, especially during the Sputnik thing there was a big push to go into science. I sort of felt it was the responsible thing for me to do. A kind of respectable direction for me to go in. Science had a certain amount of integrity to it. As opposed to, say, being a salesman or banker or something. I never felt that was really a worthwhile thing, as I still feel it's important for me to be doing a service which I feel is benefiting people in a way that's not solely related to profit making. A profession that a lot of other people, other men, have gained admiration, respect, encouragement, support from the community. I've been exposed to a lot of sort of media interpretation of the scientist's work as being very beneficial to mankind. Somebody who's just doing this work solely for the good of mankind, rather than just for personal profit.

What appealed to me is more in the sense of old science. . . . Like what the great innovators in science like Galileo and Newton and those people did, where they would sit in their lab and they would have a certain desire to solve a problem. They would go about doing it. They weren't working for someone else, and they weren't regimented to stick in one particular field. And there's a lot of glamour and excitement, I felt, about this intellectual curiosity and working on problems by yourself. Sort of following your own interests in working out problems. An independent sort of thing. I think that another thing that appealed to me was that it was a field where you could work independently. . . .

I felt that science was the socially expected thing to do. Out of all the socially accepted activities for a man to get involved in, that allowed for the most independent work.

The images of Galileo and Newton summarize Mr. Goodson's guiding model of the scientist's life: autonomous in the laboratory, away from others and able to work creatively by himself on socially valuable projects. Mr. Goodson's view of his life as a scientist was that he would not have to be exposed to the public eye and would be able to work on his own in a laboratory, without having to defend or justify his work to others:

> I had a kind of vision of working in the lab doing research on my own, following my own interest in a particular research problem . . . that I would be pretty much involved in totally myself, and it would be something where I would be branching out into whatever path seemed necessary to me in order to solve this problem. And it's kind of the old sort of romantic idea of the scientist working alone in a lab.

Here we note the emphasis on a sense of independence: Mr. Goodson would not have to ask for help or be dependent on others. This is the opposite of Mr. Markowitz, who sought reassuring control and accountability in the laboratory. Mr. Goodson hoped to find independence and autonomy in the scientist's role, plus a valued anonymity. We can summarize this pattern of self-definition as being of service and nonegocentric.

As in the case of Mr. Prezinski, the desire to be nonegocentric is strongly rooted in anxieties for Mr. Goodson about being egocentric. For Mr. Goodson, being egocentric has a strong overtone of being feminine, while to be masculine means to be selfless, responsible, restrained, and humble. This was precisely the pattern of Mr. Goodson's sex-role models and indicates his difficulties in harnessing aggression and impulse as masculine attributes. Briefly, Mr. Goodson's father was a frugal, Spartan individual who believed in the value of emotional restraint. His wife enjoyed creature comforts and also seems to have had a more aggressive outlook toward the world. Mr. Goodson can recall fights between his parents in which his mother urged his father to be more assertive at work and in meeting the financial needs of the family. As well, he can recall other times when his father would "cruelly" mock his mother for being too concerned with her own welfare and for being "hedonistic." Mr. Goodson seems to have often sided with his mother as a child. He evidences some anger at his father's restraint and aloofness, experienced as a rejection of his son's interests, enthusiasms, and dependency needs. His father's aloofness and restraint meant the absence of a strong male model to whom Mr. Goodson could turn for advice, support, dependency. He thus lacked an example of what it meant to be an aggressive male person. However, reliance on his mother for such needs—or taking her side in arguments—led to considerable anxiety for Mr. Goodson about his sexual identity, as he felt himself allied with his mother and her hedonism against his father and his restraint.

One area of rejection and uncertainty in particular was the young child's intense interest in drawing and painting, a type of self-expression his father didn't understand. As with Mr. O'Hara, the affective experience of art acquired feminine overtones. Again we see disappointment turned into virtue, as Mr. Goodson idealized his father as a model of what a male should be. The desire to become responsible, independent, and humble mark Mr. Goodson's implemented self-definition in young adulthood and is rooted in the devaluation of the selfishness, dependency, and aggression he experienced as a youngster. The interest in painting and drawing is left behind in this initial life structure, as there is little room in Mr. Goodson's world of young adulthood for the openly selfish, playful, or self-indulgent. From this perspective it is understandable why painting would not be an appropriate career for someone striving so much to define himself as a man.

At the time, Mr. Goodson says, it never occurred to him to consider something he really enjoyed as something that would do for a living. On the one hand, then, the career choice of science was rooted in parental prohibitions and images of what Mr. Goodson as a child and adolescent felt he should be. In a very real sense Mr. Goodson, like our other participants, was relying heavily on his parents for the definition of adulthood. This can be seen in the way he describes being dragged along by unacknowledged forces and obligated to his parents at the time of initial career choice: "I was never really that enthusiastic. I remember my teachers in college urging me on. My parents really encouraged me." On the other hand, we also see some effort to move out of the family. Mr. Goodson chose a career different from that of his father, and he recalls his pleasure at taking a first teaching position far from his home town and living by himself.

Mr. Lonzetti: "The Conquerer"

Mr. Lonzetti entered business school after college, obtaining an MBA and taking a mangerial position with an international firm in the energy field. The self-definition implemented in young adulthood was of himself as the doer of important work and the one who is above criticism. These aspects of self are intertwined in that the latter ensures the former. He remembers after college strong feelings of being judged and a tendency to make constant comparisons between himself and others. A career was the way to safeguard himself, to create a self above judgment or criticism, to insure a positive comparison:

As long as I can remember, it's seemed very important to be very purposeful. To define yourself in terms of some pursuit or purpose of work—important work.

The decision to enter business in part reflects the attempt to affirm or implement this self. Mr. Lonzetti entered business school with "the idea that if I don't know what to do, I'd better get myself some credentials." Credentials are an external status marker that signify his important work and that put him above reproach from others. Mr. Lonzetti comes close to verbalizing this concern with defending himself against negative evaluation when he says that an MBA provided respectability and business school was "insurance."

Consistent with the desire to be safely recognized as superior is Mr. Lonzetti's movement after college away from a major in science, which was replaced by a desire to move into the higher realms of business. This movement in part reflects Mr. Lonzetti's feeling that scientists are mere "technicians," responsible to others, whereas he wants to do "important work," directing others and getting into higher supervisory positions. The sense of self as superior, above criticism, and respected by all is reflected in Mr. Lonzetti's description of his attraction to the "knighthood" he had first sought in the sciences:

> For a while I saw science very much as a measure of one's worth. I mean the scientists were the knights. You know, they were the people that went off in search of discovery. That really primordial force behind the energy and dedication of the really famous and productive scientists. It seemed really a kind of specialized knowledge you could feel proud of and that people looked up to. As a kid, I knew about scientists because the media is full of them.

The world of business became a later means of achieving this knighthood. He thus describes businessmen as the true couriers of civilization, the social managers:

> Now I must admit to some extent that can be a way to describe me when I was younger. In terms of wanting to have some kind of prestige or be associated with people who are doing important things. All those were needs that I have that sort of dictated specific things. Like I think certainly in terms of going into business school. It was sort of accruing credentials. The more qualified I could be, the better. [*Why an MBA as opposed to some other credential?*] Oh, I think that businessmen in this day and age have access to more people. . . . If you wanted to talk about society as a kind of a living organism, the people who've got the mobility and control are the businessmen. . . . Look at the way, historically, in which ideas of one civilization to another are diffused. The role of the merchants or lines of communication in business or goods or supplies played a very important role in the way that the knowledge was transferred. I think frequently you find people with those kind of convictions or pursuits adopting the roles of

business because of the ease with which they can move about. Businessmen are the couriers of civilization, through history.

This affirmation of his "knighthood" was supported by the fact that Mr. Lonzetti picked a prestigious graduate school that was surrounded with status: "I adored my grandfather, who had talked glowingly about so-and-so who had gone to that college, and I had known people from my fraternity who had gone there. And it had a lot of prestige associated with getting good jobs and positions of responsibility."

Most important was the perceived structure of work in the business world. When he took his first position in industry, Mr. Lonzetti comments, "I was naive, I imagined a real organization for work." He had pictured a situation in which responsiblities and work opportunities would be clear-cut, with lines of status, a structure of command, and understandable criteria for advancement. For Mr. Lonzetti this would allow achievement of a sense of self as securely above others—in terms of respect and status—and as doing important work that would not be open to others' criticism and questioning, since he would follow the clearly presented rules and responsibilities for successful completion of his tasks.

Marriage, too, played a role in achieving this self-definition. Mr. Lonzetti married soon after college and chose a younger and relatively unworldly woman who appealed to him, Mr. Lonzetti says, because she needed him.

[*What was it that you found attractive about your wife-to-be?*] First of all sort of the stimulation that she offered about being willing to argue about ideas. And she was quite a good arguer. She would argue past the point of believing things just for the sake of arguing. I felt that she needed me. She's a lot younger than I am. I don't mean to make a big deal out of it but there was that kind of equality that played some role. [*How would you see her need?*] Oh sometimes in various sort of mundane things. I just had a lot more experience in doing things than she did. I had traveled a lot and I had seen a lot of places before she'd ever been there. I knew a lot about science and business, which were sort of technical areas that she felt awkward in. I had had a lot of experience building things, so I knew a little bit about how to use my hands and she didn't really know anything about that. I remember being just absolutely flabbergasted and mad when I came back one time to my apartment and we were going to have coffee and she didn't know how to make it. I just couldn't believe that anybody was 20 years old and didn't know how to make coffee. But basically it's just that I really liked her wholesomeness or something like that. She was a person who was bright, who was not in any way mangled by the world, so to speak.

Here was somebody of worth, yet who supported as well Mr. Lonzetti's wish to be clearly above others, since she, younger and unworldly, "needed me."

The young adulthood years were a time of excitement and enthusiasm for Mr. Lonzetti. The company he worked for

> had a lot of qualities that appealed to me enormously. It was advertised that you worked with a variety of talented people. People would come together to apply their insights and skills to a task. I anticipated a lot of stimulation. The pay was good, and it had a lot of prestige. Somewhat elitist, I guess. I was actually very excited about going to work there. I remember being full of enthusiasm and eager to respond to whatever anybody wanted me to do. . . . I mean, if there was a task to be done somebody just asked you to do it, they didn't ask you how you were going to do it.

In a real sense Mr. Lonzetti felt he had made it into the world of talented, superior people, with his position as a confirmation of these attributes in himself.

> I always liked being with people who were good at what they're doing. . . . In the beginning there was a feeling that the work was very important. Yeah, the feeling of doing something important was greatest when I first started. The feeling of *doing*—actively doing something important.

For Mr. Lonzetti, the hope of defining himself as superior was rooted in anxieties about being inferior—a person worthless and unvalued. In large part this anxiety derives from the manner in which Mr. Lonzetti experienced his aggression and impulse in childhood. Powerfully angry feelings toward his parents were transformed into feelings of inferiority and worthlessness. As with Mr. Anderson, Mr. Lonzetti encountered at an early age a variety of narcissistic injuries that led to the belief that his own aggression and affect marked him as an inferior, unworthy person. Throughout childhood, work—his activity and play—became a means of establishing a sense of superiority, of being above others, and achieving a safe, secure position in which he could feel protected from challenge or criticism. By achieving such a position of certain value and worth—attained in young adulthood by joining the "knighthood" of business managers—Mr. Lonzetti was able to move away from the experience of inferiority provoked by a turbulent, angry inner world. In his sense of self in young adulthood as being over and above others by reason of his important, superior work, Mr. Lonzetti is *the conquerer*.

In Mr. Lonzetti's career and marriage choice we can see both the conflict from the past and the hope for a new future. Work and marriage were perceived by Mr. Lonzetti as ways of strengthening himself and achieving a favorable, superior comparison against others, much as he tried to be invulnerable to humiliation as a child. Much of Mr. Lonzetti's young adult activities were still tied to the experiences of inferiority he endured as a child. But those activities also express the hope of being something else, and different from himself as a child. He was attracted by his wife's youth and vitality as an expression of a "wholesome" future with a "kind of equality." From his description earlier he obviously felt some delight in his fiancée's spunkiness and liveliness, and enjoyed as well being "more experienced"—he was her rescuer and conqueror, who thus showed his superiority. As with his work, Mr. Lonzetti thus was moving in two directions at once in his marital choice: wanting both someone to feel superior to and someone with whom to establish a new "unmangled" life, separate from the past. This dialectic is present in his work choice as well: seeing himself as part of the couriers of civilization that he perceives in the world of business, Mr. Lonzetti expressed the hope of becoming one who has culturally important ideas and plays a role in communicating them in the world. So, as with all of our men, the career and marital choices are expressive of a self-organization tied both to conflicts with the family and to attempts to separate and become an autonomous adult.

Summary: The Predominance of the "Wished-for" Self in Young Adulthood

There are consistencies running throughout the six case studies presented in this chapter. In general, the young adulthood career and marital choices of our group all contained, at their core, a wish to remake or redefine themselves in the mold of a more perfect image. This image is an idealization of the parental figures of their childhood and adolescence. By "ideal" I do not in this case mean the usual usage as "most beautiful" or "truthful." Rather, I refer to the image of perfection and goodness that the young child unconsciously perceives in his parents. For Mr. Markowitz, this idealized image centered around the exclusion of impulse and affect—that it is not only desirable, but also possible, for some individuals to eliminate antisocial thoughts, wishes, and behaviors. For Mr. Anderson this idealized image was largely rooted in the perfection associated with his brother's and father's verbal skill and social poise, as well as in the elimination of "unruly" feelings, thoughts, and behaviors. Again, the belief was in the possibility of actually becoming that way. Similarly, for Mr. O'Hara the perfectionist wish centered on the desire for complete acceptance and love from all; unconsciously, he believed that he could work so hard at this and give so much to people that all would proclaim their acceptance of him, sparing him from ever again feeling rejected. For Mr. Prezinski, the ideal was one of powerlessness—to become without appetite or desire and thus to be threatening to none. Again the belief was that it was possible to eliminate egocentricism and desire from one's world. So, too, for Mr. Goodson and Mr. Lonzetti: For the former, the ideal was to become completely autonomous and to work clearly for the good of others without thought of himself; for the latter, to be so competent and productive as to be invulnerable to criticism. In both cases the underlying wish involved the belief that it really would be possible to be this way—to remove all selfish motives and behaviors and to be respected by all. Each of these patterns can be traced to the struggles of childhood and adolescence; we shall discuss these patterns more fully in Chapter 5.

The career and marital decisions of young adulthood became important means of "making real" these wishes, based on images of perfection from childhood. It is for this reason that we can say that these career choices were rooted in difficulty in separation from the past at the same time as they represented attempts to separate and define onself free of these childhood conflicts the men had experienced. The self one was attempting to "make real" in young adulthood was heavily determined by anxiety over who one really was, by unconscious guilt and shame about the past, and by attempts to remake oneself into a more perfect person determined more by unconscious conflict than by personal choice.

Work in young adulthood was, then, still tightly tied to developmental conflict. For Mr. O'Hara, work was a way of redeeming himself; this need arose out of childhood experiences of feeling terribly unworthy. For Mr. Markowitz the ideal world of the scientist was in part one that would establish him as a clearly good, responsible, socially productive person— aspects of self that he was unsure of. For Mr. Anderson, becoming an expert at his work was in large part a means of triumphing over his brother and proving himself in the eyes of his parents. For these three men, work and adult life were not separate from the conflicts and difficulties of childhood but were partly continuations of them. Work was wrapped up in unfinished business from childhood rather than an enjoyable activity representing personal interest, capacity, desire, and choice, separate from the conflicts and problems of the past. So, too, for the others: For Mr. Prezinski, work was a means of stripping himself of his egocentric desires and avoiding the anticipated retribution for self-assertion he had fantasized as a child. For Mr. Goodson, work was partly a vehicle for proving his manhood. And for Mr. Lonzetti, work was a means of safeguarding himself from the anticipated humiliations from others he had experienced as a child and an adolescent. Yet we find that these choices also represented attempts at separation from these earlier conflicts: At the same time that Mr. O'Hara, for example, is trying to make his life into a gift to his parents, he also describes the university as meaning leaving home, with the possibility of a better life.

Because of this pattern of early narcissistic difficulty in childhood with attempted self-definition through appropriation of idealized role attributes (of a career or marital status), I have found it useful to conceive of the key young adulthood choices of these men as organized predominantly around a wished-for self.* Yet there are several reasons why the wished-for self expressed in these career and marital choices contained the seeds of later loss.

1. These patterns of attempted self-definition were not flexible, nur-turant, confident senses of who one is, but rather a rigid, defensive stan-dard admitting of no compromises. The roots of these patterns as efforts to compensate for intolerable or inadequate parts of self are discussed fur-ther in Chapter 5. It is important here to note, though, that the compen-satory, overdriven nature of these wished-for selves made for later disap-pointment, as they seem scarcely attainable. Mr. Markowitz divides the world into good guys and bad guys as if right and wrong were quickly, easily determined and were never admixed. Thus a person was one or the other. This is a frightening alternative if one detected antisocial, selfish, "bad" impulses or thoughts in oneself. Likewise for Mr. O'Hara: To be "accepted whole" meant precisely that—to be completely accepted and approved by all. Not, rather, to find some acceptance and caring for par-ticular aspects of self among some people; in Mr. O'Hara's fragile and un-compromising world, any rejection or rebuff meant total rejection. Thus, these self-definitions were not reassuring images expressive of values and ideals toward which the person confidently strove, able to experience some failure with humor, resilience, and rededicated effort. Rather, dis-appointments or variation in being this way meant a very deep sense of failure, without easy solace or comfort. Thus, in this group the expecta-tion and assumption about who one is and will be (the wished-for self) are grandiose and difficult to fulfill under the best of circumstances.

2. The wished-for self is exclusionary, exiling or suppressing parts of who one is. For example, Mr. Markowitz's self-definition as responsible and unbiased excluded the irresponsible and biased aspects of himself. That is, there is a sense that Mr. Markowitz did not just want to become a scientist and husband, since he laments becoming the "provider at age 12" and having to keep his nose to the grindstone all his life. And, indeed, how can a total provider take time off? In Mr. Markowitz's world that would be irresponsible. As he says, all his life he was "preoccupied with earning a living." How can someone needing to be completely socially contribu-tive justify a desire to be at times playful and not productive? How can someone who doesn't trust the "deep, dark recesses" of his mind get angry

*This strategy of examining the goal-orientedness of a person's choices and ex-perience has a strong tradition in psychosocial research. The concept of a wished-for self has roots in Adler's notion of the "guiding fiction" that underlies individual development (Ansbacher and Ansbacher 1956). More recently, Levinson has drawn on this tradition with his concept of the guiding dream (Levinson 1978). See further discussion of this point in Chapter 6.

or demand things from others with confidence? In the case of Mr. Anderson, a self-definition as socially poised, verbal, and an expert excludes his "unruly" self—the times when he is not poised but rather upset, angry, jealous, or openly competitive. A "poised" person in Mr. Anderson's definition is not someone who gets angry or ruffled—he doesn't show unpleasant feelings or assert himself in an aggressive fashion. This is the importance of the inability of Messrs. Prezinski, Anderson, and Goodson to integrate more fully their interests in the arts into their young adulthood sense of self: The rejection was broader than merely of the arts as a career; it was of devalued or frightening aspects of themselves represented by the arts. Thus, when Mr. Goodson says he was unable to find a place in his life for his artistic interests because they seemed too egocentric, he is also indicating that he was unable to find a place in his life for his egocentrism.

By rigidly excluding from awareness aspects of self that are pressing for expression yet are frightening or devalued it seems likely that the conflict continues and the probability of obtaining satisfaction in these areas decreases. Mr. Markowitz, for example, gives evidence of never forgetting what he felt he was forced to give up in becoming a provider: the playful, spontaneous, nonresponsible one who wants *not* to have the burden of family support and the life of the scientist constantly on his shoulders. And, as we shall see, Mr. Markowitz is constantly reminded and resentful throughout his life of what he feels he lost in young adulthood. Mr. Prezinski, too, attempted to banish his appetites, aggression, and sensuality. Yet the world serves as a constant reminder for Mr. Prezinski of the egocentrism and sensuality that he tries so hard to expunge from his sense of self.* What is excluded from the predominant definition of self is actually ambivalently held, since the person is attracted to these aspects of self as well as repelled by them. In attempting to rigidly expel these potentialities from one's sense of self the probability of easy satisfaction and integration of these strivings is lessened.

3. The wished-for self is actually ambivalently held as well. That is, the person is both repelled by, as well as attracted to, career and marital

---

*There is a Zen anecdote concerning two monks that expresses very well this point about the ultimate retention of what we so frantically try to get rid of:

Tanzan and Ekido were once traveling together down a muddy road. A heavy rain was still falling.

Coming around a bend, they met a lovely girl in a silk kimono and sash, unable to cross the intersection.

"Come on, girl," said Tanzan at once. Lifting her in his arms, he carried her over the mud.

Ekido did not speak again until that night when they reached a lodging temple. Then he no longer could restrain himself. "We monks don't go near females," he told Tanzan, "especially not young and lovely ones. It is dangerous. Why did you do that?"

"I left the girl there," said Tanzan. "Are you still carrying her?" (Reps, 1961)

choices that represent the wished-for self-definition. This is due to the fact that a) the choices are not rooted in personally valued, freely made decisions but rather reflect a commitment to someone else's values, and b) the wished-for self incorporates the person's negative and hostile feelings about the idealized father. That is, commitment to the wished-for self in young adulthood comes in part from the rigid, uncompromising demand that the participants experienced as children and adolescents that they be different than they were. Their attitudes to the wished-for self incorporate their anger and rage at having to be this way. Mr. Markowitz at several points indicates his anger at feeling accountable and controlled by others at the same time as he seeks their control.

At the same time as Mr. Markowitz strives to be perfectly controlled and responsible, Mr. O'Hara to make gifts to the world, and Mr. Anderson to be perfectly poised and verbal, there is built into the attitude to the career their rage and anger at having to be accountable and controlled as a child, of having one's gifts potentially rejected by these hateful, unaccepting, hurtful people, and of having one's "unpoised" inner life repeatedly rejected by parents who did not understand their son. And so, too, for Mr. Prezinski: At the same time as engineering was a means of being unthreatening and powerless, there was, like a distant echo, his anger at feeling unable to assert himself and the rage he earlier felt at being "disciplined" or "threatened." Similarly with Mr. Goodson and Mr. Lonzetti: There was embedded in their career choices deeper ambivalences about the wished-for qualities they seem so much to seek. Mr. Goodson's choice of science contains sources of frustration that echo earlier conflicts. When Mr. Goodson finds himself in situations where he is made selfless and only of service to others, he feels "taken for granted," "used," and "trapped." At such times he feels he is not being allowed to be himself—as he did when younger with his father—and the rage and anger he felt at such frustration is repeated. And Mr. Lonzetti's wish to be on top carries with it the rage at having to prove himself all the time.

4. Finally, since the career and marital choices take into account only part of who the person is, we find that such choices are often based on only limited knowledge of their field or the other person. This makes it even more unlikely that the wished-for self will occur. An analysis of the role testing and career exploration that occurred in adolescence among this group is in Chapter 5.

So we find these men entering the adult world with a strong hope of being a certain way as the result of their career and marital decisions. We now turn, in Chapter 3, to the fate at midlife of these wishes, dreams, and desires.

3

Midlife as an Experience of Separation and Loss

WHAT IS the fate at midlife of the wishes and dreams of young adulthood? We can approach this question both from a person's subjective experience of events and from an objective or analytic perspective that attempts to reveal fundamental dynamics. The former perspective reconstructs the reported experience of the midlife years, while the latter attends to the evolution of separation issues woven into ambivalently held career choices. In terms of subjective experience, when we listen to descriptions by the participants in our study of the course of their lives past young adulthood, there is a repetitive sense of individuals encountering events profoundly discordant to their expectations and assumptions. These men had clear expectations and assumptions about who they would be in a particular career or marriage, and the reality of midlife evolved in a very divergent direction. From a more distanced, objective perspective we can describe these individuals' midlife years in terms of a continued dialectic around separation-individuation, seen in particular through struggles with an ambivalently held wished-for self in work and marriage. These two perspectives—subjective and objective—come together, since the experienced loss at midlife is of the wished-for self of young adulthood. In this chapter I will first develop a perspective on the midlife years of this sample as one of separation and loss, and then turn to the dialectic around separation from parents reflected in this loss.

A Loss at Midlife

In the previous chapter we saw that the young adulthood years of the participants in our study were a time of affirmation of particular patterns of self-definition, through specific career and marital choices. These years are characterized by the investment of time, money, and energy in professional establishment and advancement, and—in many cases—the creation of a family of one's own. The young adulthood years of this group were ones of hard work and achievement. These individuals were, by external criteria, successful during their twenties, evidencing promotions and increasing responsibility in their work. At work, advanced professional training gave way to first jobs and subsequent advancement in their occupations. Yet attention to the fate of self-definition at midlife allows us to understand the loss experienced at this time, the loss of a self organized around the key work and marital choices of young adulthood, as reconstructed for each of our six men in the previous chapter.

Recent theoretical and empirical work on loss and grief has proceeded in two directions: (1) to extend our concept of loss from that of separation from concrete attachments (for example, the death of a loved one) to situations that involve, fundamentally, the (anticipated or actual) invalidation of central interpretations of and assumptions about the world in which the individual lives (Carr 1975; Marris 1975; Weinstein and Platt 1973); and (2) to extend our understanding of grief reactions beyond the proximate time of loss. A variety of studies have found evidence of loss and grief reactions among individuals in such disparate situations as urban relocation and immigration (Fried 1963; Marris 1975).

Although the precise nature of loss remains an area of some uncertainty, the primary utility of such a paradigm for the understanding of midlife lies in the attention to the impact on the individual of experiences producing dramatic alterations in the sense of self. This developing perspective sees the fundamental substrate of all losses as disruption of the individual context of psychic stability by experiences fundamentally discrepant to trusted understandings of self-in-the-world. That is, theories of loss and grief are in general essentially concerned with how individuals respond to a particular type of experience: that which invalidates or destroys the web of meaning in which we all live our lives. Within this context, situations of change in general partake of losses because the continuity of expectation and assumption about oneself-in-the-world is dramatically altered. The experience of loss arises out of a confrontation with experiences sharply discrepant to one's understanding of the world, with a resulting "crisis of discontinuity" between the sense of "who one was" and "who one will be." From this perspective, "loss" is always of oneself, not others, as the particular understanding of self that is organized around the lost attachments and commitments (e.g., to a marriage partner or career) is threatened.

This literature provides an opening to the consideration of some problems of midlife. The loss in our group is of the self affirmed by career and marital choices. The experience of loss arises out of a confrontation with discrepant experiences that accumulate during midlife; experiences that invalidate one's understanding of "who I am." Because of the accumulation of such experiences, salient understanding of self-in-the-world is threatened or disintegrated; this erosion of meaning forces the search for new interpretations to restore the continuity and meaningfulness of experience. In situations of concrete object loss, urban relocation, or immigration, the precipitant of the experience of loss is sharply located in time and easily defined (e.g., the death of a spouse, moving away from a home one has lived in for many years), while in cases of loss of self the threats to established interpretations of oneself are more subtle and intangible, but nonetheless powerful. In our group, the threat to trusted definitions and interpretations of self took the form of an accumulation of experiences that invalidated or left unfulfilled the self organized around the key career and marriage choices of young adulthood. We can conceive of this loss, then, as a slow erosion of understanding of self, rather than the more dramatic, sudden alterations of self in, for example, cases of concrete object loss.

The crisis preceding the career change (described in the first chapter) is this one of loss of self, as these men struggled with experiences puzzling to them—hard to understand, at times frightening, and at variance with their sense of who they are. In this chapter I want to describe the manner in which midlife represents a struggle with experiences discrepant to self-definition. In the next chapter I will outline different patterns of recovery from this crisis, in which—through a process functionally similar to grieving—the self is reconstituted and the career change emerges. The ways in which self-definition comes to be undermined and threatened can be reconstructed from the patterns of discrepant experiences during young adulthood and mid-life in the following case studies.

Mr. Markowitz: "That wasn't my picture of myself."

Mr. Markowitz was a research scientist through his early midlife years. We saw in Chapter 2 that his decision to become a scientist was made in college, fulfilling a childhood dream of the scientist's "ideal life" as highly socially responsible, omniscient, and nonaffective or unbiased.

When we inquire as to the fate of young adulthood self-definition for

Mr. Markowitz we find that discrepant experiences began to accumulate during the midlife years that invalidated the sense of self as one who is responsible, controlled, and impulse-free. First a confrontation with the "real" nature of science took place as Mr. Markowitz found himself in a world where—as everywhere—impulse, lying, cheating, and corruption did indeed exist. Although his descriptions of the early years in science are marked by a sense of participating in an enterprise with dispassionate men in the midst of reassuring structure and control, as Mr. Markowitz progressed in his career, a more troublesome view of the scientist's life appeared. This view was based on incidents of assistants who falsified data, bitter conflicts with colleagues, and a sense that the end-products of science were not necessarily socially beneficial. In his interactions at work Mr. Markowitz seemed especially shocked at the intrusion of human passions and conflicts into the everyday life of the scientist:

> I found one time that a research assistant was giving me the results he thought I wanted, rather than the data from the instruments. . . .
>
> One position was especially difficult. Because I was working under the supervision of the chief of the laboratories, who was not a nice person at all. There was a real scramble for power, a lot of politics. In fact there was a real clash in personalities. I was in a supervisory position. I had a section of very fine engineers. And we were intact. The man I was telling you about felt that this was a kind of threat to him, I suppose, and he set about to break up the group. To disperse them. And that was wrong. Yet he was really interested in going places in the government. I don't mind that, but in a bad way, that is, he would step on people to get where he wanted. [*How did he do that?*] Well, he would accentuate the people's mistakes. There are ways of saying to your superior that this person is a shmuck or a son-of-a-bitch or really stupid and doing it nicely so that it isn't apparent, and that's what he would do. [*Was he critical of you?*] Oh, yes, he was extremely critical of me. We had a terrible stand-off fight, I was ready to leave and there were times when we couldn't speak civilly to each other.

Mr. Markowitz also recalls his widening perception as to the uses of science:

> I began to realize the antisocial nature of the things that scientific discoveries were put to. [*For example? What were you thinking about then?*] Well it's hard *not* to think of an example. DDT—there's a good example. A completely unmalicious thing. You develop something that kills mosquitoes. It's good to kill mosquitoes. Everybody admits it's good to kill mosquitoes. In fact you can actually get rid of

malaria if you just get rid of mosquitoes. So they go ahead and they spray everything with DDT. Because obviously it's good to kill mosquitoes, not realizing that when you're doing anything on a scale that large you're going to somehow change the balance. This was before anyone knew about how long DDT stays in the ground or the effects it has on birds, fish, human beings. You never know the uses things will be put to. . . . I thought maybe it was business that was the demon. Because business was interested in profit and not in social use. I was in science because of its social use. I think somebody stated that the trouble with Western or world science or technology is that it asks the question, Can it be done? not, should it be done?

These experiences were important, we can infer, because Mr. Markowitz was struggling with similar concerns in his own life. That is, he was confronting the realization that not only science, but he himself, struggled with unruly human emotions. In his work not only were other scientists coming to be seen as "corruptible" and impulse ridden, but he himself was subject to these difficulties: Mr. Markowitz, as well as others, participated in bitter laboratory struggles, and offers of high-salaried corporate administrative posts led to worry about his own corruptibility. The "temptation" Mr. Markowitz felt to accept such offers were powerfully discrepant to his sense of himself as devoid of self-aggrandizing or antisocial motives:

I never was asked to do any antisocial thing. I was extremely lucky because I don't really know what I'd have done when my family was growing up. It's very difficult to leave a job when it's your only source of income and you're not sure there's another one. And there were damn few jobs in science where somehow it doesn't work its way into something bad. You always have the sneaking suspicion you're being compromised. . . .

I turned down offers to get into the private sector, in administration, where salaries were high, partly because I didn't care for that kind of work and partly because I was a little afraid. You can resist everything except temptation, and I really didn't want to get into a position where I was making a lot of money and then it would turn out to be very, very important to me so that I would find myself doing things that I really didn't want to do.

In addition, Mr. Markowitz not only came to see that some science may have antisocial results, but his own role did not allow the sense of social productivity he originally sought. He found himself working on the evaluation of consumer goods, a far cry from the fantasy of eliminating disease that had first helped lead him into the field. His enjoyment of the work he was doing in consumer testing was "always pulling against a feel-ing of social responsibility. Perhaps I should be pointing more directly at a social problem like working on a cure for cancer or something like that."

It is in the areas of interpersonal relationships, though, that self-defi-nition received perhaps its most severe shaking. Mr. Markowitz, com-mitted to a sense of self as controlled and impulse free, found himself ex-pressing bitter anger and rage at his wife and children. Child rearing was, by his own description, characterized by bitterness and tension between himself and his two sons. He describes this difficulty in the following mov-ing passage:

> If they were ordinary people not related to me I would feel privileged to know them. You know they're really nice. [*But there was some dif-ficulty?*] Oh! Terrible! Terrible difficulties. It was almost a standing joke. Our oldest son left the house when he was sixteen or seventeen, I think. And the speech he made was, "I'm glad to be leaving this fuck-ing house. The only regret I have is I'm leaving these poor helpless children in your care." And as each one left they would repeat the same speech. A man would have to be made of stone not to think "What the hell is going on?"
>
> I think it's normal and natural for there to be trouble between the generations, especially during adolescence. I think perhaps there may be something else at work if it strikes too deep, if it becomes too corrosive, as it did on my part. Last winter [*one son*] wrote me a very disturbing letter . . . in which he told me that he had very bad mem-ories of his childhood . . . that his memories were of like walking on eggshells when he was around me. I wasn't consistent, he never knew when I might fly off the handle and explode in rage. And he was find-ing things about himself now, and he felt impelled to tell me this. So I wrote back recalling my own memories which were just the opposite. Of course I lost my temper sometimes. But I felt that this was an im-pression but it wasn't an accurate impression of his childhood with me. I felt that if it were accurate I would have been behaving in a ter-rible way. That is, I think I'm not that kind of person. I don't think that's my picture of myself.

Note the sense of discrepancy and discontinuity in interpretation of self implicit in his comments, "What the hell is going on?" and "I don't think that's my picutre of myself." The anger and rage he expressed as a father and husband were powerfully discrepant experiences for Mr. Markowitz, as was his evolving life as a scientist. In this case the loss of self was rooted in experiences discrepant to Mr. Markowitz's organizing definition of himself as a scientist and father who had banished impulse and affect and who was a respected individual, intellectual, dispassionate, and wise. This sense of discordance is clearly expressed in his statement, "you can resist everything except temptation." By age 35 Mr. Markowitz reports the beginning of a personal crisis in which life became "pretty disorderly." He comments:

> I felt I had an incomplete way of looking at myself and looking at the world. In other words it was important for me to go into motivations, to go into the reasons why I felt certain things. You can't live a satisfactory life if you're always living it from the outside, looking on the outside. You have to turn inwards sometimes.

Mr. Anderson: "That was not my image of a husband."

Mr. Anderson entered the midlife years as a lawyer, with a self-definition organized around the attributes of propriety, expert professional status, and verbal proficiency and poise. But after several years in a law firm Mr. Anderson came to see that law was not entirely the romantic or honorable profession he had expected. His position in the firm was in the Family Law division, and, contrary to his expectations at the time of law school, he found that lawyers were often concerned less with their client's benefit than the firm's fee; that the courts were social systems oiled by judges' like or dislike of lawyers they encountered; that he was expected to participate in the social flow as well—lunches, golf, etc.—with wealthy clients; and that his own sense of honor was often obscured by his work mediating family disputes over custody and ownership in divorce proceedings. Lawyers were, then, not just elegant barristers, but also competitive individuals attempting to get ahead in an ambiguous world. Participation in such situations was discrepant to Mr. Anderson's definition of himself as "honorable" and "poised."

Several of Mr. Anderson's descriptions of his experiences as a lawyer emphasized the gap between what he encountered and what he earlier expected:

> I had a naive idea about law practice. Sure you made contacts, but you got clients because you were good. And you didn't have to play golf every Saturday or something. Or go to the right parties and belong to the right church. . . .
> I was doing very well in my law practice. About to be made a partner. But I was developing what I think are rationalizations. What I really wanted to do was to contact what I really wanted to do. Like I didn't want to really join the gold club. I didn't want to curry clients. [*Curry clients?*] Yeah, I mean develop clients. You curry favor [*laughs*] and there's a whole kind of things you sort of gotta do. Just seemed like a disgustingly neat package. You know, I had some friends. I just didn't like what I saw coming out from them.

There would be a typical pattern of the pecking order in the firm, which is how a client was handled. Everyone was really all kind of sucking around the client. Basically the same thing had to happen to be successful. To keep working with people and finally get enough trust with them to let you talk to them and eventually throw wheels for them because the more clients, the more money that the firm gets.

There weren't enough questions that I wanted to ask. Ask a partner that you're working for why his fake smile. Why the fake smile with the clients? There's no love there.

I didn't like the system. You can call me almost a radical. But I didn't like the well-oiled way the judge would award fees and if he happened to like you the fee was real good. And I would have preferred to have been on the side of a person that was exposing those— not really anything unethical, but just a clubby, nice, little "you take care of us we'll take care of you."

Plus there's a lot of prima donnas. There were two or three especially in the firm. One of the partners I didn't get along with at all. He would call me up and cuss me out for some minor thing. I can't call up the exact things, but it wasn't big. Whatever it was, it was tricky and silly but it affected me directly and I would get really sore about it. I would blow my cool, I guess.

Further, Mr. Anderson's sense of his verbal-analytic skill as a lawyer had come into question. He was successful in his work, but getting there had raised questions for him as to how expert he really was: "I was in about the middle third of my law school class. Not great grade-wise." In this regard, too, Mr. Anderson was finding that the verbal-analytic skills demanded of the lawyer were not as appealing as he had anticipated. Over time he began to confront the realization that continued advancement in his field implied commitment to activities that did not truly interest him.

A lot of my life was caught up with doing all the things I had to do in the firm or I'd lose my job. You know, in the first several years, until things began to settle down and I began to see what I had to do to keep going in the firm and become a partner. At that point I looked at myself and said, "Wait a minute! In forty years all I'll have is a memory of a lot of briefs that I wrote and things like anecdotes and funny things that happened. Everything was so verbal. That's all a lawyer does. I've always enjoyed doing manual work with my hands as well. And that's almost exactly what I expressed to one of these partners. He said, "I know what you mean." He was pointing to the drawers, to cases and all kinds of matters that come up, and said, "That's all I've got."

Rather than enjoying the "poised," "expert" life of the lawyer, organized around verbal-analytic skills, Mr. Anderson experienced other interests and urges, representing devalued parts of himself:

> I took a sculpting course at night just to try it. I did incredibly bad
> pieces. They're awful. [*laughs*] But I *loved* working with my hands.

Law had failed to define Mr. Anderson as separate from his brother,
providing undivided love and attention from his parents. While Mr. Anderson had been doing "not great grade-wise," his brother had graduated
high in his class at the Wharton School and had soon risen in the ranks of
an Atlanta accounting firm. Mr. Anderson's slower ascent toward promi-
nence was an experience very much at variance with his self-definition as
an expert, possessing skills, abilities, and social graces that marked him
both as distinctly separate from, and equal to, his brother:

> At one point when I was practicing law I was talking to my parents.
> They were visiting. I was thinking about a shift in career. I kept try-
> ing to talk to my father. I just wanted to talk it over, to air my feel-
> ings, to give him a little information about his boy. During the con-
> versation at some point I said, "I didn't do that well in law school
> anyway, grade-wise." Which was true, OK? But that was a big ad-
> mission—for me to admit that I wasn't perfect. I didn't knock off
> straight As and do everything number one in my class. He said, "Oh,
> yes, you did!" He had it in his head that of course it was so.

In this vignette we can see Mr. Anderson's desire for attention and respect from his father in his attempt "to talk" with him—to provide "a little information about his boy." These tender words, spoken by an adult
man who saw himself momentarily as a boy offering self explanation to
his father, reveal deeper meanings of the conversation beyond that of discussing Mr. Anderson's future as a lawyer. The last sentences reveal the
wish to be taken seriously as a separate person, seen for who he is, rather
than in the image of his brother. We might say that again Mr. Anderson
felt "swallowed up" by his brother. Law, in this respect, had failed to
make him into the person his parents would appreciate in his own right.
This sense of failing to establish his own place in the family—despite his
achievements as a lawyer—can be seen if the following excerpt:

> Even after we were both married I had some feelings that [*my
> brother*] seemed to love to sort of dominate a situation. He'd try to
> create an atmosphere in a group of people. Whereas somebody would
> have to come to me. I might talk to one other person but basically I
> wouldn't initiate much. He's much more developed. Or he was, you

know. A lot of extroversion. And laughing at his own jokes. Something that I would never do. He always seemed in control of everything, to be at the center.

At home, too, Mr. Anderson's inner urgings became increasingly discrepant as time went on to his belief in the social graces and "propriety." By midlife Mr. Anderson had been married several years and felt increasingly unable to maintain a "proper" and "correct" role as a husband and father. Mr. Anderson felt at times restrained by the demands of child rearing, and at times in bitter disagreement with his wife. Such feelings were difficult for Mr. Anderson, since they violated his image of a father and husband:

> My wife once said to me, "You're carrying around a lot of obligations that don't exist!" It was hard for me to be a parent and do anything else. If you're a family person, people expect certain things from you. You get home at a certain hour and it's dinner time and you horse around with the kids—that would happen sometimes and other times I just wouldn't feel like it at all. Also, I was too passive with my wife. We disagreed sometimes about how to handle our daughter. I was a sounding board but I had the feeling she'd make the decisions. I would be fairly patient. I'd listen, almost like an image, you know. I wanted to say, "I can't listen to you anymore, let's do it my way." But I wouldn't say that. I'd be immensely conciliatory and very, very careful.

Around age 35 Mr. Anderson found essential definitions of himself as an expert, highly verbal, proper, and poised lawyer and husband sharply called into question. Mr. Anderson remembers spending "more and more time at the office . . . avoiding contact with my family" but feeling equally unhappy at work. "I was operating at a very basic level, because I felt very lost at that time."

Mr. O'Hara: "The university . . . was a rude surprise."

Mr. O'Hara decided after college to pursue a career as an academic and went on for graduate training in history. As we saw in Chapter 2, he took his first job as a faculty member at a prestigious, small urban university. Mr. O'Hara's self-definition centered around being a "hero" and being "accepted whole." Being a hero meant producing great work or gifts to others for which he received acclaim, and being accepted whole meant receiving support, validation, and encouragement—for both his intuitive and emotional responses, as well as the power of his intellect.

However, by his late twenties Mr. O'Hara began to find that his life as a university faculty member was a more complex one than the "rich," "glorious" future he had anticipated. First, Mr. O'Hara found his place in the university different than he thought. He was not going to be a hero, accepted whole by all. The hoped-for reaction to his thesis—completed after several years teaching, in his late twenties—didn't occur. This thesis was a prodigious undertaking for Mr. O'Hara, surrounded by powerful expectations as to what it would produce:

> I had such an investment in my thesis that it kept me for great periods of time from enjoying my family or teaching how I wanted to teach. Actually from doing almost everything I want to do. It became such a thing, so much like climbing Mount Everest, maybe building Mt. Everest. So that when it was done, five years of my life was twisted up. Only three people read my dissertation [*laughs*] and the typist.
>
> It took an enormous amount of energy to get it done, and then when it was done I remember that there was a great release of some sort. Then I went back to the department for the oral examination. It was exciting to have it done, but it was a terrific comedown. I felt like committing suicide. I'm not very suicidal, but that's the only way I can explain it. The feeling of having put off so much, sacrificed myself physically, emotionally. I was so bitter about what had happened. All that work hadn't given me what I wanted. [*What was that?*] I'm not sure. Success, the hero's welcome, trumpets playing, for everyone to clap or something. Finally getting my father's love.

The disinterest or lack of response to his thesis was actually experienced by Mr. O'Hara as a profound rejection of his intellectual life, his masculinity, by the very surrogate-fathers whose approval and "father's love" Mr. O'Hara had been seeking.

Further, the desire to be "accepted whole" was frustrated at the university where Mr. O'Hara was teaching by the reality of constant politicking between faculty members, in which Mr. O'Hara's own status was unclear. Mr. O'Hara thus experienced a demand for divided allegiances and uncertain alliances. He recalls several experiences of secretive machinations between faculty members:

> I felt very constricted by just being a faculty member. It was a very small faculty and incredibly conformist in terms of its own peculiar image of itself. I mean it wasn't like going to a large university where there's a lot of diversity. It was extremely uniform, incredibly powerful. A small department. Intense competition between several non-tenured faculty—the tenured faculty felt frustrated by the students and therefore took it out on the junior faculty. [*laughs*] You had your allies and your enemies everywhere.

There was much bitterness, politicking, and secrets. For example, a close friend of mine, a professor from graduate school, had become chairman there through a difficult period. They really wanted this guy where I was teaching . . . they invited him to visit to find out about him, for a week, and they wouldn't let me see him—they kept it a secret from me as long as they could. [*Why?*] They didn't want us to see each other. They gave him an hour to talk to me.

Another example. I had been pretty much assured, but not on paper, that I would get tenure because I was invited to come with that. I had every reasonable expectation. What happened was the chairman, in a typical kind of politics, didn't want to be chairman anymore and the university wanted to upgrade all of its departments constantly in competition with all the other universities, and so they wanted a world-famous scholar as head of the department, and so they had to go outside of the department. They went out and got this shmuck [*laughs*] but he wouldn't take the job unless all the tenured slots not filled were his. And so they reneged on my expectations. They told me secretly and didn't even tell the others until much later. Most of them probably don't even know now how the decision was made. I was appalled at all these hidden machinations.

The failure to be "accepted whole" can be seen as well in the report of criticism and evaluation of his teaching, where Mr. O'Hara came to feel that his "intuitive, sensory approach to things" was rejected by his seniors and that he had to conform, impotently, to their demands:

The climate was so repressive. Coming in as a new teacher, they indoctrinate you into the process, and the process was very bizarre, I found. Very tight. Incredibly structured. I felt caught and molded. I was working in a school with an unbroken tradition of master-type structure. Almost everything that I wanted to talk about was forbidden [*laughs*], such as feelings. An intuitive, sensory approach to things. Just very, very forbidden. Teaching for instance, a course in medieval history, with an approach that was very different even though we had a standard source in the department. And the department had a standard interpretation—extremely analytic, very conceptualized, and everything had to be snaked in according to an intellectual model. I found that a bit boring. So destructive. I guess they figured I would be a nice person for them to mold.

I was a very popular teacher. I had lots of people come to my lectures. I was an excellent lecturer. I made love in my lectures. I really was a real spellbinder. [*laughs*]

When I arrived I found that I didn't have any courses of my own. They were all team taught. There were very few personal courses and they were all taught by the senior faculty. So there was just incredible political activity to get any kind of freedom or to get anything you had to be a toady to somebody. There was a lot of division among the members of the faculty. Totally unsupportive and really uncomfortable. It was kind of a blow to discover what was happening. I was very resentful. I felt I couldn't meet all their different demands and preserve myself in terms of my own basic personality structure. It blew my mind really. I wasn't willing to subject myself to another person's system.

Note Mr. O'Hara's sense of being surrounded by a hostile environment that will change him, expressed in such phrases as "indoctrinated" and having "to subject myself to another person's system." Once again, Mr. O'Hara found himself in the middle of what he perceived as a secretive, repressive world, in which plots, tensions, and scenarios abounded. Thus Mr. O'Hara found himself experiencing once more divided allegiances, with conflicting loyalties and a divided inner nature. Far from being accepted whole, as a man with feelings and intellect, he and his affective life were again rejected:

I felt that staying in the university meant suppressing large parts of me. My intuitive self and sensation, my images, things which were forbidden as evidence. In the humanities even, maybe especially it is even worse there. On a research and teaching level there is the same desire for some sort of scientific perfection of one's methodology, one's demonstration, proof. And so the strongest parts of myself were not, not ordinarily permissible. I thought I'd be able to teach in whatever way I wanted. Certainly I thought that after my dissertation I could write about whatever I wanted. The university was a rude surprise.

At home, too, Mr. O'Hara found his sense of self as heroic and accepted whole called into question. Mr. O'Hara was finding that the simple, accepting woman he had married had her own complexities. At times she seemed secretive and hidden as well. His wife's first pregnancy came as a surprise to Mr. O'Hara, as did a family trust his wife had access to during a period of financial stress. The everday conflicts and differences of marriage were a source of difficulty for both parties:

My marriage, our relationship became brittle. We began to share much less. I had to teach a full load and my wife became more of a housewife. Our roles became more differentiated, we grew further apart. The difficulty in the marriage was I became so learned and so verbal that I became a different person than who my wife married and I think she found that hard to deal with. She avoided issues between us, trying to smooth things over. She got very good at not complaining but it got like where if she'd just blown up, it would have been better. But our lives just got grimmer and our relationship thinner. She accepted our conflicts silently, kept everything inside. I didn't know how she really felt about me.

Note in this the sense of rejection and uncertainty as to whether he was truly valued by his wife. The failure to be accepted whole—the experience of his feelings and wishes being excluded in the family setting—is apparent in his recollection of his family's attitude toward him at this time:

The family was very resistant to hearing about how I felt. They didn't want to know how I felt. I was imprisoned in my study writing my dissertation or preparing lectures as far as they were concerned. And any attempt I'd make to talk about my feelings at the dinner table, I'd be shut up. So I really felt I couldn't be who I was. Actually I guess I married a woman who was completely uninterested in my feelings. When I discovered those days that she really didn't want to know anything about me, it was kind of a blow.

Further, Mr. O'Hara was finding that he was not the heroic, potent lover, finally, who through his sexuality had total access to—and acceptance from—his wife:

There were many ways I wanted to change her, to make her into my ideal image. But she resisted my attempts to, say, physically change the way she dressed. She was a very strong person. Resistant to any change from the outside. The reality of her was really much more complex, sometimes not satisfying. [*What did you feel was missing?*] The enchantment of her, feeling she was my muse, I had to work hard to get that. I was always supportive in the relationship, but also trying to change her. The vision was always that she would transform—and in lovemaking she would. But after lovemaking she would go back and it was always very frustrating. I would make her into what I wanted sexually and please her and that would please me and we would become briefly very close but fifteen minutes later she'd be her other self, her old self. Keeping silent, unresponsive, very into herself. Totally unaware of my feelings.

The continued presence of the slight polio in his wife's leg became a symbol of Mr. O'Hara's failure to produce a perfect gift for his wife. He "hardly noticed" this when they were courting and early in their marriage, but over time he "became more and more preoccupied with this disfigurement I saw in her." His inability to cure his wife's polio stood as an ever-present discrepancy to his sense of power, his heroic myth about himself:

> I guess I felt powerless in the relationship, powerless to change it in a long-term way. I couldn't stand that. And it was very related to the sense of powerless to cure the polio. The reality of this chronic disease transformed my power. As part of my own myth that I couldn't achieve, we couldn't achieve such a joy and union and banish it.

The frustrated wish to feel redeemed and accepted by his wife, to make his life into a gift for her and to win the approval and love he so desperately demanded is movingly expressed in Mr. O'Hara's memory of actually making a present for her:

> When I finished all of my dissertation, the last thing was that I had to write a five-hundred-word abstract. That was like getting blood out of a stone. That took two solid weeks to do and that really broke something in me. I didn't ever want to write again. I still find it difficult to write letters. And when I finished the thing early one morning, I thought of the things I used to do as a child. I'd get up early around five or six in the morning and go downstairs and make something, often out of clay. Sometimes a house. So I'd have this thing done by the time my parents got up. [*And what would happen then?*] Oh, they were very, very confirming. I mean they were very good about it and liked it. And it was often as a present.
>
> We had some clay in the basement that I had bought. I worked with it and brought it up to my wife as she woke up and gave it to her. It was my present, a gift for her. Partly, maybe, it was compensation for all the years of bitterness between us. You see, I really liked working with my hands. I was so really bitter about what had happened to me as an intellectual, as a scholar.

By midlife, Mr. O'Hara—rather than a hero with an accepted inner life—found himself in a secretive, mysterious world similar to that he had known as a child: "I felt like a child again . . . a reexperiencing of not being accepted and being different and asked to be something other than who I was." The concern with who he wasn't is linked to the question of who he was: Mr. O'Hara had failed to become a powerful man with an inner life acceptable to all.

Mr. Prezinski: "I thought I was dead."

Mr. Prezinski gives sharp illustration of the role before midlife, in young adulthood, of threats to his sense of self. Mr. Prezinski entered young adulthood with a self organized around *nonsensuality* and *nonsalience* expressed in a career choice of engineering. His most characteristic complaint about his young adulthood years during the 1950s—how "boring" they were—offers a clue to his early, continuing struggle with experiences discrepant to his sense of self.

Mr. Prezinski took his first job with a multinational corporation, at a branch in Puerto Rico. The easy life in Puerto Rico, a new experience for the son of an immigrant family from Chicago, was a mixed blessing for Mr. Prezinski. He participated in a lot of activities in Puerto Rico: learning how to fly, living by the ocean, buying a car. While the opportunity to learn more about his urges and appetites may seem like an engaging experience, it was not entirely so. After several years in Puerto Rico, Mr. Prezinski decided that the "material stuff was no good":

> I mean I had everything I wanted. I had a sailboat. We had all the material things; there were a lot of women, and I didn't have to work too hard. After a few years I decided all of this material stuff was no good. I needed something more basic. So I volunteered to go to Japan. I wanted to get rid of all that crap that I had, the car, boat, that whole life. I wanted to go to Japan because I felt that Japan would be more cultural, and spiritual. I wanted to study meditation.

Mr. Prezinski asked to be transferred to a company branch in Japan in order to study "spirituality" more carefully. Material stuff, Mr. Prezinski says, is a "bore." We can see Mr. Prezinski's decision to leave Puerto Rico as in part reflecting his struggle with the sensual and with experiences that appeal to his affective life. The decision to move to Japan—toward "higher" spirituality rather than "lower" materialism—in part reflects the continued safeguarding of his self-definition as nonaffective and nonegocentric. The interesting thing about this transfer is that obviously engineering was not serving as an effective shield against Mr. Prezinski's inner life—he was finding himself filled with desires and appetites. An indication of this can be gained from Mr. Prezinski's comment about a vacation in the Caribbean:

> I didn't have a very good time. There was tremendous sensuality on those islands. I was aware that it was very sensual. But I didn't really deal with it properly. The tropical climate, the smells, were just so sensual. And there were women that were so primitive. So basic. And I partially realized it. And then on the other hand, I was sort of looking down on them. You know I had a holier-than-thou attitude about them and that was too bad. I regreted that much later, having been like that. Having been so unable to be loose. I couldn't make any progress. [*What kind of progress do you mean?*] Well, being more of

a human being and less of a machine. Which I thought I was. I guess maybe I didn't realize until later how machine-like I was.

Note again in this interview segment the presence of a stimulating experience exemplified by the tropical ambience and the existence of "primitive" women, and Mr. Prezinski's reaction of anxiety and the movement away. Further, note that Mr. Prezinski neither ignored, accepted, or forgot about the invitation represented by the women. Rather, he was both attracted and repelled by them at the time, and upset by this reaction. Mr. Prezinski's own attraction to such women and the "sensual" opportunities they represented, were for him discrepant experiences. The intensity of difficulty for Mr. Prezinski around experiences appealing to his affective life are a signal of his continued exclusion of aspects of self and his attempts to safeguard himself against constant discrepancies derived from the perpetual, ceaseless invitation of the world to sensual pleasure and egotism. Boredom is understandable, in this context, as reflecting a blockage of the ability to experience freely. Instead of the lure of "primitive" women and "materialism"—opportunities where he would have to expose his sensual, egocentric desires—Mr. Prezinski in the 1950s moved toward what he calls "superficial" relationships and a nonacquisitive style of life. Thus Mr. Prezinski comments on his "superficial, detached, muddled" relationships of the fifties and laments his failure to respond to several women interested in him. He recalls feeling "stifled" and "blocked." This is understandable in terms of his inability to allow affective expression and the need to suppress his feelings and affective life. In order to safeguard his deep belief in himself as a person without desire or appetite during the fifties Mr. Prezinski displayed patterns of (1) leaving the situation of such invitations (as when he transferred out of Puerto Rico) and (2) locating such desire on the outside, in other people ("primitive women"). Thus "boredom" results, since Mr. Prezinski is unable to freely express appetite and desire for fear of retribution from others. How can someone attempting to banish his affective life expect to feel very much?

> I didn't have a sense of friendship with people. I didn't even understand that very well, really. Real friendship I always considered sort of threatening. And the fact that my work was very logical and abstract tended to color everything else. There wasn't much in the way of feeling or emotions. The human things, I would just rule those things out. Like rule out emotions and feelings.

Mr. Prezinski was transferred to Chicago, not Japan, where he continued to work for the company. It was not until 1964, when Mr. Prezinski was in his thirty-fourth year, that he experienced a real crisis. Mr. Prezinski reports the experience in terms of feeling "dead," of dying inside. He reports feeling as if he had lost touch with intuition and human things, that "rationalism was my religion" and "my whole life was abstract." The feeling was one of inner emptiness and isolation, cut off from the real world: "I wanted to see some of the results of my work, I didn't want to just sit in my office." This experience is captured dramatically in the following passage.

I became really discontented in my engineering work after a while. Because I felt it was unrewarding and boring and monotonous, and not what I really wanted to do. It just came to a point when I finally realized that I couldn't do engineering anymore. I couldn't keep track of the numbers. I was making so many mistakes that I had to leave. There was something that was happening to me and I didn't know what it was. I was really scared because I didn't know what was happening. Why I wasn't able to work because it was simple stuff, I mean I did it hundreds of times.

I believed so much then that everything could be understood by rational logic, intellect. I think my whole world became so abstract that it was crazy. And I think it practically destroyed me. Because it was so empty. Everything was just empty of any kind of humanity and life. [*Can you give me an example?*] Well, I was practicing engineering and here I was in a large room with a lot of other people at desks. Very quiet. No radio. And you sit at this desk all day. Calculating various things. I was in structural design. It got to the point where I couldn't deal with it anymore. I couldn't do it. I started making a lot of mistakes. And this is the final touch. I did all this calculation and stuff. I never saw the job, before, during, or after the construction. I never saw the results of my work. It was like it didn't even mean anything. All those facts and figures were absolutely imaginary. They probably were. And so I had no contact with reality. That was absolutely the limit. I couldn't go any further.

I thought I was dead. I felt that all the school I had gone to, they were putting more nails in my coffin. They were ready to kill me. They wanted to do me in. Now I know they weren't. I mean it sounds paranoid because they didn't mean to do that but that's what they did. [*How were they doing that?*] Well, by abstracting everything that was worthwhile in my life. It was just awfully hard on human beings to sit there and do those things day after day. And then also the fact that I never got out and actually saw the results of the work. It all seemed so abstract. And that was part of my working life but also part of my inner life too. Well, whatever there was of my inner life.

Note first that the central crisis described is one of an "empty self," the inability to feel and respond; he "felt dead." We can see that the "empty self" experience Mr. Prezinski reports is one logical result of the deadening of his affective life, characteristic of his self-definition as weak, powerless, and unable to have a real effect in the world. His inner sense of weakness, tendency to give power to others, and anxieties about intrusion made any deep emotion or feeling very difficult for Mr. Prezinski. I refer to an "empty self" because for Mr. Prezinski an initial life structure built around the avoidance of salience and impulse had led to the drying up of his affective life. Fearful of being depleted by others if he strikes out on his own with novelty, impulse, or playfulness, Mr. Prezinski reports feeling "literally dead." For a person who interprets the world in terms of its possibly critical, intrusive nature, who hides from others because he feels unable to defend his psychological boundaries, it is not surprising that the material rewards of a successful job in engineering are not satisfying, nor was Mr. Prezinski able to form close, personal relationships with others, especially women.

Given Mr. Prezinski's strong movement away from sensuality and self-assertion it is also not surprising that such a crisis of feeling dead inside developed. Yet in order to feel dead inside, you must be aware of what it means to feel not-dead inside. My belief is that Mr. Prezinski was feeling most empty inside at this time, in his thirties, because he was being confronted most strongly with his appetites and desires. As he says, "I couldn't keep things down and every once in a while they'd crop up." These things cropping up were discrepant experiences for Mr. Prezinski, since they invalidated his sense of self as without self-centered urges and desires. Mr. Prezinski's feeling of being dead is symptomatic of intensified feelings of being alive—a resurgence of appetites and desires discrepant to self-definition. There were at least two sources of discrepant experiences that confronted Mr. Prezinksi with his own egocentrism and appetites at this time: (1) the appearance of a "strong" woman in his life in the early sixties, and (2) the sociocultural climate of the early sixties.

Mr. Prezinski first found himself confronted with appetites through a strong figure in his life, a dance student named Barbara. She was very involved in the aesthetic activities of underlying interest to Mr. Prezinski, and he found himself very attracted to those qualities in her. He took coursework in art and was again reminded—through her—of his own desire for self-expression and assertion.

> Barbara really opened up my life. She opened up a lot of doors to all the things that I felt I was missing. She was primarily a dancer but also an artist. I really admired what she was doing in art. We went to drawing classes at night. And I really got into art. Again. I got interested in a lot of things through her. I went to exhibitions. There was just that other side of life altogether. That side of culture and not just science or engineering. I guess that's when I started drifting away

from engineering. I had feelings I didn't understand. Wanting to study more in the arts, feeling sick of my job.

When I first met Barbara there was some aspect of my needing her. Barbara had all these qualities that helped me out in social situations. She would be much more apt than I was. She would do the right thing. Really carry me through some of those things. I guess I learned to depend on her in social situations. She put me in touch with a lot of my feelings. I realized in going out with her that there were a lot of things that I had taken for granted that I ought to re-think. I always liked art but I didn't know people who were into such things. It's hard to pursue something all by yourself. She helped me.

Painting courses were a powerful reminder of his own joy in art and his "strong" inner life. We can see Mr. Prezinski struggling with his resurgent interests, wishes, and desires in the following material, as he describes his life and work in the early sixties:

I knew I was getting more and more interested in art, I knew things were happening. I knew that I wasn't satisfied with my life. I knew that I wanted to make some changes and I didn't know exactly how. I didn't want to do what I had been doing in the past. I wanted to shake off the past. I had to do something that made me feel that I accomplished something. I wanted to see the results of my work. I didn't want to just sit in that office making design calculations or something I never saw and never will see. Something that was so abstract and had no meaning for me. I wanted to know somehow where it fit into the whole scheme of things. Whatever I was working on. I wanted to know about that. I wanted to have something to say about it too. Not that I wanted to be an autocrat, but I just wanted to see the wholeness of it all.

But I was scared. It seemed so bold and audacious. It seemed too daring to think that I might do art. I couldn't imagine that I could carry that off at that time, like my whole background was against it. Like what right did I have to go into the arts? I guess I had a lot of "shoulds" pumped into me from my early days. Like, you should make a living, and I had this education and I should use it. I said to myself that what I should do is quit and do my art. But I couldn't quite come to that conviction. I mean I had the idea but I couldn't deal with it at that time. I'd say, "Well, I think I just have to wait it out." I actually began to work harder at my engineering job.

Finally, Mr. Prezinski's confrontation with his appetites was occurring as well through more generalized "strong figures"—the civil rights movement of the early 1960s. Here again we see the role of powerful figures supporting further growth and development in Mr. Prezinski. These figures, though, are more abstract than specific people. This participation in civil rights work carried with it the central experience of the small becoming powerful:

> I remember cutting out all the clippings. One was about Allen Ginsberg, the beatnik. This was in 1963, I remember. He wasn't very fashionable, he was considered odd. But I was attracted to that and yet I felt fearful in my usual way, that I couldn't be like that. I wouldn't know how to deal with it, but I felt there was something good in it. I thought I was inadequate to be so free and strong about yourself. I mean I just felt I couldn't do that. I remember a march on Washington in 1963. I considered that a good development, that blacks were going to get their civil rights. I felt this was going to be a marvelous change in the country, that we were definitely down the path of giving civil rights to all minority people. I remember that demonstration, feeling so powerful. I wanted to express my anger. I wrote poetry and I remember even doing some sketches of that march.

While he says he felt "inadequate to be as strong and free, like Ginsberg," these models of perceived power had an impact on Mr. Prezinski, as a vehicle for his aggression and impulse. Significantly, he remembers writing poetry to "express my anger," and sketching appears in the context of powerful affect. Under the impact of these reappearing interests and desires—from the stimulation of strong people and social events— Mr. Prezinski's sense of self was being eroded. The presence of his appetites made for heightened rigidity, and it is in this context that we find a turning away from these parts of himself. We find renewed anxiety about his efforts at self-expression: "Maybe I felt too inflated with my own importance, trying to do too much. . . . I had a lot of doubts about myself." As he recalls, Mr. Prezinski's reaction to his own efforts at self-expression were to renew his investment in his engineering job and to "work harder at it."

Mr. Prezinski had hoped to rid himself of his inner life, of his sensual desires, of his affective response to people and things. This his work could not do, as Mr. Prezinski's inner life refused to go away or disappear. Mr. Prezinski's discrepant exprinces lay in the continued presence of his appetites and desires and his inability to be truly "lost" in the world of engineering.

At midlife, the nonegocentric self of young adulthood was threatened as Mr. Prezinski was struggling with the twin desires to be "dead," or without his resurgent inner life, and "alive," integrating his affect and appetites more fully. By the middle sixties Mr. Prezinski says he felt "like I had to do something, but I didn't know what. I felt I wanted to . . . experience something. . . . I wanted to go someplace where I could experience something. I felt I had to get out of my job, away from Chicago. I remember my feeling was to get out. To escape."

Mr. Goodson: "It didn't live up to my ideals."

For Mr. Goodson the young adulthood years were spent training to become a physicist and in pursuit of a wished-for self, characterized by service to others and nonegocentric motives.

Mr. Goodson took a position as a research fellow in Germany after graduate school and it is here that discrepant experiences began to accumulate. First, neither science, nor he himself, was as autonomous as he expected. Mr. Goodson doesn't find the scientist's role to be anonymously autonomous. Indeed he found himself a part of someone else's laboratory and accountable to that person:

> That's a problem with science where you're more often working as part of a team in a small specialized area with other people. The small specialized area is really the thing that restricts people working in science who really want to do something important and make some real contribution to help people's lives. [*Physics was a disappointment to you then?*] Yeah. The way it was a disappointment, it didn't live up to my ideals. I never got into a position working by myself, solving important problems. There was always someone else above me choosing a problem, and they'd direct me. I couldn't really get personally involved in the problem. I had little personal desire to do the work. It was almost like doing a job for somebody. I didn't like it if people found something at fault or if something was wrong, I'd take it personally. Like a personal criticism of myself.
>
> I didn't have any real emotional interest in the research. It was purely something that I was doing under the direction of someone else. It was a kind of drudgery. I only did it during the hours that I was working there. When I wasn't working there I wouldn't even think about it. It was just like a nine-to-five job.

In this situation Mr. Goodson had to defend his decisions and his work. He found himself feeling angry and uncomfortable in response to the normal criticism and daily structure of work in a scientific laboratory. These responses were at variance with his self-definition as "of service." His own anger and dissatisfaction at not being able to be independent were discrepant experiences to his sense of self as of service.

On the other hand, Mr. Goodson also found himself not as truly independent and original as he thought:

> I realized later all through my education in science, that one of the things that's gotten me through has been hard work, but not creativity. I didn't like to strike off on my own. When I ran up against problems that involved creative thought there were some problems that I just could not do as well as other people. In fact that was one of the things I began to feel after I got out of school and started doing science with other scientists. There your achievements were based more on what you really knew and how you could think independently and originally about scientific problems.
>
> I had a desire to not do something that's completely done by me but rather something that didn't have my name or my stamp on it. That starts on someone else's initiative. Part of me doesn't like to get too personally involved or to say that it's a personal opinion. I'm uncomfortable with projecting myself in my work. I feel I'd make a fool of myself by exposing myself or failing at something I tried to do.
>
> I remember when I was in Germany doing research, I was working on a problem of my own and I would talk to my supervisor and he would say, "Well, it would be interesting to look into this particular area." So I would start looking into that area but what I would do is start doing whole series of experiments. And rather than going off on a new direction, or further direction, I would sort of build up information. Just a large amount of experiments. And then I often wouldn't take the time to sort out and think through what the data implied as to do next. I realized at many points I had collected too much information. It was just very confusing to try and sort it out. I was just hoping that maybe by sheer volume of information that I could make some conclusions with the help of somebody else, like my supervisor. I would tend to wait for help, and that bothered me.

We can understand this as in part reflecting a desire on Mr. Goodson's part for direction and help in his laboratory work. Here Mr. Goodson is brought into contact with his dependency needs and his desire to take from—not just give to—others.

To summarize, Mr. Goodson found himself having to work with others and this produced two kinds of discrepant experiences: (1) the necessity to defend his work and (2) the desire for help from others. Both of these experiences were difficult for Mr. Goodson because they threatened his definition of self as "of service" (e.g., nonassertive and nonaggressive) and "nonegocentric" (e.g., not making demands on others, that is, not needing their help).

Further, Mr. Goodson found himself not truly committed to the painstakingly detailed, independent research of the scientist and not entirely drawn to the reality of being of service to people in this way. As with Mr. Anderson, we have the sense of someone not truly enjoying or committed to the work he was doing. This is implied in his statement "I didn't like to get personally involved," and can be seen in a research assistant's comment reported by Mr. Goodson:

The truth is that I was a very halfhearted worker so far as doing research was concerned. It was only on the urging of the laboratory director that I would go ahead and do something. Even when I was working in the lab doing experiments, a lab technician once made the remark that she couldn't imagine how I had got that far in physics because I was always making mistakes doing labwork. My heart and mind really weren't in it.

Clearly valuable work of great social importance was not immediately forthcoming. His work was of a very detailed, painstaking nature and Mr. Goodson comments that "after the Ph.D. I realized how esoteric it was." Once again, as with so many of these men, we find a sharp discordance between expectation and reality:

I felt when I was in graduate school, that it was just necessary for me to get the Ph.D. in order to get a job doing science work. Then after I finished, I began to realize that this Ph.D. would only lead to doing research in a lab which would be very specialized or teaching at a university, or doing research in a very esoteric, specialized field. I just realized then that the connection to something useful to mankind was very far removed. [*What kind of usefulness did you hope to have in your work?*] Well, doing something that would lead to, say, some, either some medical usefulness or some environmental improvement, something that would make people's lives better.

Mr. Goodson took a teaching position in a university medical school in the United States, seeing this as a more humane, contributory area of the sciences:

When I came there it was to work with a professor of biology, involved in medical research and teaching, because I wanted to make a move into something more related to human interests which I hoped would be in the medical fields. And that would be a move toward a more humanistic study. But again the work I did was very specific in one isolated little topic. I really didn't have much heart for it.

In part this move safeguarded Mr. Goodson's threatened self as "of service" in the face of his own disinterest, dependency needs, and difficulty asserting himself.

Both Mr. Goodson's perception of the nature of science as not entirely socially responsible and his realization of himself as not entirely interested in science were at variance to the sense of himself as "selfless" and "of service." Another discrepancy lay in the twin demands of dependency and assertion in the sciences—that he was not anonymous but rather had to defend his work and that he needed to be able to ask for help in his work. Both of these were threats to the sense of himself as not needing or dominating others, being rather of service.

Further, Mr. Goodson's sense of self as nonegocentric—that is, without selfish interests and desires for dominance and aggression—was encountering discrepant experiences in other areas. Mr. Goodson began to have experiences indicating a desire to be not just socially contributory and selfless but more socially dominant. He had an affair with his secretary, finding the experience very much to his satisfaction:

> In Germany there were relationships where I felt that we both really fully enjoyed it and I didn't really have an insecurity about it. [*What happened there?*] Well, I started going out with my secretary [*laughs*] and we spent a lot of nights together and then we went on several camping trips together. After that I began to feel that I overcame a lot of my inhibitions about sex and I started having a lot more sexual experiences.

There is a general sense of social adventureness and exploration in young adulthood, missing from Mr. Goodson's college and graduate school years:

> [*What was your time in Europe like?*] I was traveling around more, meeting people who weren't connected with the university. Going to parties, going over to people's houses for dinner, going out to bars with people, playing darts and other games with people in bars. Going to concerts, traveling in Europe a little bit. It was just doing a lot of nonacademic things. Also it was the first time that I'd ever spent free of taking courses and studying for courses. I wasn't in school during the day. In other words, when I'd leave the lab at night I was just doing whatever I wanted to do. That was my first exposure, developing a real social life. Getting to do things with people on a social level. And I was also starting to do art work again and the art work developed in a style that was the first time that I was really happy with. And I would spend a lot of time doing that instead of doing the work in the lab.

Mr. Goodson credits this exploration and initiative partially to the completion of his B.A. and Ph.D. requirements and the fact that he had more time on his hands than in graduate school. Significantly, painting reappears as an activity at this time. This is similar to Mr. Anderson, to Mr. Prezinski (after Barbara and painting lessons), and—as we shall see— to Mr. Lonzetti, all of whom were confronted by some older, almost forgotten dreams and aspirations at midlife in the guise of "new" interests and desires. These new interests and desires brought with them old questions and challenges: how to assert and "make real" those parts of oneself. For Mr. Goodson, painting and his interest in it brought along old questions about his egocentricism and selfishness, very at variance with his self-definition:

> Working on art is sort of bringing your own ego or your own self into the limelight. I have difficulty accepting that sort of ego glorification. I remember all the attention I would get when I showed people my artwork, and I'd feel uncomfortable.
>
> It is, and was, difficult to tell myself it's OK to spend a block of time doing art. It's that old thing, the conflict between my feelings toward art being basically something which is enjoyable, almost like play, conflicting with my feelings of responsibility. That I should be doing something that's not totally enjoyable. Doing work. I don't feel comfortable indulging myself for long periods of time. I would get guilt feelings about it.

Further, upon his new job in this country, a girlfriend provided important lessons about his pleasures and tastes. This was a love affair that continued for several years, and, as with Mr. Anderson and his wife, this relationship served as an important source of information for Mr. Goodson about himself:

> Paula also taught, in the humanities. And we started going out together and starting getting into a lover relationship. And she was into a lot of things that I hadn't been exposed to before. Like she had traveled around the world and she was into a lot of different kinds of foreign cooking and liked to dance and appreciated a lot of fine things. She wore really nice clothes and was concerned about her appearance. She was also more attractive than most of the women I had gone with up until that time. So I was really excited about that. Like here was the first woman that I was going with that I really felt proud of being with. And she got me really interested in a lot of her friends. Like I got to meet her friends and we would spend time with them, and through those friends I got to meet other people.

Experiences further discrepant to the sense of self as nonegocentric come from an encounter group where—through this supportive social milieu and (for perhaps the first time) real interconnectedness with others— Mr. Goodson learns some things about his feelings toward his family:

These encounter groups, people would always talk about really deep heavy feelings and I really enjoyed that, even though a lot of it was painful. I was feeling pretty frustrated about being all bottled up. I was dating Paula and we had a number of breakups with each other. And during one of those it was that she said that I never expressed really what I was feeling or that I just couldn't express my emotions to her. And I realized at the time that that was something I had been like during high school, during college and grad school, and I knew that at some point in my life I have to deal with the reality of being able to show my emotions and talk about them. And I figured that my relationship with Paula was important for me to want to do something about it right then. And here was the opportunity.

Mr. Goodson had been having experiences discrepant to the sense of self as not being angry or dominating toward others, or selfish, and as not needing help, support, or direction from others. A mounting crisis developed, as summarized in his painting *Turning 30*:

I remember a picture I did was called *Turning 30*. I was looking back on my life at that time thinking about what I felt that I had missed. It was a picture of a man wearing a black suit and a tie. His head was kind of a misshapen blob and his feet were roller skates like he was on a treadmill or somebody was pushing him and he didn't have his own sort of feet to stand on or his own feet to determine what he wanted to do. And in the background were some paintings. One of them was a landscape of a road going back into the distance. Everything was kind of tilted and jumbled and sort of in disarray. [*How would you interpret the picture?*] I felt like it was expressing the conflict within me. The man wearing a tie and wearing roller skates was part of me that was being pushed on blindly by my own internal sort of pressure or feelings of responsibility to society. The ease of being conventional and doing what was expected so that I wouldn't be hassled or have doubts about whether I was all alone vs. the picture in the background which was sort of getting out into the country where there were no people around, no objects, just the natural landscape. And just sort of like escaping and being an artist. [*Was the age of 30 significant?*] Yeah, it was the phrase about "you can't trust anybody over 30," and it was just an age that was kind of symbolic of the loss of youth or the loss of purity. You know all the things that were bound up in that phrase, "you can't trust anybody over 30." What was meant I believed, was the change that was taking place in some people as they got older as they began to settle down and accept a job that maybe didn't correspond to their ideals that they had when they were younger. Or that was sort of copping out in the eyes of younger people.

The overt content in the painting and his discussion of it reveal that Mr. Goodson feels he didn't accept a job corresponding to his ideals. While there are many meanings to Mr. Goodson's painting, one underlying theme is a feeling of being trapped in a self about which he is uncertain. "Am I who I think I am?" Mr. Goodson seems to be asking.

Mr. Lonzetti: "You needed to spend so much time at the maintenance of your position."

Mr. Lonzetti left college with the decision to obtain an MBA and afterward found a position in an energy corporation as an executive in a research and planning division. He married in his early twenties. By his middle twenties Mr. Lonzetti exuded a sense of excitement and enthusiasm as he organized a sense of self around being above others and doing important work. During his late twenties he established himself at his company. His marriage was sound and he received support and acceptance from his wife. A child was born. At this time Mr. Lonzetti enrolled in a photography course with an exciting, energetic, well-known teacher and reactivated an earlier interest in photography, dating back to adolescence. He describes his experiences in this way:

During summer I was really sort of casting around for something to do and I heard about a course that was being given. I really wasn't at all sure that I wanted to spend the money. I decided just to take the chance. And it was one of the most important things I did. There was a guy who I know who gave the course. It was an intermediate photography course that showed certain techniques in the darkroom. The main thing was that I soon realized that this guy who couldn't explain a damn thing about what he was doing or how to do it—I had all these technical questions—still knew exactly what he was doing. And I really began to like him and to see that there was something. And through him in a very indirect sort of way I then began meeting other photographers. I took these advanced photography courses. And that exposed me all of a sudden to thinking of it as a kind of art form that had associations with other art forms and which opened up all kinds of imponderable questions.

Over time Mr. Lonzetti's interests and success at photography began to emerge forcefully. He took and then conducted workshops. Mr. Lonzetti's business training may have been of some advantage as he sought out and obtained commissions and showed off his works. Several encouraging reviews of his work were published. The appearance of photography in Mr. Lonzetti's life was important because it changed, in itself, part of the world for him: Mr. Lonzetti was now confronted with the fact that he had an avid interest in an activity which demanded engagement of his aesthetic sense, and yet provided ambiguous standards for evaluation of progress. This was a source of discrepant experience because it constantly reminded him that he was not totally committed to the "important work" of business consulting, and it cast him in the role of student, dependent upon others. Mr. Lonzetti needed to feel as if he was doing "important work," and photography, as one of the arts, had for him an air of "frivolity" and "self-indulgence":

> I remember an early assignment in the very beginning of the course where the teacher asked everybody to find some object that seemed to have some nice qualities to it like a cup or saucer or candle or something. And just look and stare at it for twenty minutes, and there are some prescribed conditions, and see what happened to it. And I did that with great fervor and I reported on it in sort of objective ways. He criticized me severely for not saying how I felt but sort of as though I were detached in a way that I'd spoken. I sometimes felt like it was a weakness that there weren't more important things to say than just subjective responses.
>
> A big problem was lack of confidence in photography. And it wasn't confidence about my real interests. It was confidence about being judged by other people.

For Mr. Lonzetti, then, his increasing interest in photography was at first a threat to his fundamental self-definition as a superior person, above others, doing clearly respectable and high-status work. The discrepant experiences involved in his work in photography were (1) being a student, with flaws and inadequacies, like us all, rather than clearly superior and above others and (2) producing subjectively defined, personally rooted work rather than work rooted in clearly definable objectives, standards, and values.

Further, problems at work began to develop during Mr. Lonzetti's early thirties. He experienced increasing boredom at work, with impatience at the heavy social component of his life in the company. While he had anticipated a clear "organization for work" with recognized lines of authority and established procedures for accomplishing tasks, he instead found a strong informal structure and friendship network at work. The social emphasis and the interpersonal demands and ambiguity this presented were a real problem for Mr. Lonzetti.

I felt an incredible waste of time. To go into work and to see the kinds of questions that people are raising about solving some problem or to see what I infer is really a great social sort of transaction going on where people are satisfying certain needs they have to be involved or to participate or to get recognition that really are consuming everybody else's attention and energy.

Or all kinds of monkeyshines to maneuver one into a better position or to put somebody else in who's a friend in place of somebody else. I very much resented being with people that I'm supposed to be helping or working with when I see that they're not very motivated as far as the problem solving is concerned. The other things are of no interest to me except that I know that they are of great interest to the person but which I regard as sort of maintenance functions. [*What are some of those other things that don't have to do with the problem solving?*] Well, people are brought together, for example, to work on a certain problem in a meeting. And they cannot put themselves into the problem. They can only think of its repercussion for themselves. Anything that changes their present position is something to be sabotaged.

Lots of people that I knew I felt engaged in monologues that I just sort of sat and listened to. Monologues are where a person essentially is telling something about himself and carries it beyond the point of clear and obvious interest to other people to whom he's speaking. And the other quality is that it's not a discussion that involves other people or benefits at all from the reaction of other people. Every time in a group of people together, and you know I would be under enormous pressure to get something done and things usually end up such that a lot of time is spent, I would say, in monologues.

There were a lot of matter-of-fact issues that are all pretty stupid in my opinion. But if you're with a group of people like that you have to some extent come to terms with them. These are all maintenance issues. The maintenance of your position beyond doing the work that suggests itself. A collateral, an ancilliary preoccupation. Whatever seeks to create some kind of a bond. [*What's wrong with that?*] You mean what's wrong with the function of going around to people and spending time talking about things and whatnot? I say it's a waste of time.

Note the attention again to position and the need of having to defend or protect oneself during social interaction, expressed by "monkeyshines to maneuver one into a better position" and a concern with "the maintenance of your position." Mr. Lonzetti distinguishes his work from his social relationships. He refers to the social interactions derogatively as "maintenance work" and means by this the effort required to keep things going, the everyday give-and-take of the real world. These demands strained Mr. Lonzetti's resources for dealing on an interpersonal level with people, as he felt socially ill-at-ease and had difficulty with the everyday give-and-take of his company. Such interaction drew him toward people and made him vulnerable to them, thus bringing him closer to the anger and resentment and fear of humiliation that he carried with him since childhood. Having to carry out his "maintenance work" at business, Mr. Lonzetti found he had to sacrifice his sense of self as being engaged in "important work":

> There are things that happened a lot. Being with people for longer periods of time and meeting and going out to dinner afterwards and whatnot. Where they would be talking about things that were important to them, but it's just that I wasn't interested in those things. I wasn't faulting them but I just didn't identify myself with those things very much and I found it hard to maintain an interest.

The impact of experiences calling into question Mr. Lonzetti's sense of self as an "important figure" and an "authority" is vividly captured in just such an episode at work.

> Once I was asked to make some organizational change in a unit of our company. A manager of the unit I was transferred into as an advisor had not participated in the decision to bring us in at all. It had been imposed upon him from above. And he was an intelligent, very articulate fellow who had lived by his wits in this big corporation and had done some things by really pushing himself on other people and made commitments for the corporation that were, I think, at the time very sort of speculative but ambitious and bold decisions. You have to admire him. But that basically he ran this unit by withholding information. And he was a tremendous spokesman for whatever ideas he wanted to advance.
>   But the omissions and the selectiveness with which he did that were egregious in my opinion. And in the course of time a lot of that began to come out and other people that didn't know much about the business were discovering a lot about it that they didn't know. But all along the way this guy was fighting it. He was doing everything he could to sabotage my work. [*How was he fighting it?*] Oh, in some cases it would be sort of modest attempts to discredit the methodology of my work—you could find places to question. And at other times, you know, he would find ways to contradict me in terms of things

that I might have said earlier. There were meetings to discuss my report and to clarify what had come out. There were instances where people wouldn't show up from the unit or we would get into arguments with this guy about the data where the corporate leaders knew exactly what happened. They knew this guy was attempting to sabotage the work but didn't say anything. They were letting the cats and dogs fight it out. I felt like a hired hand—brought into the unit to fight. I certainly didn't feel like an authority, there to do some work. I resented that enormously. I didn't feel that I should be involved in that.

The disappointment in Mr. Lonzetti's sense of who he is resulting from his experiences at work is captured by his comment that he felt like a hired hand rather than an "authority." The status and worth of an "authority" are clear and accepted by all; a "hired hand" must constantly fight for his position without any sense of security or status. Boredom is the predominant affect reported by Mr. Lonzetti as produced by the need for this kind of "maintenance work." This is the second time boredom has appeared prominently in a subject's account since Mr. Prezinski reported it as well. What is the meaning of boredom for Mr. Lonzetti? Significantly, Mr. Lonzetti dates his increasing boredom with work back to the time when a report he gave to the company leadership was criticized and he had a hard time defending it:

My enthusiasm for the work began to wane as time went on. It seemed to me that the results of my work were not very important. That is to say I increasingly had questions about whether the services I was doing were anything that was very good for people in the first place. Now I must say that I also had some feelings of inferiority, as my report to the corporate leadership got towards the final conclusions and I was responsible for the technical work on the one hand as well as presenting the report to the company. That business of going around to the highest executive to present some of the results and I ran into people with a great deal of technical knowledge that in a more specialized way exceeded my own. And I didn't have anything to be ashamed of, but always felt a little bit that way. Know what I mean?

Sometimes I felt I couldn't answer people's questions completely. And in one instance I remember going to a meeting I walked into a group of really hostile people. The company was in something of a transition and there were people who were sort of taking a personal interest. Eventually the group sort of began arguing with me about technical details. And it bothered me most because I felt that it didn't matter what I answered or didn't. It was a question of just trying to embarrass us or discredit the project as a whole. The real thing being transacted, you see, was not the resolution of a technical question. And that upset me a lot. I just felt bad as work seemed shitty to me. And under those circumstances I'd rather not deal with people.

[*What were your feelings?*] That I was in the middle of a group of people who were fighting about different things and that I was really someone innocent but a ploy in the whole thing and that my actions were not having any great bearing on the result. I'm trying to be honest about this. After that I became more and more detached, increasingly. I wanted to let people know that what I was doing is very important and they all ought to think more about it. But that seemed a much bigger effort than I wanted to make.

Embedded in this experience of being put in a hostile situation and having to defend himself was a sharp threat to the sense of himself as worthy, productive, and above criticism. Mr. Lonzetti deals with this situation by distancing himself from the experience, locating the blame outside himself in seeing his role as an "innocent" one and essentially feeling bored with the entire experience. No overt rage, only surface boredom, but we can infer that the experience brought him close to the rage he felt in such humiliating experiences and thereby close to the inner feeling of inferiority warded off by his sense of self as superior and above criticism. Boredom is thus serving analogous functions in the cases of Mr. Prezinski and Mr. Lonzetti. For Mr. Prezinski, boredom masks inner anxiety over his appetites, for Mr. Lonzetti, anxiety over his rage and feelings of inferiority.

The discrepancies to Mr. Lonzetti's self-definition were rooted in experiences broader than this single episode. The structure of work was a problem. Mr. Lonzetti had difficulty with the large social investment required because of the informal structure of the firm. Further, advancement was not clear-cut, and Mr. Lonzetti found the reward structure ambiguous and the importance of his work unclear to others:

A long as you don't do very badly nothing happens. And if you do very well not a lot happens either. So there's not a great deal of punishment and there's not a great deal of reward either. And if you have a need for a great deal of reward or a need for achievement you probably won't be content staying there very long. You'll want to go somewhere else where the measures of success are more blatant. Certainly the remuneration and visibility with respect to doing well didn't increase for me.

The balance between "maintenance work" and "important work" also suffered, for Mr. Lonzetti, in his experience as a father and husband. Being a parent demanded maintenance work—taking care of the children and relating to his wife—and these needs also threatened Mr. Lonzetti's sense of being a knight or courier on an important mission. He discusses this primarily in terms of his work in photography:

> I would say that until after I was married, or until I had a child, I used to feel every year that as I got older I had more freedom and more control over opportunity, that I had more of an ability to put myself in a position where things very interesting were happening. I felt more liberated every year I got older, until marriage and family.
>
> The idea of a family clearly has aspects of it that are maintenance. Worrying about their security. I don't mean that that's a great preoccupation, but I think twice about what I can do given their presence or responsibility for them. If I were by myself I'd feel like I could easily live on a lot less money, for example, and I certainly would be more inclined not to have a house. To have a more impermanent kind of livelihood I guess. Having children has created an enormous drain of time and energy. On a petty level it's working in the darkroom lost in something that I'm doing and then somebody yells at me, to help them, in some very trivial way. I mean it isn't as if the house is burning down.

We see, then, definitions of self threatened in at least three areas: photography, work, and family. For each, this self-definition as above others and superior is threatened by experiences indicating his vulnerability and by experience demanding that he be the opposite of above and superior: more engaged with others, giving, and (even if only temporarily) less above them—needing their help and dependent on their support. Each of these experiences is discrepant to Mr. Lonzetti's sense of self. Yet if he is not who he thinks he is, who is he? Mr. Lonzetti describes himself in his middle thirties as concerned "with knowing yourself well. . . . I felt, perhaps more than most people, that I didn't know myself as well as most people." He was feeling "a lot of anxiety and acute questions about what I should do in my work."

The Wished-for Self at Midlife: A Dialectic of Separation

To this point I have been describing the subjective experience of midlife as involving a powerful discrepancy between the anticipated and the real. This discrepancy involved a threat to the kind of self one hoped to be, a loss of the wished-for self we reconstructed from our participants' accounts of young adulthood.

From a more objective-analytic perspective we can see the discrepancies of midlife as representing in part a continued ambivalence or dialectic around separation-individuation. Note in these individuals' descriptions of their career evolution through the midlife years a sense of their having to be a certain way. Mr. Anderson speaks of "obligation in marital contracts," Mr. O'Hara of having "no choice" at work or home, and Mr. Goodson characterizes work as "like doing a job for somebody." These statements are clues revealing these men's ambivalence toward the wished-for self. Experiences consistent with the wished-for self bring with them the anger and resentment, jealousy of others, and great expectations for what is forthcoming that accompany the inner feeling of having to be a certain way, without free choice in the matter. This resentment of being forced to be this way is reflective of the introjected nature of these men's adolescent–young adulthood patterns of self-definition. It is also perhaps analogous to their childhood feeling of external pressure repressing their "true" selves. Yet rebelling or changing or attempting to not be that way brings with it anxiety over the consequences of separating from parents, doing it on one's own, defining oneself in a new way for oneself. Thus both alternatives—being a "good boy" or being "rebellious," in Mr. Anderson's dichotomy—are ambivalently held. This sets the stage for a cycle of conflict during midlife, as the feelings of anger, rage, and resentment lead to anxiety about these feelings and renewed commitment to the defensive, wished-for self, with resulting increased resentment. The figure below represents this dialectic or "cycle of conflict" around separation-individuation.

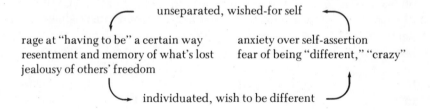

Let me illustrate this cycle of conflict around separation from idealized images of parents and self in our case studies. Mr. Markowitz, for example, reports strong feelings of anger and resentment during the central years of child raising. Having made career and marital choices with a heavy feeling of responsibility and accountability, Mr. Markowitz expresses a recurrent feeling of having sacrificed important aspects of himself as a result of having to be so "responsible" in family and work matters. He describes having become "responsible at age 12" under pressure of the family; of having married right after college, as if it was not his choice; and he emphasizes how important it was for him to do "useful," "socially contributory" work. The heavy sense of responsibility he felt both at home and at work is communicated by his "nose to the grindstone" image discussed in the previous chapter. He felt always "concerned about being a failure financially" and thus pressed himself hard at work, afraid of losing his job if he slacked off or asserted himself to his superiors. He mentions at several points his fear of being fired from his positions because of challenges to his bosses, as if self-assertion invariably brings fears of rebuke.

The family in particular emerges as a heavy burden. Mr. Markowitz's discussion of the early years at home emphasizes his worry over his family and all the frightening possibilities: children's illnesses wiping out the family savings, not having a job, the children not turning out "right." For Mr. Markowitz, the family was a task demanding heavy involvement and great effort. The role of play, spontaneity, and enjoyment is rarely mentioned. Children in Mr. Markowitz's description are "objects" who look to parents as guides. There is a heavy burden in both the work and family for Mr. Markowitz. He discusses the "terrible consequences" of making a mistake in science, in that people may be misled. In the family, too, much depends on the "strong father image." As Mr. Markowitz says, he was unable to combine the roles of lover and provider.

We see in this a circle of conflict, a dialectic, in Mr. Markowitz's rigid, idealized sense of himself. The self-definition as responsible, useful, and socially productive are not confident, reassuring guides to action and hopes for the future; rather they are overbearing, uncompromising demands admitting of no ambiguity or failure. In Mr. Markowitz's discussions of young adulthood these ideals have an external air, as if they were not rooted in his strong sense of himself but rather originate as the terms of a surrender agreement with more powerful others. Thus the air of anger and resentment running throughout his account, the feelings of deprivation, jealousy of others, and some social isolation. The jealousy of others and resentment Mr. Markowitz feels at having to be always responsible and useful is alluded to only faintly and indirectly. We note these feelings in his description as an adult watching a young pianist at music school:

> I realized there were things people developed, and it was well known, and I hadn't the slightest idea about it. One time I went to a graduation exercise in Boston, at a music school. A technical school devoted to training people to be musicians or artists. And there was a sixteen-year-old girl doing a Mozart piano concerto. Mozart is one of my favorite composers. And she was playing it beautifully, she was not only playing it beautifully, she understood Mozart, she *knew*. At sixteen she knew what Mozart was saying—it was something that had taken me thirty, forty years to find out and I'm still in the process of finding out. So at the same time I was enjoying her performance I was resenting her—the fact that she was such a prodigy. That it had come to her, and perhaps as prodigious as Mozart was himself. And

this also, this element is always present. Admiration tempered by a kind of feeling of resentment.

Note in this, too, his feeling of having been held back in his development, expressed through the comparison to a sixteen-year-old girl who "knew what Mozart was saying." Mr. Markowitz felt he was still in the process of understanding Mozart although he was many years her senior. Further, Mr. Markowitz recalls wanting to take more time off from work, but not being able to let himself. When Mr. Markowitz gives expression to a long-standing interest in music and the theater it is described in terms of its usefulness to others and as if it were almost a chance occurrence, without his active participation or choice. Finally, there are more direct undertones of anger at all he's missed in his life, of the ways he has been misled and disturbed by significant people in his life:

> Towards the end there at work, my wife noticed my resentment. She knew I liked to play the flute and it was getting so that if it was a nice day outside I would feel a little resentful, you know you get the feeling that man wasn't meant for this. One of my great projects is to work the industrial system so that a person retires when he's young and works when he's old, when it really doesn't matter. If you maintain a kind of objectivity, as if you had just come down from Mars and everything was strange, it becomes very difficult to go through the motions of what people have to do to get along today. It's like the old children's story called "The Bear that Was." The bear is convinced by the people around him that he's not really a bear. And they absolutely convince him. They show him for instance a bear in a circus. The bear in a circus is riding around on a bicycle with a funny hat on. They say, "Obviously if you were a bear you would be riding around on a bicycle with a funny hat on." And finally they convinced him he was not a bear.
>
> In my family my mother was very strong. My father was rather weak. She had very strong ideas and a sense of family and she posed these ideas. They were wrong, they were wrong. She felt that in the family you should have a responsible man. And my father was not that kind of person. But I was there you see, so really I became strong and responsible even though I was only twelve years old. It took me a while to work it out. I have some very important ideas about mothers and sons. I started really thinking about it a couple of years ago when I saw a production of *Coriolanus*. . . .

At this point in the interview Mr. Markowitz leaned forward in his chair and described to me the plot of *Coriolanus*. This play by Shakespeare is the story of a charismatic Roman general whose mother persuades him

not to attack Rome; they both know he will then be killed by his own rebellious army. With great feeling Mr. Markowitz describes the penulti-
mate scene in which the mother, on her knees, finishes her appeal to her
son. Coriolanus stands with his back to her, facing the audience.

> And in the most anguished tone he says, "Mother, what have you
> done to me?" But what I heard in the theatre was a universal call of
> all sons to all mothers: "Mother, what have you done to me?" It was
> such a revelation! [*What do you feel was done to you?*] As you grow
> up and recognize attitudes, you start thinking about them and if you
> can correct them. And you ask, "Where did I get this feeling from,
> where did I get that from?" Yeats did the same thing. He has a line
> that says, "No man has ever had enough of woman's love or children's
> gratitude. . . ."

We see here the ambivalence toward the initial self-definition itself, and
the circle of conflict that evolved at midlife. Underneath the strong feelings of duty are strong feelings of being owed things for all he has sacrificed and given up in the process. Mr. Markowitz draws on two powerful
works of art to communicate his feeling that "women's love or children's
gratitude" must make up for all that has been "done to me." Being accountable and responsible, then, brought with it feelings of anger and resentment about what he feels was missed. This in turn produces anxiety
and worry over his true nature with a resulting holding on to the self-definition as accountable and socially responsible, with eventual return of resentment and feelings of what was owed to him. Further, Mr. Markowitz
was not able to share the load of family and work by looking to others for
help, by acknowledging his fears or anxieties, or by feeling less centrally
involved, since others were precisely the ones to whom he felt accountable.

A similar cycle of conflict around the ambivalently held self-definition can be seen in the case of Mr. O'Hara. The heavy feeling of responsibility at having to redeem himself and to produce perfect gifts for others
breeds strong anger and resentment, resulting in greater need to redeem
himself. The heavy sense of expectation and responsibility Mr. O'Hara
felt in having to give gifts to everyone can be seen in his feelings about his
wife's polio and the rage at not being able to transform her. In the family,
Mr. O'Hara describes the great expectations built into marriage:

> We didn't want a church wedding but that was part of the compro-
> mise with my parents that we would be married by a minister. And I
> went through it not being aware of how much of a compromise it
> really was for me and for my wife. In terms of the contractual quali-
> ty, the Christian wedding. [*What was the contract?*] Well, the vows

you make. The contract got very mixed up with my Christian background. The relationship was really quite free of that. I sort of cava-
lierly went along with it but I think that because that was the way the
marriage was contracted, ultimately it changed our relationship, the
marriage. I began to feel responsible for providing for her and all of
that and she should take all my shit, be with me in my adversity and
all of those things you swear to.

　　After I left my job, I felt really guilty about what I felt I was doing. I was reducing my family's standard of living and making very
clear that I wasn't going to send the kids to college and if they wanted
to go they had to pay their own way. So that I was giving up slowly
piece by piece—reneging on pieces of a contract, a conscious contract
of marriage and children based on my parents' expectations. So that
was very painful to give those up and feel that you're failing. But it
was the survival of me and I knew that there wouldn't be anything
left of me if I kept up this contract.

　　There is a great sense of work and effort that Mr. O'Hara must put
into the situation in order to redeem himself in this area and to make
things right. Again, the university and family are oppressive environments for this person, demanding great effort and work. We can hypothe-
size strong investment and work leading to resentment, followed by anxiety and renewed effort and gifts to others. The heavy investment Mr.
O'Hara makes in redeeming himself and making gifts for others can be
seen in his repeated report of feeling that he had sacrificed so much of
himself in his career and marital decisions. The heavy work making gifts
to others then demands a great gift in return. Mr. O'Hara feels that he
sacrificed so much to make the gift, and within his own world he does.
Then he demands a great, unambivalent response from others—they
should like and accept him. This sets him up for great disappointment, as
can be seen in his rage at the university faculty and their underhanded
dealings and his anger at the contract of marriage. Thus the cycle of conflict: giving gifts and sacrificing so much led to the demand for response
and acceptance with resulting anger and rage at not getting this, with resulting increasing isolation and feeling cut off and rejected by others. Mr.
O'Hara's isolation in his family and at the university can be found in his
feelings of the family being "very resistant to hearing about how I felt," as
he felt with his colleagues that "everything that I wanted to talk about
was forbidden . . . such as feelings."

　　We can see Mr. Anderson's ambivalence around separation from an
idealized self-definition in his comments about being perceived as the
"good boy" in his law firm yet having a more "rebellious" streak. The
image of the good boy carries with it the burden and responsibility Mr.

Anderson felt at having to be poised and proper. In his world of law Mr. Anderson could not blow his cool, even in the face of ordinary provocations. That is, his critical feelings in difficult situations violated his image of self as poised and unruffled. Mr. Anderson was very sensitive and aware of the necessity of acting properly. He had difficulty tolerating situations where he felt obstreperous or different. Yet, of course, Mr. Anderson had such feelings at home and work, as is evidenced by his numerous criticisms of experiences in both spheres: "everyone was twitter and sucking around the client;" "why the fake smile with the client," "one of the partners I didn't get along with at all;" "I wanted to say . . . let's do it my way." He thus felt he had to be the good boy yet wanted to be more. He reports strong feelings of being swallowed up by the system, as if becoming what he wished for apparently meant giving up parts of self. In the family, too, Mr. Anderson felt under pressure to be the good boy, and he reports all the obligations he felt; the responsibilities of the father role kept him from other things. Ironically, as with all our men, Mr. Anderson was most tied to the rules and regulations of what it meant to be a husband and worker because of the rigid, uncompromising nature of his idealized self-definition. So we find Mr. Anderson feeling angry and resentful over being "mesmerized" by systems and having to be the good boy, yet then feeling anxiety over his bad, unruly, overly serious, unworthy side, with a resulting wish to prove himself responsible, poised, correct, and proper.

And similarly for the other men. For Mr. Prezinski, the social isolation probably increases his sense of frightening power and being potentially out of control. He has an incorrect view of his own power—as either totally powerless or totally powerful—and his psychological isolation from others probably contributes to his inability to learn differently. Mr. Prezinski also experiences the heavy responsibility of having to be "egoless" (perfect). Feeling controlled and powerless by near omnipotent parents, he feels and expresses anger and resentment. As well, there is envy at the powerful who have it so much better than he. Again our cycle: feeling empty inside and so controlled by others results in deep thirst for what he feels he has missed, very strong feelings of wanting things and very strong feelings of resentment/anger/destructiveness toward the controllers and disappointers. A result is anxiety about his impulses and the compensatory wish to feel controlled and powerless. As with all the participants, the depth of his renunciation of his appetites and impulses only makes him long for these desires and appetites all the more, and to feel greater resentment at what is lost and disappointment in what is actually achieved. Mr. Prezinski sets the stage for strong disappointment in others and rage at them because they haven't come through with what he wants.

Mr. Lonzetti and Mr. Goodson are similar in the cycle of conflict:

The heavy burden of having always to be on top certainly restricts Mr. Lonzetti's enjoyment and satisfaction at work, and the ambivalence that he feels toward this ideal self only increases the need to be that way. There is a sense of Mr. Lonzetti's not doing work for himself—he reports feeling like he can't get into it, that it feels not important. Further, he feels resentful of people who can be sociable. The underlying ambivalence can be seen in his feeling of having been cheated in a variety of situations. The result is greater resentment, anger, and anxiety without any place to go, plus feelings of being rejected, humiliated. Mr. Goodson displayed constant resentment over missing things in trying to be a good boy and his work in science not really being for him. This is evidenced in his lab assistant's remark and his constantly taking time off. The ambivalence toward being of service is evidenced in his feeling of people constantly taking advantage of him—he has to be a certain way and feels other people don't really take his needs into account. Note both these men's psychological isolation. In Mr. Goodson the feeling is that other people are jealous and critical of him; for Mr. Lonzetti they are judges and critics. In different ways for both men other people are potential enemies.

Again we find some consistencies in developmental issues among very different men and work situations. For each of our men I have tried to analyze in this section the separation problems of the midlife years as permutations of the following psychological dimensions:

1. The heavy burden of having to be a certain way, resulting from the introjected nature of an ambivalently held wished-for self. Each of the participants had a very narrow, tight image of what it meant to be a "good boy." As a result, these men were not very creative or exploratory in resolving family or career problems within the work or home setting itself. Having to be a certain way meant limited experimentation within these settings to find new ways out of old binds.

2. The resulting oppressiveness of work and family situations, which bred different kinds of anger and resentments at missed opportunities and the inner experience of external press, contributing to already existing anger and resentment at not having been "allowed," in adolescence and young adulthood, to define themselves in a particular way.

3. The strong sense of being owed things in return for the great effort and sacrifices made. This set these men up for great disappointments in both the responses of others and their own achievements. Note, too, in this last element the seeds of a certain social isolation, leading to difficulty in turning to others for aid and support in the process of resolving problems in the workplace and at home.

We can bring together our objective and subjective perspectives on midlife in the following manner. Young adulthood was the time of implementation of a wished-for self; at midlife experiences discrepant to this self accumulated, reopening separation issues only partially resolved earlier in the life cycle. The result is a potential loss at midlife of this "I" and the necessity to grieve for the lost self at midlife in order to reconstitute a sense of self within an altered intra- and interpersonal world. In the next chapter I discuss the process of reconstitution of self at midlife and the career change that resulted for these men at this time.

4

Grieving for a Lost Self
at Midlife

How do people come to terms with the reality of their achievements and situation at midlife in the face of the wishes, dreams, and fantasies of young adulthood? Implicit in this question is a more profound one: how do people grow and learn from their experiences? These questions form the focus of this chapter. The last chapter described the process whereby experiences in adulthood served to erode the dominant self-definition of the individuals in our study. In this chapter I explore the impact of these discrepant experiences and the manner in which self-definition was reconstituted in this group.

Understanding the impact of discrepant experiences will offer a perspective on growth and change in adulthood. A major goal of this chapter is to describe some of the markers of growth and change in adult personality. To do so I focus on three aspects of the maturation of self in adulthood:

1. Increased learning about self and an increased capacity for an internal dialogue about one's experience;

2. Increased recognition of the complexity of self and others;

3. A richer capacity for autonomous choice and decision making in one's life.

There are strong theoretical reasons for examining how our men have evolved from young adulthood to midlife in regard to these particular dimensions. Each dimension is emerging as an important marker of growth from studies of adult personality and development. A deeper understanding of one's own motives, needs, and conflicts is the kind of learning about self I am referring to in adulthood. Such self-understanding and learning is taken as a marker of adult growth in the theoretical writings of Erikson (1959), Maslow (1962), and Wheelis (1958), as well as the empirical work of Lowenthal *et al.* (1975) and Vaillant (1978). I am particularly interested in the maturation of the capacity for an "inner dialogue" concomitant with such self-learning. I mean this term to encompass a reflective attitude toward oneself and the ability to examine and comment on one's experience. Such capacity is evident in some men in our group at midlife and less so among others. A second emergent marker of growth and development in research is the increasingly complex perception of others and oneself. This means that other people (particularly parents, siblings, wife, friends) come to be seen as complex figures encompassing many different attributes, motives, needs, and conflicts separate from self. Perry (1970) in particular has presented rich evidence for the increasing differentiations of self and others, with the ability to see multiple viewpoints and tolerate conflicting perceptions as a key aspect of maturation from adolescence to adulthood. Support for this can be seen in research on aging (Neugarten 1968). Certainly, clinicians often take as a major goal of therapeutic work the increasing rich and well-understood perception by the person of his parents, spouse, children, and siblings as real people separate from him with motives, desires, and needs of their own. Finally, the capacity to make decisions and choices in a flexible, confident, responsible manner is a major focus of Perry's work (1970), and is an implicit theme in the work of Vaillant (1978) and Levinson (1978) when they focus on the evolution of careers and family life in their samples of men during midlife. Again, clinicians often attend to the manner in which their client approaches decisions and the feelings of choice in their life (or absence of such feelings). The capacity to bring affect and intellect to bear in major decisions, to see and tolerate the complexities of decisions, and to "freely" choose (while acknowledging the limits of any choice) is a key marker of the evolution of self.

Given the reports of the men in our group, there are strong empirical reasons for focusing on each of these three dimensions. Our men generally date the time of profound emotional crisis as beginning around age 35–40. In this group we find the attempt at recovery or reconstitution extending over a period of years, culminating in a stable resolution from which the career change emerges. Some individuals seem to have come out of the crisis at midlife with evidence of a changed perspective on themselves and others; others seem not to have been deeply affected by these events. This is evidenced from retrospective descriptions of midlife experiences, from the perception of self and others, and—in some cases—from the account of decision making around the career change itself. Some of the men seemed to have learned much about themselves and the world from their difficulties in career and marriage at midlife. This learning is reflected in a deeper, richer perception of important figures and events in their life history. The answer to the question, Who am I? seems to have changed and broadened, as these individuals show greater awareness and integration of aspects of self. Other participants seemed to have found out less about themselves from their experiences at midlife; here the sense of self seems unchanged from that of earlier in the life cycle. These patterns seem to me to reveal different ways in which individuals have coped with the discrepancies of midlife and reconstituted self-definition.

Describing the dimensions of change is different from understanding how it occurs. That is, we can ask, What are the dynamic processes of change separate from the way such change becomes manifest? By offering a conceptualization of the nature of grieving, I hope to show the utility of this paradigm for understanding the dynamics of growth, learning, and change in adulthood. The following section discusses the relevance of grieving to the evolution of self and careers at midlife.

Two Tasks of Grieving Work

We can identify in the literature two interrelated tasks that form major challenges of "grieving work": (1) reestablishment of the stability of interpretation and assumption about self in the world, and (2) integration of ambivalent feelings surrounding the lost person, place, or thing. While the work of those attending to loss as the failure of trusted assumptions about self has emphasized the first task, traditional psychoanalytic formulations of grieving have emphasized the latter (Freud 1964; Pollack 1961). Such psychoanalytic formulations trace problems in mourning to the inability to acknowledge ambivalent feelings of love and hate, anger and dependency surrounding the lost figure. As a result the gradual "decathexis" of the lost object is stalled, and patterns of chronic, inhibited, or delayed grief reactions appear as defenses against these frightening, ambivalent feelings that emerge as a consequence of loss. For Marris (1975) and others, chronic, inhibited, or delayed grief reactions are seen more broadly, as attempts to deny, suppress, and generally defend against painful discrepancies in one's understanding of the world. Yet in reality the first task of grieving work cannot occur without the second, as integration of ambivalent feelings toward the lost object are an essential step toward restoration of a stable sense of self. Loss and grief can therefore be considered as a two-stage phenomenon in which there is first the disruption of trusted interpretation of self in the world, followed by the emergence of a complex of ambivalent feelings toward this lost self. In the previous chapter we explored the nature of the "disruption" as an encounter with experiences contradictory to or at variance with established understandings of self and world. Such breakage in fundamental understanding of self can be painful, yet this disruption—the ambiguity or uncertainty of self-definition—brought with it a further challenge. Underneath the ambiguity of self-definition at midlife lay earlier ambivalences toward the threatened or lost self.

These men first encountered experiences discrepant to their self-definition at midlife; in confronting such discrepancies they were brought face to face with their underlying uncertainties and ambivalence about self, avoided or suppressed in first getting into the adult world, and earlier as well. Mr. Markowitz, for example, first found himself repeatedly in situations that threatened his sense of self as a fully responsible, wise, impulse-free scientist and husband (the accumulation of discrepancies that threaten the loss of self) and then was confronted with the underlying uncertainty about "who I am" dating back to childhood. This involved his anger and rage at feeling accountable and "controlled" and the presence within himself of "antisocial" aggression, jealousy, and rage. Or, for example, Mr. Lonzetti found himself at work in situations that eroded his sense of superiority. One specific situation involved intense criticism of a report he made to executives of his company. This experience of criticism not only created an uncertainty about Mr. Lonzetti's knowledge of himself as superior, but also then touched on his own underlying uncertainties and feeling of inferiority. To acknowledge discrepancies in self-definition for these men meant, as for us all, opening up a long trail of deeper and deeper questions about self. In the case of Mr. Lonzetti, for example, we can reconstruct the following kind of sequence: the report was criticized ⟶ my work is being attacked ⟶ am I as good as I think I am? ⟶ is the criticism of me valid? ⟶ how good am I? ⟶ I feel rage. Why? ⟶ I feel inferior. Why?

Mr. Anderson, as a final example, was confronted at midlife with the fact that he had not really separated from his brother in his parents' eyes. Yet the true confrontation was with the fact that he was not really the socially facile, poised, "perfect" person he wanted to be. Underneath these experiences lay Mr. Anderson's devaluation of his inner life—the belief that his impulses and emotions were worthless and marked him as imperfect. In losing the self-definition organized around their careers, all our group had a confrontation at midlife with aspects of self excluded from awareness since adolescence and earlier. Some men's description of discrepant experiences thus carry with them a sense of the return of conflictual aspects of self. As Mr. O'Hara commented in the last chapter about his difficulties as a faculty member in a university: "It was a reexperiencing of feelings I had as a child." A key focus for our analysis of development at midlife is the manner in which these individuals cope with the reemergence at this time of the earlier ambivalently held aspects and potentialities of self.

"Holding On" vs. "Letting Go":
The Process of Reconstitution of Self

Marris (1975) argues that there is a form by which the process of reconstitution proceeds, and it is an ambivalent one, involving an oscillation—over the course of months or years—between the desire to rigidly hold onto the past (preserving unaffected the threatened sense of self) and that of letting go and rushing into the future (abandoning entirely the threatened sense of self). Grieving can be seen as a process of moving between these poles in a series of attempts at gathering new information about the self in the world, trying on new roles, and testing possibilities. The key to adequate grieving is keeping the ambivalent oscillation from premature closure: Individuals who can tolerate both the initial painful discrepancies of midlife and underlying ambivalences are able to experiment and obtain new information about self, thus finding new roles and objectives and reconstituting self. The process of reconstitution can thus be seen as a time of self-exploration and self-testing. When the process is not short-circuited, the result is restoration of the continuity of experience by reconstituting the sense of self independently of the past; one integrates who one was then with who one is now and will be in the future. However, when the process of grieving ends prematurely—because of inability to tolerate either the initial discrepancies or the underlying ambivalence that emerges—it is usually built around one pole of this ambivalent oscillation; rigidly holding onto, or letting go of, the past. As self-definition becomes threatened, we can see the competing, ambivalent desires of "grieving work" in our participants' reports. Some men describe years of denying difficulty at work or in their marriage (holding on rigidly to their interpretations of self and thus denying any discrepancy), others talked of making small, tentative changes and feeling reborn or "like a new person" (thus verbalizing the hope of quickly letting go and thereby avoiding the underlying problems in self-definition).*

Both these patterns of holding on and letting go are, then, an attempt to safeguard a threatened self. By rigidly excluding the discrepancies in

---

*This is again similar to reports from recent studies of the duration of grief reactions beyond the proximate time of loss. In his classic study of traumatic loss, Lindemann (1944) conceived of grief as an "acute" syndrome. His assumption that the grieving reaction to loss was of brief duration and disappeared rapidly has come under closer scrutiny, and many studies of loss (widows, urban relocation, immigration) have found the pattern of recovery to extend over a period of months and years (Marris 1958; Parkes 1972; Glick et al. 1974).

Note also that we are taking the process of resolution to be closed or finished by the time of the career change. However, this may not be true in all cases—the career change may represent only a way station on the road to reconstitution, and the process of resolution is likely still in progress, to different degrees, for all participants at the time of the interviews.

understanding of the self in the world, the threatened self can be maintained. This helps us understand reports of boredom in the years at work
before the career change as part of the attempt to hold on rigidly to a
threatened self. For Mr. Lonzetti and Mr. Prezinski, boredom served to
protect against discrepancies to their self-definition. Boredom, in this
sense, anesthetizes or wipes out feelings that threaten the person's sense of
self. Both men report boredom during experiences that provoke aspects of
self at variance with who they think they are. Boredom becomes a signal
of a paralyzed inner life; it is the tip of the iceberg of concealed emotions:
in the case of Mr. Prezinski sensual, pleasurable desires and appetites, and
for Mr. Lonzetti angry and rageful ones. Boredom safeguards the wished-
for self by buffering it against these experiences. The feeling of rage and
frustration Mr. Lonzetti experiences in these situations are not acknowledged and thus he need not confront the anxieties about inferiority that
lurk under the surface. The same is true for Mr. Prezinski: The buffer of
"boredom" means that appetites need not be acknowledged, and thus the
established order need not be called into question.

Our major concern, however, will not be with the process of grieving
but rather its resolution. The data obtained from retrospective interviews,
taking place within a single short time period, lack detailed description of
the full course of reconstitution. Given this telescoped, retrospective bias,
we can most appropriately analyze grieving in this group from the perspective of its resolution. From our vantage point three to ten years after
the career change and its preceding crisis we will, then, assess how the
process of reconstitution of self at midlife has resolved for our men.

Two Alternate "Ideal" Patterns of
Reconstitution of Self at Midlife:
Sculpted and Foreclosed Resolutions

In this section I construct two "ideal" theoretical types of resolution
at midlife, based on the discussions above of grieving as a process of reconstitution of self. These resolutions should be seen as ideal cases in that they
define the two extreme points on a continuum of resolution; in real life
most people will probably fall at intermediate points between these ex-
tremes.

The keys to our analysis are the ambivalences that form the major
challenge of reconstitution: the ambivalent response to ambiguity/dis-
crepancy and the ambivalence toward the self. Does the individual allow
a full resolution of these ambivalences—fully exploring the discrepancies
of midlife and underlying ambivalent feelings—or is there a premature
foreclosure of the grieving process, settling on one pole of the ambivalence
and effectively denying the loss? In the first alternative, the loss is
confronted—with some pain and over considerable time—more or less directly; this ability to assimilate new information about self in the world is

coincidental with what we usually think of as growth. The second alternative is effectively a denial of experience; behavior and thought are thus serving more defensive ends (protecting against conflict too painful for the ego to deal with). This is a more neurotic, no-growth situation.

We can, from this, articulate two different theoretical resolutions at midlife:

1. *Premature (foreclosed) resolution.* This alternative has to do with the foreshortening of the ambivalent oscillation between holding on and letting go by forming a resolution around one of these poles, and is characteristic of chronic, inhibited, or delayed grieving. In this pattern, the discrepant experiences are not dealt with directly, but rather distorted so as to avoid the sense of loss. In terms of our two-stage model of loss we find defensive distortion either at the level of initial discrepancy or in terms of the underlying ambivalence and uncertainty about self. Since the ambivalence of loss has not been fully explored at midlife we find that the degree of differentiation in these individuals' perception of the complex experiences of life is affected. Rather than perceiving key persons (including self) and events at midlife in a reflective and balanced manner there is a tendency to concrete thinking, to see only one side of situations or persons. Premature resolutions can also be seen in decision making at important choice points at midlife. Since the discrepant experiences have not been integrated as information about oneself, decision making is without a sense of internal responsibility for behavior and a careful stock taking. *

2. *A fuller (sculpted) resolution.* In this case the alternatives of quickly letting go of the past and rigidly holding on are forestalled and greater exploration of these alternatives occurs. We find a fuller integration rather than distortion of the loss, an acknowledgment that the initial project of one's life has gone awry, with some painful implications for oneself and family. Since the loss is accepted ultimately for what it is—information about oneself—and greater experimentation and testing of possibilities occurs, we find a more measured, differentiated appraisal of the key figures and events at midlife, and movement into the future in which the new information about self is taken into account and used, to some measure, in the decision making process. There is thus a "sculpted" quality to this resolution. This term, drawn from Jacques's (1965) discussion, captures the sense of forming and reforming the final product or resolution, involving an interplay between oneself and the outside world (new information resulting from discrepant experiences). Resignation and detachment result from this loss, combined with greater reality testing, as ambivalently held parts of oneself are acknowledged and integrated.

---

*These dimensions bear some similarity to the affective, cognitive, and behavioral components of effective response to challenge and stress described by coping theorists (see Hamburg 1974).

We can summarize our loss and grieving paradigm for midlife, presented over the last two chapters, in the following manner:

Loss: ⟶ *Grieving Work:* ⟶ *Resolution:*
(*reconstitution*)

Accumulation of discrepant experiences that erode the wished-for self	Ambivalent oscillation between attempts to *hold on* and *let go,* marked by: efforts to integrate ambivalent feelings, search for help, experimentation, "testing of possibilities"	Sculpted or Foreclosed

Further Discussion of These Resolutions:
Empirical Observation through Content
and Structure of the Interview Data

This section presents in more detail the nature of sculpted and foreclosed resolutions. The discussion focuses on the empirical observation of such resolutions in the interview data we have available.*

First, a caution. Our two alternatives of sculpted and foreclosed resolution serve a heuristic function as models or guides identifying the kinds of processes and outcomes in evidence during the reconstitution of self at midlife. However, it is important that the either/or nature of this distinction not be overstressed, as if individuals can be easily classified as either sculpted or foreclosed resolutions. The individuals in our group of career changers are, rather, differing mixtures of tendencies toward foreclosure and sculpting. All of the individuals display some (sculpted) openness to their experiences at midlife and some (foreclosed) turning away from them. That is, no person completely distorts or totally integrates his experiences at midlife; rather, all the men have, to varying degrees, learned some les-

---

*There are two major empirical approaches to interview data: attention to content and structural features of interviews. The three dimensions of the interview discussed in this chapter—defensive distortion of discrepant experiences, degree of differentiation of perception of self and others, and quality of decision making—are aspects of interview *content*: what the person tells us about his life history. The Methodological Appendix discusses aspects of interview structure in differentiating foreclosed from sculpted resolutions at midlife. Interview *structure* refers to how the person talks about his life history: the organization of his life story during the sessions; who, how, and why he starts and stops talking; the relative attention given to particular topics and events, the relationship between interviewer and participant, and other aspects of the manner in which the person constructs his life story during the interview sessions.

sons about themselves at midlife. Likewise, no one has a completely full and differentiated view of key persons and events at midlife, nor a totally simplistic, undifferentiated view. And, rarely is decision making completely without a sense of responsibility for one's actions, nor often characterized by a full responsibility for it. We do find, however, that people indicate in the interviews strong tendencies one way or the other—toward greater or less distortion/integration of discrepant experiences, differentiation of key figures, and informed decision making. On this basis we can conceive of particular individuals as representing sculpted or foreclosed resolutions. Yet we must not be misled into conceiving of these resolutions as fixed, easily distinguishable achievements; the complexity of individual functioning reveals, rather, a dialectic of back-and-forth development in which forward growth toward more complex, reconstituted selves (sculpting) alternates with backward movements toward simplistic, less fully reconstituted selves (foreclosing). Thus, those men identified as sculpted resolutions contain tendencies toward foreclosure as well, and foreclosed individuals usually evidence some integration of their experiences at midlife.

Distortion/Integration of the Midlife Experience

Our first content dimension has to do with the integration of ambivalent feelings at midlife. In focusing on what the individual reports from his past, we can first ask, How does the person conceive of his discrepant experiences at midlife? Is midlife seen as a time of learning about self, or is the person's attention directed elsewhere, without integration of the discrepant experiences into the person's sense of self? The latter reflects a rapid rejection of the discrepant experiences through defensive distortion of them; the former a fuller integration and acceptance of these discrepancies. A foreclosed resolution is characterized by such defensive distortion, sculpted resolutions by greater perception of the relevance of midlife to the self.

We can look at the interview from two perspectives in arriving at some conclusions about this. First, how does the person describe the discrepant events of midlife? Here we are concerned with the person's description of the past. Secondly, what is his explanation at present—that is, in reflecting back at the time of the interviews—for these midlife difficulties? In relation to this first perspective we might note, for example, Mr. Lonzetti's discussion of his difficulties at work described in Chapter 3. There was a strong focus on the inadequacies of the people and situations around him. Much of his description concerned the "incredible waste of time," the "maintenance work" involved, and the "people fighting about things." By contrast, he paid less attention to his own role in the discrepant events of midlife. He discussed minimally his own motives, feelings, and inner experiences; he was "an innocent pawn." At times Mr. Lonzetti did acknowledge his own role in his dissatisfaction at work, but he emphasized throughout the ulterior motives of others, the enormous drain of a family, and the deficiencies of his corporation. Contrast this with Mr. Goodson's reports of his work experiences in his laboratory in Chapter 3, wherein the role of the self was more central. This is exemplified by such self-observant statements as, "I didn't like to strike off on my own," "I would tend to wait for help." In this case the discrepant experiences are seen generally for what they are: experiences in the world that contain information about self as well as others. We find greater description of the impact of experiences on him, his own active role in the creation of these experiences, and his responses in these situations. In the distortions of foreclosed resolutions the meaning of these events is circumscribed, restricted to their implications for other people or external institutions. This can be seen as well in terms of our second perspective. Here we are concerned with the personal explanations of the individual, after these events, for their career change. Individuals usually have some retrospective understanding or accounting for why they carried out their career change. This is usually interwoven into their discussion of the past rather than in response to a direct question. Mr. Prezinski and Mr. Goodson stand as contrasting examples. In his explanation of the career change Mr. Prezinski's attention is directed to the failure of engineering to interest him, and he denies any feeling of loss in the decision to leave his first career. He rails at the "narrowness" of the 1950s and the stupidity of the "men stuck in their fucking professions," as if the historical times or particular jobs were the sole source of the problem:

I guess I was really stifled, in this country. By everything. Things in the fifties were really not very good, really a square time. In my generation people were really not with it at all. They were just into their material things. They were such asses. . .

In terms of orientation to the discrepancies of midlife, we find that Mr. Prezinski does not see midlife as essentially containing information about himself. It is rather about the inappropriateness of some professions and of other peoples' problems. This can also be seen in his descriptions of his feelings and experiences, as described in Chapter 3. When describing his boredom at work in engineering, Mr. Prezinski said: "I felt a change would be good. So the next job I looked for was where I could experience something." In this comment, the ability to experience things is attributed to the place, not the individual. This perspective runs throughout Mr. Prezinski's discussion of his life history, and is consistent with his personal explanation of his midlife experience of feeling "dead" as attributable to the "square" fifties. Although at times Mr. Prezinski does center on himself, the predominant role of the self in his descriptions is responsive or passive—usually being acted upon by, or responding to, the deterring environment in its many forms. This emphasis can be seen very clearly in Mr. Prezinski's discussion in Chapter 3 of his anxieties when considering a career change: "My whole background was against it. What right did I have to go into the arts? . . . 'shoulds' were pumped into me from my early days."

Mr. Goodson's personal explanation of his midlife experiences, on the other hand, contains some attention to the role of the "I" in his experiences. In the following examples note how his account focuses to some extent on the role of inner experiences—his values, feelings, and motives—in helping to shape his behavior:

> The career change is to some extent related to this conflict between letting myself play and doing things that are responsible: the "I should" thing. . . . There's a clear split between the responsibility, the conventionality vs. the play, unconventionality. And I sort of feel like it's something I'll always have with me. [*What are your thoughts about where that comes from?*] Some of it is conflict between what my mind is telling me to do and what my heart feels like doing. My mind is bringing in a lot of these "shoulds," these feelings of responsibility that I got during the process of growing to the age where I am now. And my heart lets me be playful. It's the part that sort of takes over and gets me out of my head. Gets me to stop worrying. And it's the part that's acting when I'm really having fun and thoroughly enjoying myself.

In Mr. Goodson's discussion we find as well at times attempts to shift or foreclose the focus of his midlife experiences to the outside world. He comments at one point that science was "a disappointment, it didn't live up to my ideals," as if the structure of science was solely at fault. Further, Mr. Goodson's description above of the "clear split" within himself is actually two-edged, locating the conflict both within and outside him: his mind is subtly associated with the "shoulds" of other people, determining his behavior and opposed to his "real" desires—those of his heart. This is a useful metaphor for Mr. Goodson's own inner struggle to reconcile different motives and needs, yet there is an undertone that the "real" origin of his behavior lies in external forces or in motives and beliefs passively given to him during childhood, as when he refers to "these feelings of responsibility I got during the process of growing up."

This admixture of foreclosed attention to the external determinants of behavior and a sculpted focus on one's own inner ambivalent motives and desires is revealed in Mr. Goodson's discussion of his painting *Turning 30* in Chapter 3. On the one hand he centers his discussion very much on "the conflict within me," his "own internal pressure," and the pain of "looking back on my life at that time thinking about what I felt I had missed." Yet note that the person was being pushed by others, with "his own sort of feet to stand on or . . . to determine what he wanted to do." Further, art is equated with an escape from a restrictive environment, a work situation that had failed Mr. Goodson. Thus, along with the active role of the "I" in Mr. Goodson's account of his midlife runs a passive stance in which the problem is located primarily in a restrictive, faulty work and social environment.

To summarize this dimension, we find that in both the kind of description and kind of explanation of midlife the role of the self is central: Is the meaning of events for the self attended to, understood, and described, or does an attenuated and diminished self emerge from the person's description of his midlife experiences? Such defensive attention away from self characterizes foreclosed resolutions, while attention to the personal involvement of the self in events around oneself—a prerequisite for learning and growth—is a marker of sculpted resolutions.

Differentiation of Figures and Events

Secondly, how fully explored or differentiated do we find key figures and events at midlife? As a result of the exploration and testing of self and world following the loss of familiar understanding of "who I am," how filled in and complete is the person's perception of self and significant others, particularly parents, wives, siblings, and co-workers? Efforts toward assimilation of the "loss" in sculpted resolutions are marked by more synthetic perceptions, attempting to reconcile contradictory experiences and motives, while attempts at foreclosure involve black-and-white thinking that reflect the goal of defending against loss by excluding painfully ambivalent feelings. New insight from the experience of midlife should lead to greater awareness of self and others. We can think of this process of differentiation in terms of a figure-ground metaphor as described by Perry (1970). Individuals strongly embedded in an undifferentiated family environment may emerge over time as sharper figures in their own right, separate from the "ground" of their family. We find in some individuals' interview material extreme stereotype, vagueness, one-dimensionality, and lack of exploration in their discussion of key figures in their past, while other men indicate a fuller reconciliation and integration of the past in their portraits of significant others. Mr. Prezinski's discussion of the "papier-mâché" co-workers he left behind in engineering is an example of the former perspective:

[*What was your world like?*] It was very limited. Most of my friends were engineers or architects. I didn't know many creative people. It was a very narrow world. I made my friends where I worked. I think

I was well enough liked. But they were basically the same kind of people as I was. Maybe there wasn't enough diversity, so I could see other ways of living.

[*How would you describe those people?*] Well, I would say this: that I wouldn't want to be friends with them now. Whenever I meet some of my ex-classmates, I mean it is so unbelievable. Those people were like papier-mâché. I just didn't believe that those people were the same people that I went to school with. I couldn't make any relation, any friendship. And I couldn't fudge the relationship. I didn't feel like making it up. You know, pretending I really liked them. I just disliked them. I just felt that they were so empty. I didn't want to have anything to do with them. I mean they're so brainwashed by the whole system and they're so goal oriented and money. . . . They're so completely Americanized. They're so brainwashed by the whole commercialism. By the whole country, you know? They go for all this stuff. The whole thing, they love all the shopping and everything else. Big fat cars, and stuff I can't believe. It's all papier-mâché, it's all junk. There's no commonality with them anymore. . . . I feel like shaking it off. That epoch, the fifties, that was a bad thing in terms of people in the United States. They were really square, really square. They were about the deadest generation around. What did they call that generation? The quiet generation.

The essention point here, for our purposes, is that there is so little exploration by Mr. Prezinski of what is shared by these people and himself. This is true as well, as we shall see below, of Mr. Prezinski's involvement with his parents. Instead there is a stereotyped characterization and a cutting himself off from these figures. They are psychologically unavailable for his further exploration or learning about self. Mr. Prezinski attends very little to his motives and reasons for becoming an engineer, to why he didn't know any "creative" architects and engineers, what needs, values, and beliefs of his own were fulfilled by his being a "quiet" part of a "quiet generation." In such perceptions we can see the ambivalence of change still "split" and thus foreclosed or avoided—there was nothing of value in his initial career, his peers were "papier-mâché," and (see below) his parents were "wrong." In Mr. Prezinski's undifferentiated perception of the past nothing important about himself was represented by the "way I was." Midlife discrepancies are thus foreclosed by removing the necessity to look at one's experience. This is consistent as well with Mr. Prezinski's emphasis on the external determinants of his behavior. The cause of his feeling "dead inside" is located squarely with the "dead generation" around him.

We are concerned here with the degree to which people and experiences at midlife are seen in a reflective and balanced manner, as opposed to a tendency toward concrete thinking, to see only one side of situations or persons. The latter is evidence of difficulty in tolerating the competing desires and motivations of the ambivalent oscillation that is grieving. Is there evidence of a rigid, stereotyped perception that indicates an unexplored ambivalence or more complex, differentiated perceptions of self and others? Do we find evidence of more complex perceptions in the present than seemed to characterize the views of self and others earlier in their lives? For example, have perceptions of parents become more complex and rich? This is a particularly important dimension of the degree of differentiation of key figures. In Chapter 2 I noted the roots of the young adulthood self-definition in difficulties around separation from parents. Grieving the lost self of midlife in part involves separating more fully from the childhood, idealized images of parents around which these men's self-definition was based. In terms of differentiation we must inquire into both the conceptualization or understanding of one's parents and also the behavior toward them. Is the person dealing with his parents at midlife differently than he did earlier in his life? And has his view of his parents changed as both he and they age, whether his behavior is different or not? Some people indicate little change in their relationship with their parents, or their perceptions of them. Thus, in the following interview excerpt from Mr. Prezinski, note that there is little evidence of increased learning or separation from the idealized figures in the past. Mr. Prezinski's perception of parents seems neither more complex nor sympathetic than that of his childhood. This account of his parents and childhood is still organized solely around a sense of things being done to Mr. Prezinski by these powerful figures:

> My background was such that my parents didn't give me any support in terms of art. Whenever I did drawings or anything like that they would think I was wasting my time. I should do something useful, like engineering. I was just very overprotected. The whole world seemed threatening—I wasn't ready to cope with it at all. I never had any training, my parents never showed me by example how I could cope with the world. My parents tried to squelch whatever creativity I had by telling me everytime I did something that it was no good. . . .

> [*End of first interview*] That kind of summarizes my life pretty well. I don't know what else I could say. [*Are there other things that you feel are important for me to know about your life?*] I don't know, that's about all I can think of. The only other thing is I guess the response of my parents was very negative to anything I did. That held me back for a long time. I always felt whatever I could do would be worthless. That was probably something that held me back from trying a lot of things. That everything I did was garbage, which my

mother still holds today. She still if I come home dressed in a strange way—I have sandals and I might have a pair of shorts on—my mother's all upset. She's wondering what the neighbors are thinking. It's so ridiculous. That's typical. So I've had to struggle against that kind of thing.

The mother and father are presented in these excerpts solely as negative figures relating hostilely or unsupportively to Mr. Prezinski. He does not mention positive aspects of his parents (for example, the strength that allowed them to establish themselves as immigrants in this country), nor does he understand their perspective (for example, reasons why they—as immigrants—might have been fearful about their son's future and so might have pressured him to succeed), or discuss his own roles in these conflicts (why he had not learned to cope with the world more fully). In adulthood Mr. Prezinski fails to exhibit a deeper understanding of his relationships with his parents; he still responds like a kid to his mother's feelings about his clothes. There is clearly no change in his understanding of the parental function—Mr. Prezinski perceives the parental role as essentially to give the person all he needs to get on in the world. He holds them responsible for his being, as when he says that "I never had any training . . . my parents never showed me," "that was probably something that held me back." Essentially, Mr. Prezinski blames his parents for not being perfect enough—not giving him all he needs to get on in the world. There is no sense here of seeing the limitations of parents, the realization that everyone has to cope with great pressures in adulthood, and that we all feel limited at times. He reacts to his disappointment with anger and decries his father for not asserting himself in earlier times, and for becoming "weaker" as he ages. Mr. Prezinski implies it would have been easier for him if his father had been able to change, to stand up to his mother.

I like my father in a lot of ways. He was sort of weak, not very assertive. He sort of went along with everything my mother did. My mother was the dominant person, much more vigorous. Stronger. She made all the decisions. My father did provide for the family, but I think she made most of the decisions. She's very stubborn. She wants her own way and she usually gets it. My father never asserted himself in any of those situations. My father would only occasionally lose his head and take off his belt and run after us and we'd run like hell. We thought that was amusing. He would just act every once in a while very irrationally. And most of the time we just couldn't care. My mother would be very inconsistent. Indulgent one moment and very strict another. Oh, she used to threaten to send us to reform school, too. Can you beat that? Here I was a model kid, and she'd scare the shit out of me. That must have really impressed me greatly. Because that was an awful thing to do to a child. I was very terrified.

[*What did you do that she would say . . . ?*] Oh! It was so minor that I don't even remember what it was. It was like I was just being stubborn about something or another. It was so ludicrous, out of proportion. It wasn't as if I'd done anything significant. I can't even remember. Maybe I didn't eat my breakfast or I didn't sweep the sidewalk or something crazy. My struggle has been getting over my family life. It was awfully confusing. Because I couldn't make sense out of the world, I guess, and I felt that the world was basically unfriendly, and difficult to deal with. And that I was completely inadequate to deal with it.

Mr. Prezinski's present lack of further differentiation in his perception of parents is a major indication of the failure to explore and integrate unresolved aspects of his life history. The essential point is that he is still very much tied to his parents, with a great investment in what they are like; only a change in them will enable him to become different. Further, his account of his behavior toward, and relationship with, his parents at present describes a repetition of his childhood conflicts with them, giving us a clue that Mr. Prezinski has not resolved some of the conflicts that led to the original young adulthood self-definition.

[*I was curious about the reactions of your parents to your decision to leave engineering?*] Oh, my parents were very upset that I left. And it took them quite a while before they would stop talking about that. They kept harassing me. Yeah, every time I met them they would get down on me about that. At first they thought I was going crazy or something. Going nutty, going into the arts. What the hell was I doing that for? But that was the whole attitude they had towards it in the first place anyway. Right? "It's crazy, what are you wasting your time on that for? Are you going to make any money on it?" I had no idea I was going to make any money on it right from the beginning.

[*How did you deal with their harassment of you?*] Oh, I guess I just got angry and harassed them back. I didn't deal with it very well. I just got angry and I shouted at them and they shouted at me. Back and forth. Until we all dropped of exhaustion. I guess I just found myself caught in the same childhood situation in which I was the child. I was acting like I always acted as a child. I felt regression.

[*How did you feel as a child?*] Well, I felt like a child being chastised for doing the thing the parents didn't like. I was just stubbornly holding out. I was even kind of unsure of myself during the whole thing. [*What were you unsure about?*] Well, I just felt as I did when I was a child. And I was wondering about my decisions and everything, but I didn't admit it to them. I mean I had enough problems trying to deal with these new things anyway. That surely didn't help me in any way. But there was nothing they could do about it. They no longer really influenced me a lot personally. I just ignored them. I just said, "I want to do it, that's all." I didn't listen to anything they had to say.

This continued conflict and Mr. Prezinski's childlike account of separating from his parents, exemplified by his statement that he "just ignored them . . . didn't listen to anything they had to say", indicate that he is still psychologically bound to these ambivalently held figures. Yet he also exhibits some insight about his behavior toward parents: "I was acting as I always acted as a child." In order to note one's childishness, one must have a conception of what it means to be "not childish" in relation to parents, to perceive them and behave toward them in a more autonomous, adult fashion.* This provides us with further illustration of the mixed nature of resolutions in real-life cases. Even while Mr. Prezinski's behaviors and perceptions of his parents indicate that he still relates to them like a helpless child appealing to larger, more powerful forces, his foreclosed pattern of differentiation is accompanied by some insight and awareness of his regression.

The lack of greater differentiation of parents is indicative of a foreclosed resolution, while a more differentiated picture synthesizing strengths and weaknesses, rewards and disappointments characterizes sculpted resolutions. Mr. Goodson illustrates this more sculpted perspective on parents. His interviews show evidence of much learning about his parents over time and an increasingly complex, "realistic" perception of them. He portrays the sense of increased complexity in a previously undifferentiated perception of parents when he says:

My brother and I were talking last night about our parents, and he made the comment that when we were kids we really didn't have any adult models besides our parents to make our values on or make choices so far as life style or career. I never realized that that was true and for the longest time I really sort of was the same sort of person that my parents were. And that may have had some influence on determining what sort of direction I wanted to go in so far as career.

He is able to consider the similarities and differences of his parents as he notes:

My friend Joan made a remark that my mother was much more light hearted and sort of pleasure loving than my father who was more serious.

*Note, though, that the insight is not accompanied in his description above by any sense of conflict between his childlike regression and more adult behavior toward parents. It is therefore probable that these vignettes are not isolated incidents of "childishness" but rather typical, habitual patterns of interaction and thus indicative of a more foreclosed stance to his midlife discrepancies.

Also Mr. Goodson clearly separates aspects of himself from those of his father:

> My father's a very practical person, and he's never really had a feeling or appreciation for the arts or for music or for literature. He doesn't have that kind of intuitive response to it. It's sort of something that he really never developed an interest in. And that may have had some influence on the fact that it wasn't part of him so that never became a part of me until I just discovered it on my own.

Uniting positive and negative features into a balanced whole, Mr. Goodson sums up his perspective on his parents with: "a pretty good image and a valid one . . . but . . . limited."

Perception of self is the reciprocal of perception of parents. Thus, correspondingly, we can ask whether there is a broader, richer perception of self than that which characterized the participants' young adulthood sense of self. Here we are focusing on the change in differentiation of self that has occurred over time. For some this change does not occur. For Mr. Prezinski, undifferentiated perceptions of the past mean that questions of why he became involved in his initial career, what he shares in common with his friends, the meaning of his relationships with his parents, remain unanswered. This can be seen in terms of differentiation of self, which is still organized around the young adulthood image of himself as "weak" and "powerless" in the face of strong others:

> There was a whole period when I didn't want anyone to know that I had changed professions. I guess because I didn't go to art school I feel myself sort of inadequate. I couldn't do it, or someone was going to tell me I couldn't do it. And I had no right to do it. I have no right to be an artist, because I didn't go to art school or some kind of crazy thing.

Have there been any changes over time in Mr. Prezinski's perception of self? How much is Mr. Prezinski now able to acknowledge his aggressions, urges, and appetites now, as compared with earlier in adulthood? This material indicates that Mr. Prezinski's picture of himself hasn't changed as a result of his midlife experiences—he still perceives himself as weak and innocent of aggressive or self-aggrandizing motives. His self-definition is still rooted in conflicts with parents, and his underlying attitude to devalued aspects of his own subjectivity is unchanged. This can be seen clearly in his earliest memories, which stress over and over again his feelings of smallness, weakness, and "innocence" in the face of a powerful world:

> I guess I've been reactive most of my life. I can remember when I was a little kid I was always thinking creatively. I built a house once out

of boxes and crates. Well, I only partially built it. And I had other half-baked ideas when I was a kid. I mean I just didn't have the technical knowledge to know what I was doing but I guess I was maybe about five or six and I remember collecting pieces of sidewalk. You know, they tore up a concrete sidewalk and were just throwing it away. So I collected them, I got a bunch of them together and I thought I would powder it and make cement out of it again. Of course I didn't. I pounded away and I got a little bit of stone together.

A powerful underlying theme in this memory is the futility of his own efforts. He "pounded away" and all he got was "a little stone." Not only was he weak, but the outer world was destructive and overpowering:

But my parents also tried to squelch whatever creativity I had by telling me everytime I did something that it was no good. What I made was garbage. And they kept threatening to tear it down. And my father would never help me. Like I had gotten to the point in building my house where I needed a little help, and I knew I couldn't ask my father because he wouldn't help me. [*What would he do?*] Well, he would just simply say, "Tear it down, it's just junk." And I needed help. It was beyond my capacities. But I felt that if I had just a little help I could get over some of the problems involved. I'd see all the big kids and they were doing something. So one day I came back and the house was gone. In a way I breathed a sigh of relief. I was really happy it was gone because then I wouldn't have to defend myself. You know, by having this absurd structure. I just felt that I finally got it off my neck. I had to defend myself because they just wanted to tear it down. I just felt relieved of that burden. I'd just forget it. It was gone and I won't have to do anything about it.

It is not surprising that a child might feel like a "cork on the ocean" (as Mr. Prezinski described himself in Chapter 2) who is "unable to cope." What is of interest is that Mr. Prezinski still feels and perceives the world in this manner. For Mr. Prezinski childhood is the root of his problems. He still has not separated from the sense of himself as a childhood victim, at the mercy of those larger than himself. In keeping with this self-image, we find that Mr. Prezinski continues to search for powerful people whom he can turn to for help and support. As he says, "It is so hard to do things alone," and we find a succession of figures in his life history who, through their strength, enable Mr. Prezinski to do what he wants—particularly his wife and certain of his friends.

Mr. Goodson, on the other hand, shows increasing awareness of aspects of self, particularly those earlier devalued. Note the reciprocal process of differentiation of others and learning about self seen in this discussion of his parents.

One thing that happened in this group therapy I was in was that I started becoming aware of the side of my mother's and father's differences in personality and the fact that I had idolized my father so much. And one of his traits was that he was very non-emotional. He didn't cry or ever show any physical signs of affection like hugging and kissing. And I started doing this in the group and it came out how much I was angry at my father for some of the very qualities that other people found were getting in my way. Like not being able to talk about my feelings or show my emotions or be physical with people. And I remember one time when I would get so angry at my father during one of these sessions that I punched a hole in the wall and then I went home for Christmas after about a year of the group and confronted my father with these feelings and this anger and this real . . . actually, more disappointment in his sort of not being emotional and not being warm.

[*And Your Mother?*]

I remembered times when I was a child where my father put down my mother for being emotional. During this period I began to realize that I was at fault, or I was blind at the time, that I didn't appreciate that emotionality. So when I came home at Christmas, I really told my mother how much I appreciated her for her emotionality and did a lot of hugging and kissing with her and crying with her and sort of feeling very much siding with my mother and her qualities that my father lacked.

As Mr. Goodson becomes more aware of his parents' particularities and differences, he becomes more aware of his own nature and the various ways in which he is different from his parents. He first describes a strong sense of identification with his parents, particularly his father: "I had idolized my father so much." This is a thought elaborated on elsewhere when he says, "I was really emulating him to a large extent, and a lot of the things I did as a kid were things that he did or things that he encouraged." This overidentification begins to break down when Mr. Goodson is able to confront and express anger toward his father for his lack of warmth. Mr. Goodson becomes aware of his own emotionality and is able to accept aspects of self that were earlier warded off as "too feminine," those parts of himself that reminded him of his mother. Thus, Mr. Goodson's discussion of his parents portrays the sense of greater separation from a previously undifferentiated relationship and acceptance of more differentiated aspects of self.

Note that a tempering of perfectionist fantasies is related to the increasing differentiation of self, parents, and others at midlife. The failure to differentiate more completely one's parents means that the person holds on tightly to his perception of perfection in the world. For example, in

Mr. Prezinski's case the parents remain powerful people who have great strength and wisdom to give to him, and Mr. Prezinski is angry that they fail to do so. Since this perfection is still ascribed to parents, it is likely that others will be evaluated against the same perfectionist standards. This sets the groundwork for great disappointments in others, as well as the continued hope for such perfection in oneself. In other words, the failure to differentiate parents from the childlike image of perfection means that one continues to hope that he too will be perfect in some way. *

Our examination of the degree of differentiation of figures and events in the interview material thus focuses on the exploration of the internal and external environment with "testing of possibilities" so as to find new, satisfying roles and opportunities that allow reconstitution of an altered sense of self ("identity"). In attempts at premature or foreclosed grieving, the inability to tolerate the initial discontinuity or emerging complex of ambivalent feelings makes such exploration difficult, and we find less evidence of this testing and searching in the real world during midlife. †

A picture of the person's information-seeking capacity and the manner in which he is able to test and search the environment in this way can be gained from their observed receptivity to information about himself. In particular, what does the person's language in the interviews tell us of his self-awareness and self-observant capacity? How able is he to connect motive to behavior and to establish links between different events, figures, and experiences in his life history? How eager is the person to do this? Mr. Prezinski's limited receptivity to information about self, and limited capacity for self-observation, are revealed at times by his language in the interviews. Repetitively, he will comment, "well, I guess that's it . . . I don't know what else to say," "that's about all I can think of," "it's hard to go on . . . I don't know what else to say." And his lan-

---

*This tempering of perfectionist fantasies does not seem to be an either-or proposition. We find a lessening or change in such fantasies, but not necessarily the absence of such wishes.

†The focus, in essence, is on whether the individual has tolerated an ambiguity of understanding about self at midlife so as to allow uncertain aspects of self to emerge. This is an essential aspect of grieving—new emotions, beliefs, values, and attitudes are made real and integrated in a reorganized sense of self as the older, outdated self is laid to rest. Yet this involves the reexperiencing of the previously warded-off aspects of self reflected by—and embedded in—the discrepant experiences of midlife. The alternative is to hold on or let go rigidly to threatened understanding of self so as to allow for no acknowledgment of the discrepancies of midlife. Psychological defenses are important means of safeguarding a threatened self—they distort experiences so they no longer call essential self-definitions into question. We saw, for example, the function of boredom for some of our participants. Defenses operate differently to split ambivalences and remove the painful feeling of contradictory wishes and desires. Boredom and denial, for example, serve to blot out our experiences while projection and externalization "split off" the threatening part of an ambivalence, exiling (locating in the outside world) the

guage shows how little exploration of long-standing problems with his wife has occurred:

> We've separated now. I guess that's a problem that I have to deal with. I don't know if I love her anymore. I can't make up my mind. We have so many strong bonds. It's really hard to break. I just don't know what to do about it. We've been separated a year. I'm really confused about that. I can't quite think of it plainly and straight. I can't even get my mind to focus on it very long because it's so confusing to me. I can't even understand how I could be at this point, you know? Not thinking. I don't know if I can overcome it. I just don't know how to feel about this problem. I guess the way I'm dealing with it is by not doing anything. Hoping that something will become clear to me.

Mr. Prezinski's comments, "I can't get my mind to focus on it" and "I can't even understand how I could be at this point," illustrate his befuddlement and the marked degree to which the marital situation is unexplored, unintegrated, and isolated from the rest of his life.

By contrast, Mr. Goodson's language shows his receptivity to information about himself and his ability to establish linkages across different events and experiences in his life history. This positive receptivity is seen in his references to significant others, "my brother and I were talking last night . . ." and "my friend Joan made a remark." Mr. Goodson is able to use information from others to stimulate his own thinking about self. His curiosity, thoughtfulness, and willingness to explore his history are indicated by his language and demeanor at several points in the interview:

> I've thought about ever since I've made this career change, back into the past about what sort of clues I might have had from the past as to what, you know, might have prompted it . . .
>
> . . . I often try to recall . . . the number of times that I've tried to think back.

---

unacceptable wishes while we hold onto the threatened self-definition. Some markers of the defensive distortion of a foreclosed resolution thus become such defense mechanisms as externalization, denial, and intellectualization. *Externalization* locates conflictual aspects of self outside, in other people or institutions. With this mechanism the person locates the conflictual material "out there" splitting the problem from the self and fixing the responsibility on external situations or individuals. *Denial* means that discrepant experiences are not acknowledged as valid; often ambivalently held parts of oneself are not acknowledged, or are seen as no longer applicable or valid. Finally, *intellectualization* means that conflictual aspects of self are described in nonaffective, distanced terms, without appropriate affect.

When my mother puts that pressure on me. Let's see, what's the feeling I have? . . .

(I try) to sort of get in touch with what I feel is going on inside rather than what's going on outside of me.

Decision Making

As our last perspective on the reorganization of self from interview content, we can examine the person's decision making at midlife. How do the key choices of this time reflect the manner in which the person has dealt with the ambivalences and discrepancies of midlife? Do such decisions emerge out of the explored ambivalences and make use of new information about self in the world, or do they reflect a rigid foreclosing of ambiguity and uncertainty, an attempt to hold on or let go rigidly to threatened self-perceptions? The decision-making process about which we have the most information is the decision to change careers, and we can focus on the descriptions of how this change came about for the men in our study. Does this decision emerge out of the confrontation with and integration of ambivalences, or from a sense of rigid foreclosing and safe-guarding behavior?* In more integrated resolutions, because the midlife loss eventually comes to be seen as containing information about oneself, there is resultant learning and growth, from which important life decisions emerge. Decision making reflective of attempts to foreclose loss does not have this underlying sense of growth since there is less self-learning or attempt to bring new information about oneself to bear on the problems of one's life. Two of the markers of these alternate contexts of decision making are as follows. Choices made within the context of a sculpted resolution reflect a fuller accounting of who the person is; decision making in the service of foreclosure is exclusionary or a partial solution, without a sense of internal responsibility for behavior and a careful stock taking. Individuals thus differ in the degree of acceptance of the responsibility for or the consequences of their midlife decisions. Further, descriptions of choice points differ in the degree of thoughtfulness and appropriate delay that appear. Some people, by inclusion of these elements, give strong indication of decisions based on detailed conscious or preconscious consideration of who they are in the face of new information and experience:

> I really thought a lot before leaving my position with the firm. I thought a lot about "what do I really want?" I remember during that

*Note that this perspective implies that the process of resolution is closed or finished by the time of the career change. However, this may not be so, and the process of reconstitution may still be going on at midlife for some participants. The discussion of decision making during the career change that follows is meant as reflective of foreclosed or sculpted tendencies, and should be understood as illustrative of a viewpoint applicable to other kinds of decisions.

Christmas vacation, I considered all the angles I could think of. Talking with my wife, mostly a lot of searching within myself. I talked to several artists I knew. Just thinking and walking and talking a lot of time, I thought of a college English teacher, and I thought of a guy who had been in music at high school and I thought of the kind of letters I wrote, how much I loved the language. And it seemed to come together a bit. It came together in terms of making things. Giving things shape of a certain kind that seemed to matter to me.

In the protocols of other men, evidence of such careful self-assessment and decision making is absent. Thus the person may describe choices as arising out of the interplay of external or random forces, with himself as merely the passive object: "The career change was an accident really. I guess there was no real reason. It wasn't really correlated with anything, I guess." Or the person may reveal rapid or isolated decision making procedures that exclude opposing considerations or that obscure questions of underlying motive and desire entirely. Such a precipitate, unexplored resolution can be seen in Mr. Prezinski's decision making around his career change, as recollected from the perspective of our interviews. Here is an illustrative description by Mr. Prezinski of decision making at the time of the change from his engineering job into the arts in the middle sixties:

I didn't ask anybody at work for advice because I knew what their advice was going to be—that I should stay. It was a hard decision, the kind of decision I knew I had to do by myself. I wasn't thinking of asking anyone. I mean I could have, like I could have asked the head of our section at work. But I didn't want to appeal for help.

I didn't see my boss face to face either, I did it by phone. I didn't want to have to go through persuasion. I had made up my mind. I knew what I wanted to do. So I called him up and explained it. I knew that would put him at a disadvantage. First of all it was a surprise. And I know when I came back to my office to pick up my stuff, one guy was there. He was a good friend of mine and he asked me about my leaving. He was very nice and he didn't try to persuade me. He asked if there was some reason that he could help me with, if I was in trouble or something like that. But I told him I thought it all over and I didn't ask for any advice because I felt I had to make this move myself.

I had come to the conclusion that this was my last chance for the arts. There'd be simply no time. You have to put a lot of time into engineering. There would be no way back into the arts. And something told me that I really should try the arts.

In these descriptions note two elements important to our purposes: (1) the sudden unreflective nature of the decision (described as a "last chance"), without evidence of careful stock taking and (2) the defensive, "closed off" nature of Mr. Prezinski's refusal to discuss or explore the deci- sion—as if questions of motive and reason were being avoided. The refus- al to talk matters over, in this case, stems more from the desire to foreclose exploration of the situation and self-examination than from the confident certitude accompanying either the acceptance or responsibility for one's decisions. Thus, Mr. Prezinski is more concerned with putting his boss at a disadvantage and achieving a surprise than obtaining advice or getting help.

Two Polar Resolutions: Mr. Markowitz and Mr. Anderson

This section presents two illustrative case individuals, with the goal of pulling together the diverse dimensions of sculpted and foreclosed reso- lutions of loss at midlife discussed to this point. This discussion illustrates tendencies toward our two extreme resolutions: Mr. Markowitz illustrates a foreclosed resolution and Mr. Anderson a sculpted one. Before begin- ning, two disclaimers. First, I mean these alternatives as "ideal" cases, ex- emplifying the end points on a continuum. No one in this study fits clean- ly and precisely into this typology, which I present in dichotomous form merely as a heuristic device, to make more apparent the trends involved in different patterns of reconstitution. Discussion of Mr. Markowitz and Mr. Anderson is meant merely as illustrative of tendencies in one direction and the other; as with all participants, each has elements of both alterna- tives in their resolution.* A second disclaimer: Sculpted resolutions should not be perceived as necessarily "better," in the individual case, than fore- closed ones, though in the "ideal" personality we would see sculpted reso- lutions as better. The confrontation with ambivalences about self, skim- ming close to primitive wishes and anxieties, may be beyond the capacity of the individual, or not in his best interest given the "reality" of his par- ticular life situation (work, economic, family, or other demands). The movement to safeguard a threatened self may in some cases be precisely that: life saving or self-preserving. As Nieztsche pointed out, we at times need "life-saving illusions" about ourselves. The discussion that follows, then, is less oriented toward differentiating "good" from "bad" resolu- tions of midlife losses than in showing the various ways in which individ- uals cope, as best they can, with situations of ambivalence and change, as

---

*There is an artificiality to this notion of "resolution"—taking a phenomenon (human growth and development) that is inherently in process, fixing it in time, and then claiming that the snapshot taken from what is really a motion picture is truly representative of the phenomenon under study. However, I do this as a "heuristic" to allow discussion of a complex process and to sharpen the conceptual tools used in analysis.

well as indicating the possible consequences that flow from these different patterns.

Mr. Markowitz: "We have an infinite number of ways that we can deceive ourselves." Mr. Markowitz left his government position to study acting in New York City. In reaching this decision Mr. Markowitz was able to draw on accumulated savings and the fact that his wife was employed as well. Mr. Markowitz was pursuing an interest of many years in making the transition, as he was a regular participant in amateur theater in his community. Over time Mr. Markowitz began drawing regular roles in the theatre. He remains married.

In relation to orientation toward the discrepant experiences of midlife, we find that for Mr. Markowitz the "encounter with affect" at midlife is not seen as containing information about himself. This can be seen in his discussion of the events of midlife in the preceding chapter. We find a diminished self in his description of his experiences: a narrow and restricted picture of his own feelings, motives, and beliefs, with the central actor in the life history in a passive role. Mr. Markowitz's account of his life history through the midlife years is framed essentially in terms of the problems with the social institutions of science and the family; accounts of his own inner motives, experiences, and responses through those years appear much less frequently. His feelings and reactions are not central to the account; rather the focus is on what other people did to him, or the disappointing nature of other people and institutions. Mr. Markowitz's own motives and hopes in his experiences are not discussed at all, despite clear indications that he was centrally involved. He can only describe encounters: "We had a terrible stand-off fight . . . we couldn't speak civilly to each other." Mr. Markowitz was a clear participant in this angry struggle and must have had some intentions of his own, but he does not mention his own judgments, decisions, motives, or feelings. Instead, the focus is on the malevolent motives of those around him: "He set about to break up the group . . . he would step on people to get where he wanted." We also find impersonal or distanced perspectives in which motives and emotions are masked characterizing Mr. Markowitz's descriptions of many events: "a lot of politics," "a real scramble for power," "a real clash in personalities." Similarly, some of the discussion of his midlife difficulties is presented at the level of metaphor, with the relationship of self available only by inference. An example of this is his story of "the bear that was" discussed in chapter 3, page 94. In regard to difficulties at home, Mr. Markowitz tells the story of his problems as a father from the perspective of his family, and rarely clarifies his own feelings and emotions. That is, he recounts the difficulties with his children in terms of his children's behavior and speech, which seem to occur in a vacuum with Mr. Markowitz only a dim, passive figure.

In Mr. Markowitz's account during the interviews of both areas of

discrepant experience at midlife, work and family, we can only gain hints
of his struggle with his own feelings and emotions—his desire for advancement in science; his anger, resentment, and jealousy of his children;
his "antisocial" aggression. He states his own feelings and perceptions ob-
liquely: "you always have the sneaking suspicion you're being compromised," "you can resist everything except temptation," "he never knew
when I might fly off the handle and explode in rage". Only rarely does
Mr. Markowitz directly describe his own anger, resentment, and envy of
others. In other words, the attentional focus for Mr. Markowitz is away
from self and toward external events.

Consistent with this is Mr. Markowitz's personal explanation for the
events of midlife at the time of the interviews. Mr. Markowitz explains his
career change and family difficulties—loci of the crisis at midlife—as essentially resulting from the faulty structure of the institutions of marriage
and science. He focuses his attention on the failure of science and mar-
riage/family with, again, little discussion of his own role and involvement
in the events and experiences of midlife. He experiences a sharp devaluation of science and the crisis is located "out there" in the very nature of
science and marriage; not just in the way science might be practiced but
in its very structure. He compares science to Arthur Koestler's fallen idol,
The God that Failed, and bitterly criticizes it as an antisocial activity
lacking humanity:

> Is there something about science that leads men to do antisocial
> things? I got to thinking about that. And I thought "of course there is,
> the whole training of science." Because the evil we're talking about is
> the evil of being antisocial. Now the one sure way of avoiding that is
> to be able to put yourself in someone's place. Empathy is the word I
> think of. Now, the scientific method is precisely the opposite. The
> method of science is to take your problem and abstract it so that if it
> were occurring in some far reaches of the universe away from people
> it wouldn't matter at all. The solution would be exactly the same. So
> you abstract everything that you feel has no bearing, is not a function
> of whatever parameter you're measuring. So that is where the habit
> starts. The scientific method which I absolutely revered as the way of
> finding out the truth is seriously flawed. You cannot think of science
> without thinking of it as a human activity. And where is the humani-
> ty in the scientific method? There is none. It doesn't enter.

Mr. Markowitz's comment above that "the evil we're talking about is
the evil of being antisocial" is poignant. This touches on his own struggles
with feeling antisocial—an angry scientist and father. Yet the referent to
his phrase is not himself—it is "the whole training of science." As he says
at a later point, his difficulty at midlife was "just a failure in my mind, of
science."

Although Mr. Markowitz remains married, parenting—a major source of discrepant experience marked by considerable intergenerational tension and hostility—is seen as part of the socially defective institution of marriage, which is structured in an "antihuman" way. In relation to his children, the schools are sorted out for particular criticism; the locus of parenting difficulties is located as well in the "repressive" educational establishment that "demands conformity":

> I was in contact with the school system because my kids were in the school system, and from beginning to end there was nothing but trouble. The teachers were not in any position to respect anymore and with good reason. The instruction was just terrible. I don't mean all the teachers were like that. But enough of them were so that it characterized the school system. And finally I came to the conclusion that it was doing more harm than good. I know certainly my children were much more curious and open before they got into school than after they got out.
>
> I felt that my children, that the more creative they were in school the more trouble they got into. I realized that there were influences at work demanding conformity. And after you read a book like *1984* you begin to see even more insidious ideas going on which are becoming less and less farfetched as we get closer and closer to 1984.

The conflict is shifted to these passages from his difficulty with his children—his anger and resentment at their freedom and options for the future—to a conflict between his children and the schools, in which the intolerance of his children's "creativity" and expressiveness is found in the teachers, the instruction, and the school system in general.

At one point Mr. Markowitz touches on his own difficulties in the family with the comment that "the kids tell me that . . . there was an insurmountable wall between us . . . there wasn't any kind of feeling." Now this is a very powerful comment, providing an opening to his angry, resentful feelings of having been controlled in his family, of having been too involved, of having become "responsible at age 12." Mr. Markowitz alludes to this when he goes on to say, "I felt that they were first of all a responsibility. I had to take care of them." He then focuses on the nature of science, not himself:

> In any scientific field, you have to keep up with it. There's a huge amount of stuff to be done. The thing is that the way science works for most people I know, most good scientists, is like an itch. When you have a problem that won't yield, you can say, "OK, it's five o'clock. I'll go home." But the fact that the solution to that problem occurs to you at three o'clock in the morning sometimes means that it's there all the time nagging at you.

I suppose in a sense the troubles with the kids may have been an inevitable result of my outlook on science. Science should be a verb, I believe. I was playing a parent role . . . I fell into this father's role, without realizing it, the role of the parent. That's what makes life difficult in the family. That's why I think perhaps the family is finished in our society.

Note in the excerpt how the emphasis in this discussion of work and family shifts from self, the "I," to science and the "parent's role." There was an "insurmountable wall" between his children and himself because of the amount of work in his field, and he "fell into the father's role." Mr. Markowitz says that he changed careers because of the flawed nature of the scientific method and the scientific enterprise. The lessons at midlife were not about his own anger, jealousy, resentment, and competitive ambition; rather "it was just a failure . . . in my mind of science."

This explanation for his midlife experiences allows Mr. Markowitz to repair the discontinuity in self-definition by locating the discrepancy "out there" in the nature of science and marriage. These external institutions are the locus of corrupting, antisocial pressures, and the disappointment was with these choices, not with himself or his behavior. Without debating the validity of Mr. Markowtiz's critique of science, marriage, and schooling in our society, we can wonder if something is not left out of his account of his midlife history, particularly since what is attributed to other people and institutions so closely resembles parts of himself that are not acknowledged as such. Who, for example, was attracted to "corrupting" executive offers? Who at times behaved in an "antisocial" manner at home and at work? As we shall see below in our analysis of the differentiation of self at midlife, Mr. Markowitz's perception of who he is contains no acknowledgment of these aspects of self. We can infer the questions about self that are avoided: Why was I attracted to tempting ("corrupting") executive offers in the sciences? Why so much anger at my children? Unacceptable, ambivalently experienced aspects of Mr. Markowitz's inner life are externalized and "split off" as science becomes the locus of unacceptable impulses and feelings actually found within himself. In this manner the initial "crisis of discontinuity" (the "failure" of science and marriage) is externalized as well, and the ambivalence of change foreclosed as Mr. Markowitz rigidly lets go of the attachments and commitments in this area. To summarize, we find a variety of defensive distortions of Mr. Markowitz's discrepant experience at midlife. Through a combination of projection, devaluation of "split off" parts of the past, and denial the discrepant experiences are defended against and the experience of loss avoided.

In terms of differentiation of figures and events in the past, we find evidence of little change in Mr. Markowitz's perception of self or others as a result of his midlife experience. This is a further indication of constricted learning or personal development that emerges from the crisis at midlife. In terms of differentiation of self, Mr. Markowitz is presented in the interviews in an unexplored, relatively undifferentiated position as he is usually impulse free, innocent of the anger and aggression found outside of him in the external world. He comments:

> My picture of myself is as a fairly ordinary person. I guess I've had the same emphasis on truth telling as my father had. I never told a lie to anyone. Starting with the time they could understand me, I treated my kids always with great respect. There are times of course, like with everyone when one loses one's temper. But I didn't think that characterized my behavior.

Mr. Markowitz's "picture" of himself has shown relatively little enlargement or gain in complexity as a result of his experiences at midlife. His self-definition has remained relatively unchanged in the face of contradictory experiences. In this regard, Mr. Markowitz resembles Mr. Lonzetti, in that the perception of himself is as an "innocent pawn" through his midlife experiences. References to an unchanging sense of self since childhood are revealing. Mr. Markowitz says at one point, for example, "ever since I was a kid I've had an emphasis on . . ." and "I felt *very early* . . ." This unbroken thread of self-definition extending back to childhood implies, in this case, a marked lack of differentiation and separation.

Further, Mr. Markowitz's picture of his parents has not evolved very much either. He compares himself with his father very often, stressing the similarity and continuity between himself and this figure.

> My parents were fairly opposite. My father was reserved all the time, my mother was emotional and affluent, and somehow I grew up with the feeling that my father's way of living was the right way. That it was good to be in control, to be analytical, to stand aside, to stand away and look at something. Because when you got emotionally involved it got distorted—your view of things. My mother was a volatile, enthusiastic person who didn't really care too much about how she looked, how she appeared, what impression she was giving. She easily cried, easily laughed. My father, I never knew much about him. He wasn't a person to tell you things about himself, how he felt. Perhaps he had been brought up with the idea of being strong, that perhaps emotional display was a kind of weakness. And I identified with him I suppose. . . .

The statement, "I grew up with the feeling that my father's way of living was the right way," indicates this continuity between the father-

son. While Mr. Markowitz's ability to make this observation implies some
sense of being set apart from the father and family basically the influence
is accepted and Mr. Markowitz doesn't question this rigid emphasis on
"the right way" as one of always "being in control." Note too that Mr.
Markowitz's discussion soon gets vague: "I never knew much about him,"
"I identified with him, I suppose." These latter comments are indications
of Mr. Markowtiz's relatively undifferentiated and unexplored picture of
his father. Throughout the sessions we find little exploration or acknowledgment of the differences between himself and his parents. We find, as a
result, little questioning of his parents or increased understanding in Mr.
Markowitz's perception of them:

> I never really got to know my father too well. He was not a man that
> was easy to talk to. In the enthusiasm of youth I had made several at-
> tempts and had been rejected. We had a lot of conflict when I was
> growing up. Say into my teens. It was only later on when I felt secure
> unto myself that I was able to approach him.
>
> With a parent especially it's difficult. Whether you've rebelled or
> not, there's still the huge weight of authority because there's a person
> who has lived so much longer. In fact has manufactured you. And I
> wasn't thinking so much from the standpoint of knowledge, but more
> of just a kind of emotional security. It must really be deep-seated, in
> the process of being born and in growing up, the maturation. And al-
> though you may speak very strongly, it takes a long time when you're
> speaking to your parent before you're speaking on even terms. Just
> even terms. And it's just as hard for a parent to do the same thing. . . .
>
> It was pretty tough, in fact, when my father died, at age seventy.
> I felt really bereft because I didn't really know the man at all. He
> never, never would let go of his control, to speak. I had to get inklings
> of what he felt, listen in between the lines. And I felt so sorry for
> him. But the main feeling was of terrible loss because I had never
> come to know him. I doubt if anybody had.

This material indicates that little real exploration of his relationship
with his father took place when he was still alive, nor has such an exploration occurred in Mr. Markowitz's mind since his father's death. Note the
absence of any shift or deepening of understanding of his parents, or of
any change in conceptualization of the parental role. Mr. Markowitz's
father remains an idealized, godlike figure. He speaks of never feeling on
an equal footing with his father and reveals below a childlike definition of
the father's role with his reference to the "parent-godlike syndrome." The
father—his own father—remains an unexplored psychological mystery to
Mr. Markowitz at present, just as he was a mystery to his son in childhood.

For Mr. Markowitz the father is still an awesome, idealized figure. We see Mr. Markowitz's difficulty in acknowledging ambivalent feelings toward his father and in challenging this figure in the following excerpt from the interviews. At first Mr. Markowitz reveals some real difficulties with his father as a child, then shifts focus to his mother's role in this exchange, and becomes angry when pressed about his feelings toward his father:

My father's older brother had become a college professor. And his older sister had become a lawyer. So here you had a man who made his living working for other people, he never made very much money. And this was important. He just was never very sure of himself. I had grown up with a dislike for my father, a hatred at times. With dislike, suspicion, wondering what kind of person he was, and I realized later this was the result of what my mother had told me about him. Not exactly told me but implied. For instance, she broke up several friendships he had, from early days when he was a boy, with other boys, and the implication I got there was somehow they had homosexual overtones or something like that. That was what I got, perhaps she didn't mean to put that in my head, but that was what I got, that it was wrong for a man to put his friends in an important position. His family was what needed it. And I thought so too, as a child. [*You were angry because he wasn't there?*] No! It was my mother who was angry, and she was very vocal with me. [*I thought you agreed with her?*] Well, yes, my mother told me, what does a child believe! I felt that she was indeed being put upon and abused. OK?

The continued awesome role of his father—not to be criticized—can be seen in some of Mr. Markowitz's earliest memories, where the "reverent" position of authority figures is fondly remembered, as is the son's "accountability" in such situations:

I think that the older members of my family had this feeling for humanism. My grandfather's brother, for instance, was a philosopher! He was looked up to by the rest of the family. I used to play chess with him. . . . I was very young, small, but I remember the first time he came into our house; my parents' house. He went to the bookcases immediately. And he looked and looked very intently, and he said there was one philosopher that was missing. He was really shocked that we didn't have him in the bookcases. I was ashamed of myself because I never even heard of him.

There was always a social concern. We had many learned philosophers in the family. People who were not involved in business who were looked up to and were placed in a very high position in the family. There are people that I barely knew, only as a small child, but I remember the feeling and the atmosphere, which was one of reverence.

Mr. Markowitz's conception of the family and the father/parent/husband role is, then, still rooted in childhood perceptions as to the responsibility, power, and demands entailed.

The whole parent-godlike syndrome. [*How is parent godlike?*] . . . Just on earth the father is the disciplinarian. He tells the children what to do and what not to do and also just how far they can go based on the law and what have you.

His mother is presented in a stereotypically positive light, a person who approved "of everything I did," in sharp contrast to his feelings of being "raised to be responsible at age 12":

"My mother has always approved of everything I did. I could walk down the street bare-assed naked and she would figure out some good reason why not only I should do it, but everybody else as well. So, never any doubts about her."

In his discussion of his own role at midlife Mr. Markowitz reveals a primitive, childhood view of the father. And this is the source of continued conflict for Mr. Markowitz, guided by such a demanding, unrelenting image of what it means to be a father or husband or parent. He continues to feel anger and resentment at the prison he has made for himself. The rigid standards he has ambivalently accepted are revealed in his comments that he became "responsible at age 12" and felt it was "wrong to put friends in important positions." We find little tempering of the implicit perfectionist fantasy—that we can be completely correct and wise, without antisocial impulse—and the idealization of others as models or exemplars of this wished-for self.

In general, we find that the facts of midlife are rarely presented by Mr. Markowitz in their full complexity. Of course his perception of science contains elements of this, as he progresses from a sense of science as an "ideal life" to his claim that it is an "utterly immoral activity." In his twenties love had presented no alternative but marriage; now marriage is a discredited institution. Most of his life was spent as a member of the "establishment" primarily concerned with earning a living, yet, we shall see, for Mr. Markowitz the counterculture now possesses a monopoly on morality. In all these perceptions "good" and "bad" are sharply split and easily identified, a situation evidently of importance to Mr. Markowitz. We can see similar black/white thinking and simplistic perceptions in relation to significant figures: males, primarily father surrogates to whom he is potentially accountable, are idealized—they are "godlike," "geniuses." Further, Mr. Markowitz's perception of these figures—like that of his father—is usually organized around a single dimension: their highly moral nature. One such figure is described in the following manner:

> Our wrestling team in college was coached by a tremendous man. A man who believed that it was more important to be a good person than to win matches. And we simply worshipped him. He was everything that was good, considerate, dignified. He loved all of us. He walked as if he were God, erect.

Toward his children, Mr. Markowitz denied negative feelings despite the "corrosive" relationships; they are presented as very good—no description of the provocative or difficult behavior to be expected of any child is presented at all. This reveals a black/white, childlike thinking: the "good guys" are pristine, clear, godlike, and "everything that was good," while those not among the enlightened are without redeeming virtue. When discussing those in the latter group, Mr. Markowitz has difficulty in seeing their side of the story or admitting to opposing considerations or extenuating circumstances. Mr. Markowitz's colleagues in the scientific profession are stereotypically dismissed: "There was something that was very special about science, a question of selectivity, or certain people were attracted to science, people who were most easily corrupted." Note that these figures—other scientists—are the corruptible ones, not Mr. Markowitz himself. Furthermore, Mr. Markowitz's childlike view of males and females still remains, as there is a black/white split between impulse control and impulse expression. As a child Mr. Markowitz associated (as the split between his parents implies) emotions and irrationality with females and control and rationality with males (see Chapter 2). He touches on this in the following comment:

> In school, I had no coeducational learning experience at all. It led to some screwy ideas of mine about women and how apt they were in learning things. I thought most of the women I came in contact with were not too interested in the kind of things I was. That is, in concepts and philosophical ideas. That men were intellectual and women were not.

This dichotomy continues into the present, though, as Mr. Markowitz indicates considerable latent distrust of the motives of women:

> If you're interested in finding out about the physical universe you must have accurate measurement. But there are some people who

aren't. Like a woman who I just met for the first time yesterday. I'm working on a new show. Her relationship to reality is vaguely approximate. I was getting instructions from her on how to do certain things and I realized that she didn't have a clear idea she could show me but she couldn't write it out or she couldn't tell me because they were vague in her mind. In her body they were fine. She just didn't give a shit about how accurate she was.

Taking all this material on defensive distortion and differentiation of key figures together, we can see the combination of projection, denial, and splitting off of devalued parts of oneself and the past through which Mr. Markowitz holds on tightly to threatened definitions of self. Mr. Markowitz continues to believe that ideal models of "the right way" to behave still exist—godlike fathers and teachers, "geniuses" of scientists and perfectly accurate, responsible males.

Consistent with this attempt to hold onto a lost self we find little indication that Mr. Markowitz puts himself in self-testing or exploratory situations. The only situations of potential learning and testing of self that appear—for example, the following visit to a psychiatrist—find Mr. Markowitz in an adversary or defensive position:

> There was one time when I went with one of the children who needed psychiatric help to some kind of counseling. My wife and I went, just the two of us, to speak to a prestigious man. He said earlier, "I called you opinionated. What did you think I meant by that?" And I said without hesitation, "Having strong opinions." No bad connotations at all in my mind. I guess I think of myself as a good person, one who without thinking about it will do good things. [*What do you think the psychiatrist meant now?*] I thought he was rather annoyed with me in retrospect because I didn't recognize his authority, I considered my opinions as good as his. Well, as soon as he answered in the past I realized there was a criticism of me. That, my goodness, it was actually wrong for me to question his ideas.

For Mr. Markowitz the world is an essentially hostile place and the dominant feedback that seems to occur in his interactions, as he describes them, are "attacks." Given such perceptions, one can understand Mr. Markowitz's difficulty in tolerating ambiguity in self-definition. Further, Mr. Markowitz's stated receptivity to the discrepant experiences of midlife is low. After a long, highly abstract discussion about the nature of science, I put the question to him directly:

> [*It is easier for you to talk about science than to talk about yourself?*]
> Probably it is, yeah. I was brought up not to talk about myself. I was

brought up in the James Thurber school. Get out of there. Stay out of there. Thinking in terms of one's own mentality, mind, or motivations or emotions. To him and to me too it was an indulgence, a mark of egotism. There was in my mind a feeling of fright, perhaps terror. Of what I might find out. Not talking about myself but in thinking about myself. Thinking about what, for instance, what Hopkins calls "cliffs of fall." The mind has "cliffs of fall." To me there's a picture in my mind of a precipitive cliff—it's almost unreal. And he had a lot of trouble too. Hopkins. So I was brought up in that tradition. Kind of a strong silent person who doesn't fool around with thinking about himself—goes ahead and does what has to be done. Sounds like an old movie. *Beau Geste* or one of the more recent ones—*Bridge Over the River Kwai.* Do you remember Guinness in that? Any of the private eyes for instance—Bogart. He doesn't deal with any kind of introspection at all. He looks around and he sees what has to be done, what it is. He doesn't have any thoughts about his interaction with what's going on. It would never occur to say, Bogart in *The Maltese Falcon* to question whether what he's seeing is true. Or whether his state of mind might affect his observation. He would just forge ahead.

At another point Mr. Markowitz indicates his attitude toward introspection with his comment: "We have an infinite number of ways that we can fool ourselves. Especially about ourselves . . . I think it may be very valuable to examine your own motives, your insides, your thinking, your emotions. But not from the standpoint of actually finding out about them."

Mr. Markowitz's difficulty tolerating contradictory or conflicting perceptions or impulses can be seen as well in his descriptions of situations of decision and choice. Thus, Mr. Markowitz's explanation for the career change as an accident and his comment that his bureau closing offered a needed excuse to quit are indications of difficulty linking behavior to motive. Describing himself in college he speaks of "a whole generation steered into science." He says of himself, "I never knew I had a choice." Repeatedly, situations of choice are described in terms that indicate a closing off of full consideration of different options and competing motives. Mr. Markowitz's description of the manner in which he decided to purchase a home against his socialist principles is an illustration. Mr. Markowitz humorously relates going to a bar and getting "completely drunk" before signing the papers at his lawyer's office:

I was supposed to go to the lawyer's office just after lunch. And they had to point me in the direction. [*You weren't looking forward to it?*] I was pretty bombed. That's right. I wasn't looking forward to it. And I didn't open my mouth, I just wanted to get through with it.

We see here the attempt to wipe from consciousness what he is doing, when competing desires are at play. His explanation for why he went ahead to buy a house though feeling strongly that private ownership was immoral is that he "had to." His account of his immediate post-change situation carries with it the sense of an abrupt, noncontemplative decision: "It was like a leap across a chasm into darkness. It took me two years just to feel that it wasn't bad just to sit around and think about a problem or something."

Mr. Anderson: "I realized I didn't have to make it all fit together." Mr. Anderson is an example of a more complete resolution of the grieving process. The "sculpted" resolution in this case can be seen, first, in Mr. Anderson's perception of the discrepant experiences as primarily revealing things about himself. He was not as verbally facile as he had hoped, nor as socially poised. He was unhappy in his marriage and he acknowledged difficulties asserting himself with his wife as well as fulfilling the father's role. For Mr. Anderson midlife is perceived as a time when the initial, young adulthood self-definition is not working. This can be glimpsed in the manner in which Mr. Anderson describes the events of midlife, as presented in Chapter 3. Throughout, the focus is on self, his role in these events, and his inner reactions to them: "I didn't want to curry clients," "I would blow my cool," "I wanted to say, 'I can't listen to you anymore.' " This contrasts with the general framing of Mr. Markowitz's description of his midlife experiences, in terms primarily of the external events and with a diminished self in the discussion. While the description of events focuses on his dissatisfaction with law and his marriage, these fundamental problems of midlife are seen by Mr. Anderson in the context of his personal life. We find Mr. Anderson's perspective emphasizes his own difficulties as the locus of the midlife problems:

> [*What other kind of things were going on in your life at the time of your difficulties in law?*] I was very hard to be around, and my wife was doing pretty well, with me. But I think it must have been very hard on her. So we were not getting along awfully well. And without assigning fault, I would say that it was descriptive of me. I think a lot of the problems with my wife I carry with me as a problem and it's something that I couldn't sort out. Especially then, perhaps not so much now. But on a Sunday afternoon, the kids want to go out and go to some state park or something like that. And very often my head would be elsewhere, doing art.
>
> My wife and I talked about the separation a lot. Because having me around is going to be upsetting. I'm this far into sculpting and I was then thinking of myself as beginning to become a professional. Just because of the way I am it's demanding a lot of my energy. I was

not going to go back to something I had, let the art dribble through my fingers. And I would maybe teach some and earn a decent living. It wasn't enough for me because I was getting to be a real ambitious bastard in a certain way. Ambitious in the sense that to invest that amount of time in something that I really loved and then to let anything interfere with it. I was really that insistent.

As might be expected, Mr. Anderson's personal explanation of his experiences emphasize the active role of the self and the relevance of events in his career and family to his interests, choices, and desires:

I don't think if I had loved the good parts of law that I would have put up with it. Fundamentally I was in an activity even the best parts of which didn't interest me. I felt more and more that I was doing it just because it was something I ought to do.

Now I realize something that was told to me at that time. Maybe I just wanted to live alone.

We find, then, little evidence of defensive distortion of the discrepant experiences of midlife to alter their real nature. There were problems with the field of law, but this is not the whole story for Mr. Anderson. He is able to acknowledge the role of his own desires, motives, and values in his career and marital decisions. The problems of a law career are not presented as the sole reasons for his dissatisfaction, rather Mr. Anderson states that much of law did not really interest him, just as personal motives were at play in the divorce.

Consistent with this, there is a relatively differentiated perception of key figures and events at midlife as well. We find a measured perspective on Mr. Anderson's career in law and failed marriage, in sharp contrast to the attack on science in the case of Mr. Markowitz:

[*It sounds as if there were something about the motives of lawyers that . . .*] Yeah. Yet it's not across the board. No I don't agree with you. It's not lawyers. I felt quite close and a lot of respect for maybe a half a dozen lawyers in the firm. . . .

Some of our friends were quite shook up by our separation and divorce. They want to blame somebody for the split. They tried to find ways of making my wife look bad—it must be somebody's fault. Because marriages don't split up unless it's somebody's fault. And they can't seem to understand that we like each other. And I respect her. And we don't want to live together.

There is also a more differentiated perception for Mr. Anderson of the similarities and differences between himself and his parents, his brother, and his wife. Mr. Anderson was confronted at midlife with information about himself and his family—specifically his parents and brother—that his attempts to obtain his parents' love and attention, to really separate from his brother in their eyes, had failed, both because of who he himself is and who they are. We can see the impact of these experiences in Mr. Anderson's increased psychological separation from these figures. First, we find more of the language of change in regard to these figures during the interviews themselves. This is exemplified in such figures of speech, as "*I began to realize* . . . ," "I could *see* that . . . , " "it *dawned* on me." More importantly, Mr. Anderson seems more aware of the multidimensional, complex nature of others, and some of the ways he is different from the formerly idealized figures he had earlier tried to emulate. For example, when discussing his experiences at midlife, we saw in Chapter 3 that Mr. Anderson alluded to his frustrated desire to have his father appreciate his accomplishments. His father's failure to do so in a convincing manner led to an increasingly realistic perception of this figure: "He was carrying around an impression of me that he made up himself." In further discussion of his father found in the following passage, Mr. Anderson indicates insight into the manner in which he had previously not truly separated from his father.

I sort of lost touch with my parents, for several years when I was married. Whenever they would want to find out about me, my parents sort of would go through my wife. It was kind of funny in a way, but sad in another way. I don't think they understand how the machinery of questions works. I don't claim to either, but they don't feel too comfortable about asking. I can never have a sustained conversation with them, even now. I have to prepare myself for not having what I call a conversation in balance. Often now I'll write down what I want to talk about. My father typically would ask just the number of questions to illicit the information that he wants at the time. And then it's over. Out comes the newspaper.

I can remember from being a kid. It would be like I have about fourteen more things that I would want to say. And I still am conscious of running on when I'm not sure someone is interested. I'm sure that probably hurt a lot. I can remember a couple of times just from playing music. I'd play heavy stuff like Beethoven or Gershwin or Brahms—I loved it. And dad would be sitting there reading and my mother would be trying to talk to him and we were all in the same room. I'm over by the record player or something. And finally I couldn't stand it. It was time to go to supper and I was just so enthusiastic about this music. And a couple of times I just rambled on and on. And it wasn't good because somehow I didn't get a good feeling from them. There was no response.

And my father was for me a tremendous authority figure. When he spoke, there was no questioning. My observation was not so far off, generally almost always others have said that about him—that somehow, without being unpleasant, when he speaks he doesn't expect anyone to challenge him. And I know that my perception was not unique. I sort of checked that out. And even as recently as this year with my wife, he was somehow kind of a frightening person. In that he has strong ideas which he doesn't say much about but when he speaks.' And I treated him with more respect than was healthy. [*As a child?*] Yes. It was all falling down, from him to me. And I discovered it in this group therapy sessions. One of the guys that was running it said what was going on. It was very upsetting. Because it was unflattering to me. It punched a hole in this feeling of being pretty OK. But I realized that it was probably true. And that was to quite an extent a transfer of the authority I felt to my father to any other figure—an employer or teacher or something. I have to be very careful about that. Because I think my behavior in the past in certain ways towards authority was based on satisfying him.

In this excerpt Mr. Anderson is able to verbalize his dependency on his father and the degree to which he had remained tied to this important figure in his life. Further, Mr. Anderson describes some of the weaknesses and foibles of his father, filling out our picture of Mr. Anderson's feelings toward this man, beyond the single dimension of caring expressed in the last chapter. The acknowledgement by Mr. Anderson of his father as in part an unhealthy "authority figure" for his son contrasts with Mr. Markowitz's continued idealization of a "godlike" figure with "the huge weight of authority." Further, Mr. Anderson's complex perception, incorporating knowledge of his father's failings and strengths contrasts with Mr. Markowitz's more simplistic perception of his father, organized around a single dimension of morality and with a comparatively unknown quality. Note, though, that Mr. Anderson has not entirely separated from his father. While he acknowledges some of his father's limitations and developed behaviors to cope with them (such as when he writes "down what I want to talk about"), he is angry at his father for not being the way he wants him to be and his upset at his father's not listening has some of the character of a demand that he be different.

Similarly, Mr. Anderson seems to have gained some psychological distance from his brother. Again the perception is balanced and sympathetic, dominated neither by completely positive or negative features. Thus, in the following passage Mr. Anderson tempers his criticism of his brother.

I've given a little bit of a false impression about my brother. That doesn't make any difference to you, but it does make a difference to me in terms of being accurate. He does have a breadth of understanding and he's not just competitive and trying to manipulate all the time. But I still never see him when he's at a disadvantage. I never hear him say, "I don't know." That puzzles me. I have much more respect for what I don't know than he shows that he has. In other words, there's a certain mystery about things. And I don't mind that, I think he minds it. So he'll always have a comment. Like I loaned him a sculpture of mine. So they made a special trip here. I was arranging that on the phone. . . . It was not the greatest neighborhood—people get jumpy in here—they're used to living in the suburbs. And I was describing the atmosphere around here with the depressed economy and people out of jobs and stuff. And he had a phrase that he must have thought up. "The tension rises as the haves have more and the have-nots have less." It's like he has the *mot juste*.

He doesn't pretend to be perfect and try to control everybody. He's a pretty good guy, but I also see him trying in larger groups to end up by dominating. I saw it in my parents' fiftieth wedding anniversary a year ago last fall. He's the one who makes the toasts. And he loves it. And I felt good finally. It used to bother me—"Why can't I do that?" But I talk to people one or two at a time and I get my kind of presence. I was able to get much more objectivity on it and he came very close to looking like a clown to me. I'm not swallowed up in the thing.

I saw my brother getting a lot of attention in earlier days. And I couldn't growl and whine and sigh a little bit I guess if I felt he didn't deserve that much. And all those horrible nasty feelings. Now I feel that if he wants to get it that way, that's not really my concern. And as long as people don't praise him too much to me, it's OK. I get a little tacky about that still. For example several Christmases ago, there were several old people that knew him in the earlier days and gathered together for the occasion. They were talking about him, *ad nauseum*. The thought flickered through my mind that I could just keep that coming—this is a nasty thing to do—but just keep it pouring out of that person. "Yeah, yeah, more, more . . ." until it went sour.

What is Mr. Anderson saying here? The second paragraph reveals that elements of the sibling rivalry remain, as Mr. Anderson's envy of his brother's verbal facility, and the attention it gets him, is still evident in his discussion of "le mot juste" and his brother's desire to "have the exact thing that will summarize everything that is right." Yet we also find an ability on Mr. Anderson's part to separate himself from the feelings of worthlessness and loss of identity underlying his envy, as when he comments that "I felt good finally . . . I get my kind of presence . . . I can feel myself over and above the situation." His comment that he is "not swallowed up in the thing" and his behavior described in the second paragraph stand in direct contrast to the painful adolescent memory of being completely dominated by his brother and lost in his parents' appreciation of his sibling rival. These passages contain evidence both of progressive separation and change amid a regressive failure to separate from this idealized figure. Mr. Anderson sees some issues between himself and his brother, conceptualizes his brother in a more differentiated way, and indicates some behaviors for separating from him. This implies some capacity for change, and can be contrasted with the parental relationship of Mr. Prezinski and Mr. Markowitz in which much less differentiated perceptions and behaviors exist. Yet this material also indicates that the rivalry still exists and Mr. Anderson is somewhat unseparated from his brother. For example, Mr. Anderson's behavior toward his brother is limited to "getting back" at him, that is, he wants to make praise of his brother go "sour" and have him "looking like a clown." And social interaction and verbal facility are modes and experiences still very much tied to the sibling rivalry with his brother. Words and social facility are now left to his brother, while Mr. Anderson has the arts and "his presence." There is in this an element of a childlike, "sour grapes" solution. Mr. Anderson has not been able to move toward a more abstract, differentiated understanding of the world, separate from his family, wherein words and being social are detached from his brother and understood as separate from this figure. These aspects of experience are, instead, still tied to Mr. Anderson's sibling rivalry. And, indeed, we still see continued conflict around words in the interviews. Mr. Anderson wonders why he works so hard at conversations, why he needed to prove his argumentative skill to his wife, and why he has this "mission" about people "listening" to him:

> My mind will tend to jump around and I'll try to manipulate the conversation to get it on something that I think is worthwhile. I'll push people into talking about something and summarizing what they said in a rather formal term and say, "Is this what you're saying but you're telling me this. I just can't make any sense of it." And more and more I'll say, "I can't understand what you're saying."
>
> I don't like to hear myself rambling or being incoherent. Last time I talked about feeling that the conversation is responsive. Even after I was talking to you I had it on my mind when I was reading something else. The fact that I'm sitting here doing almost all the talking—well it is very hard. Because I'm not asking you any questions at all. It's not the usual situation. So there has to be a sort of agreement to hold the thing in an imbalanced state. Where I'm talking and you're listening. I don't appreciate someone that feeds on the sound of their own voice. Because real communication between two people requires a lot of concentration and a lot of energy. Communi-

cation that goes beyond the verbal in any direction. Where it isn't this imbalance.

Verbal facility and expressiveness still retain elements of conflict and rivalry with his brother. In Mr. Anderson's relationship to his father and brother we see both forward progression to greater differentiation and separation from these figures as well as the remnants of conflict around separation from these figures.

Evidence of increased differentiation of his mother and wife can also be found in Mr. Anderson's interview protocols. Aspects of his mother not previously noticed have become apparent to Mr. Anderson. In particular Mr. Anderson—in a parallel to his perception of his father—has become aware of how his mother has functioned to shape his own self-definition:

> There's a kind of value instilled in me that a lot of life is doing what you don't want to do because in the family that was the main thing. I'd kind of see something impractical and I'd say, "Gee, I'd love to do this." And the answer would come back, "But you've got to do. . . ." That kind of response tends to shut you off. It shuts me off [*who was it that that would come from?*] My mother, especially. I was there two weeks ago for a day and a night. And Mom was working on something. It was not a particularly good time and thank God I have enough experience with group sessions, with talking with my wife and seeing how things are better, that I can detach myself and observe what's happening and not get all tight inside. I'd get to notice that every statement that was made by my father or me always "yes, but," or the negative. . . . She, I think, tries to take responsibility for damn near everything. It's really none of her business.

There is also an increased awareness on Mr. Anderson's part of his wife's limitations and the manner in which she is different from him:

> I thought that by just going to those group sessions, that it can work those problems out and might help the marriage. And it did in a way. But I got the feeling at first that it was mostly me. Then I began to realize that it wasn't all me and that she wasn't interested in doing any work with the group or looking at herself for some help. It's an odd thing but if you compare the two of us, when I get into a group it's very hard for me, I don't like people to get really prying around inside or to be at a disadvantage. To be naked and to have no defense at all, which is really that way you do find out things. She was much more defensive. Even though she was more talkative. I couldn't talk to you very easily this way if it hadn't been for that. It changed me some, for the better.

We find, then, a more complex picture at midlife of significant figures in his life—combining positive and negative features—as well as the acknowledgment of frustrated desires. This can be seen in Mr. Anderson's ability to accept several conflictual situations in his life, particularly guilt around separation from his children and continued dependency on his parents for their support. Since contradictory and at times painful experiences are acknowledged, some overt conflict is present. In the following three examples, Mr. Anderson discusses problems in his continued reliance on parental financial support, unresolved feelings about separating from his family, and the experience of being an art model:

It's very much harder for me after last session than it was before because it stirred up a lot of things that were sort of settled. It took me about three or four hours to sort of settle down. In the sense that some of the problems that existed then, especially in terms of my parents, exist now, you see. I'm dealing with them right now. It's in many ways a very difficult time right now. I knew that when I came that I needed financial help from my parents which I detest taking. It bothers me and I have to keep reminding myself everyday frequently that I don't have any choice. That I'm doing the best I can to change that situation.

I can feel very bad sometimes about my kids. And feel guilty about what I did. [*What do you feel guilty about?*] Well, deserting them. Because I think kids need a male. Not necessarily a father although. . . .

I do jobs that I wouldn't have ever dreamed of doing fifteen years ago, they wouldn't have even entered my head. Modeling. Jobs that are basically debasing. And the pay is very poor. I was doing it to supplement the income I was making as a teacher. And that's a very unusual contribution. There are hangups. Were in my head and are in other people's heads about the status—you're a teacher, not a model. So I don't model where I teach. If you take your clothes off, you lose your authority. . . . And having a conceit about myself that I could get a good job because of my background and my ability. And it's been very difficult. It burns me that I'm not making more money. I have to control myself at times.

In this area of differentiation, we find also that Mr. Anderson's language in the interviews indicates a receptivity to information about self, a self-observing capacity, an attention to the role of his own feelings and motives in situations, and a capacity to link experiences at different points in his life. For example, he says that "*I discovered* some very interesting things about myself," "I'm *still conscious* of that feeling, from years ago," "I *saw how (that happened)* when I brought my wife home and she challenged my father." Mr. Anderson indicates his capacity for connecting motives to behavior, past to present, in his earlier remark concerning the impact of his father: "that was to quite an extent a transfer of the authority I felt of my father to any other figure—an employer or teacher or something." And Mr. Anderson's curiosity and openness to information about self is embedded in this comment:

> Sometimes if I am questioned by someone who's thoughtful—who are those people? The woman I live with now, my wife to some extent, a couple of other people I know, when I talk to them I kind of put together what's happened over the years. A question will pop up that will sort of turn things a bit. You may see something a little differently.

More importantly, Mr. Anderson indicates a tendency to put himself in self-testing and exploratory situations:

> I was in group therapy twice for periods of about three months. It was quite helpful. What I discovered was very interesting, that I had a real anguish in me about sitting at the dinner table with my parents when I was a kid. I had a formal household. Dinner at a certain hour. You'd sit down at the table and . . . remembering a feeling of being passive. I was just simply very anxious. To the point where I carried that over for quite a while and I didn't like sitting down at meals with people generally. I loved to just sit down quietly and eat and not talk. And I think I developed a feeling that I wasn't worth listening to.

Not only does Mr. Anderson indicate a willingness to put himself in growth situations, but he indicates some receptivity to the reexamination of the personal meaning of his experience when confronted with information about himself:

> It's an odd conjunction. I had an interview yesterday with this fellow for a teaching position. He conducts an interview that's very probing. Nicely probing but he's obviously thought about ways to get you to talk about your real likes and dislikes. Then a visit since I saw you last from a woman who used to care for me when I was a little kid. And has maintained interest.
>
> She reminded me of some things. And I tend to trust her. She's a good observer. She remembered things that I had forgotten or was too young to remember.

Consistent with this, the sculpted resolution in this case is reflected in a fuller integration of parts of self previously devalued. Because of this reexperiencing of such aspects of self, Mr. Anderson was looking at midlife with a deeper ambivalence: What kind of person am I? What is the role of "unruly feelings" in my life? Mr. Anderson now seems able to acknowledge previously devalued aspects of his subjectivity, as, for example, his jealousies, envy, and resentments. Looking back on his life history, Mr. Anderson acknowledges his "jealousy" of his wife's attractions to other men, his "envy" of his brother's social poise, and his "disgust" at times with himself. Some examples follow of his ability to tolerate his feeling life, and acknowledge dysphoric affect and see himself in a new light:

> Looking back I realize how tense I was in law school. Hoping to do well, and not being terribly satisfied with my performance. I couldn't understand some of the material. That made me sore as hell. I had a great contempt for some courses developing anyway, and I had to be careful that the contempt wasn't the result of the fact that I screwed up those exams, or wasn't doing as well as I thought I really did. . . .

> Sometimes I ask too much from a sculpture. I tend if I don't watch myself to be a monomaniac about things. Go after a sculpture and sculpt and drop and expect everything from it and when I stop working I get furious. One thing I realize is that getting furious at my sculptures, I really saw myself then. Whenever I start to feel angry at what I'm doing I realize that it actually gets to be amusing. That's been very instructive. Now I don't lose my temper anymore. I feel a disgust but I say, "Give it a rest," and I'll go do something else. . . .

> I have a sardonic view of human beings. Which used to bother me, seeing how silly people are. There is a satirical view of life. I get a great energy and pleasure in seeing the silly things that I'll do. . . . I didn't used to be able to sustain that attitude of perceiving because it would make me feel bad inside. How silly people look, how silly they walk. I didn't think I was turning it on myself and I didn't think that that was fair. I think that it's honest. I love writing or literature that does that. It exposes how things are. But then over the last several years, I'm not frightened of seeing myself as pretty silly sometimes and laugh and that and still feel OK. It comes up in sculpting for example. I'll go through silly machinations about just pacing around and just fussing, and finally take about eighteen practice swings with a golf club and then hitting the ball. You have to control it, if you don't even see it. And if you can't laugh then you can never do anything about it if you don't like it sometimes.

Most importantly, we find integration of his anger, temperamentality, and strong affective responses:

> My father. He's on the exterior very calm. In trying to emulate him, I finally realized much later that I'm really not together quite that way. Volatility or feelings that I have just don't fit the mold of what I

thought he was. And what I tried to be for a while. Which was more calm and reserved. I just had all these reactions and they weren't coming out for me. I discovered that it was OK, to have that kind of feeling. The model of him seen as a separate person brought into myself just wasn't jiving somehow with feelings that I had. And that sort of came apart for me.

What had happened to me as a kid was withdrawal and isolation and quiet and alone a lot. I still learn to accept this strange curse in what I turned out to be. I'm fairly volatile, and I'm still quite unpredictable. To the point where I almost have a certain value that I put on that. The tendency to want to shock somebody a little bit, gently in a conversation, to say something a little bit different, than it might ordinarily be said. Or I get a lot of pleasure out of seeing something from a new angle and having somebody else do that to me.

This greater acceptance and integration of his inner life has allowed Mr. Anderson to harness his unruly, imperfect world of affect and impulse, accompanied by the capacity to be "physical," "impulsive," and "natural"—all aspects of self previously devalued:

[In sculpting] a certain amount of moving and gesticulation is fairly natural to me. I move a lot, I get a lot of exercise when I work. Sculpting is actually fairly physical. I like to feel like I'm performing something. Using more than just my eye and my head. More of my whole body. I work on the floor—that's a different engagement. I get tremendous excitement working in the country. [Last summer in Vermont] I could smell the air, I could hear the cows moo. I think in that sense the activity involves being in touch—receptive to everything that is happening at the time, totally in the world at that instant.

As might be expected, we find as well a tempering of the perfectionist strivings that underlay the self-definition of young adulthood. For example, at one point I asked Mr. Anderson what had earlier stopped him from being able to see himself as "silly." His reply is revealing:

[*What would stop you earlier from looking at yourself that way?*] I think probably a sense in which I should be perfect for my father or something. Everything I did was completely very very good. There are certain things that I can't do. What I do do that I know pleases people I will do in exemplary fashion. But that image somehow began to come apart. That feeling that I wasn't perfect, didn't want to be perfect, really. This perfection thing, I don't need to tell you, becomes lunacy because you can't sustain it and you're not seeing yourself. . . .

It dawned on me that day [at art school]. I'm trying to show that I'm fantastically good and that I could sculpt any kind of way you want. And I said that's trouble. It's trouble just in the world of sculpting alone, never mind more broadly. When I jumped into the decision of sculpting, I think I carried with me a feeling that I would prove myself and I guess to my father. Sculpting has taught me many things. But one thing it has taught me: If I love it then I should do it. If I don't love it, don't do it for another reason. Like proving yourself. And always failing a little.

[Sculpting] seems to demand more and yield more. Bigger failures and better successes. Plotinus said something about that: "Great work is almost always flawed because the attempt to go beyond something leads to imperfections." It pulls a lot from me and it reaches me and it excites me. Music with the sculpting is indeed another aspect of this. I have fancy ideas. I listen to Bach pieces, or jazz. I can make visual some of the stops, cadences, key changes, pauses, rhythms. I see analogies to sculpture, without fooling myself that sculpture is a piece of music. I mean you can get to thinking you're a great sculptor because you have great music, it's the whole euphoria that I was talking about. I can go to sleep and fool myself into thinking that I'm doing something. I listen when I'm getting ready to sculpt and fussing around. I'll get into the sculpting, which is always complicated. It's a time of excitement and anticipation also wondering whether the heck you can do it this time. Like the record will have finished and I won't even know it has stopped. That's when there will be a pause in the sculpting and I will realize it's quiet and I've been conscious and then it's OK. But if I'm relying on the music to kind of pick me up, audio speed . . . then. . . .

Note, too, that elements of the perfectionist fantasy of "proving" himself and being "fantastically good" remain. Mr. Anderson's reference to Plotinus's comment on "great works" indicates this, as does his struggle with the illusions of "audio speed" and being a great sculptor. To have fancy ideas that produce the euphoria that everything is just beautiful may be a residue of the childhood fantasy of becoming beautiful through his social poise and verbal facility. Going to sleep indicates a kind of dreamlike state, and is also the phrase Mr. Anderson uses to describe his feelings of being "swallowed up" as a child by his brother. When frustrated, unsure about whether he is able to achieve what he wants, during "a time of excitement and anticipation also wondering whether the heck you can do it this time," Mr. Anderson is likely to return to a fantasy image of perfection rooted in his sibling rivalry, to "go to sleep." Thus, as noted earlier, sculpting contains elements of the original competition with brother, transposed to a different arena: It is as if for Mr. Anderson each is "an expert"—his brother with words and himself with images. Yet the last excerpt indicates the tempering of, and Mr. Anderson's greater control over, this overdriven, compensatory fantasy of perfection. At times he is aware of fooling himself, as revealed by his comment that "I can go to sleep sometimes and . . . fool myself into thinking that I'm doing something," and struggles against it.

Our last dimension of growth and change was that of choice and decision making. Analysis of interview material indicates that Mr. Anderson presents and describes his decisions to change careers and, later, leave his marriage as taking place in the face of new information about himself, with careful consideration of options and pleasant/unpleasant consequences, accompanied, as well, by a sense of responsibility for his role in these decisions:

[*Tell me more about your decision to move full-time into sculpture?*] It became clear to me after just thinking and walking and taking a lot of time, that those kind of things really did matter to me. I thought of an English teacher in college and I thought of a guy who had been in music then too and I thought of the kinds of letters I wrote—how much I loved the language. It makes something. There's a shape to a letter. How I loved words, and well, this comes together a little bit doesn't it? It comes together in terms of making things.

And it turned out that at first I was still not on the beam, because I thought I'll fit that in with my academic background. My ability to write, it was pretty good and could get a lot better and I'll be an art historian. And that will fit together. It was another struggle to realize that I didn't have to fit it together. I had to do what I wanted. And if it looked like it was throwing away everything that I'd done before, and it didn't have a logical term of progression then that's too bad. It seems almost a basic human activity to try and make sense chronologically of their life.

I took time to actually search out the best alternative for art school. It was very foreign to me. It was then that it struck me that I never felt that way before. I didn't feel that way about deciding where to go to college, or what to do in college. I had a little time at home before college began. And my father would ask me, "What are you going to do?" I had to give him an answer. I couldn't say, "Well, I'm not sure." I mean I could either go to Columbia or to Yale. He never said anything. What I'm trying to describe is the way I felt. Not like a person making the choice but somehow answering to what somebody else wanted. . . . I was sure enough so that I had the guts to walk into my boss's office and say, "Sorry" and answer all the questions "Why?" And I had never withdrawn from anything before or quit. . . .

My wife was tremendously upset when I told her that I wanted a divorce. That surprised me. I was actually shocked. Her reaction was a typhoon. Boom. She just exploded. A very tremendous temper, she had. I was shaken because it was a very hard thing to me to do anyway. To call it off was hard. And to take the responsibility for being the one to do it.

The Affirmation of Self at Midlife:
Mr. Anderson and Mr. Markowitz

In these two illustrative cases, the patterns of sculpted and foreclosed resolutions of loss of self at midlife can be seen as leading to different types of reconstituted self-definition. We find continued exclusion of suppressed aspects of self in Mr. Markowitz. Part of the meaning of acting for Mr. Markowitz lies in its "counterculture" nature, as he now sees himself as aggressively fighting against the "corrupted" and guilty establishment:

I don't know if I want to get into that. The extent of my alienation from society. You see, if you do well, if you succeed, then you're doing something wrong. Because somehow you get co-opted. If you're really creative, and you work hard, and you've got a good group you will be successful. Which means that it's going to be hard to get into your affair, maybe you're going to charge a lot for tickets, and the people with a lot of money will start backing you. You'll attract their attention. And now you're a business. You might as well have sold automobiles. Almost every creative field, you can't help but watch your standards erode gradually because when you go to school in music or almost in any art form the standards that are set up are tremendous. Mainly because there are so many good musicians around you know in order to make out you have to be really good. There are ways musically of cutting corners. Of being a little sloppy so that most people won't notice it and especially if you're in an orchestra group for ten or twenty years. You find that you don't have to follow the high standards that you had when you just got out of school. . . . I take a kind of jaundiced view of what the success is going to mean to them. It may turn them into people I really don't care for anymore. A person who is not synchronized, who has gotten so much vested interest in the status quo that she can't get out in a moment. . . .

I know there are a lot of people who do have the price of a ticket for our show. But the most valuable ones don't. The people that I really celebrate don't. What's important about them is that they have broken with our Western society. Our Western society is involved in, let's say the subtext, all the time is producing for profit. Not for human need. And this poisons the well, at the source. And in order to swim in this society or to swim in style, you join them. You get a job, which is involved in producing for profit because that's the only way you can get paid. And now you take the money that you make and you buy the things that have been produced for profit, not for need. Thus you can continue the whole cycle.

We have seen earlier that blame for antisocial impulse and corruption is externalized onto the institutions of science and marriage. Part of the way Mr. Markowitz has been able to let go of the past and move into the arts is through the externalization of discrepant experiences. On the other hand, Mr. Markowitz holds on to, safeguards, constantly threatened perceptions of himself as a socially responsible, nonbiased person by splitting off his own wishes and desires. Acting in this regard has meaning in terms of accountability and control, and these purposes have been transferred from science to the theater. Discussions of his work in the theater thus emphasize the highly structured nature of drama, in which affect is expressed yet channeled and directed in a manner demanded by necessities of script and of his fellow actors:

One of the things I like about working in an ensemble group is that there's a large element of truth telling there. But it isn't the verbal, intellectual truth telling. You're doing it with the inflections in your voice, with your body and the way you move. Nobody can lie to a fellow actor or to a director. You pick it up right away. . . . The nature of the artistic process demands your offering of yourself. If you hold back you don't get anything out of it. And the people you're working with don't get anything out of it either. And they can tell right away. Did I tell you about my anger? For instance in an acting group one of the exercises is to do things. OK, do anger. And I got up there, and I couldn't do it. The teacher said, "That's OK, very few people can do it." We're taught not to express anger because it's dangerous to express anger. You might actually not be able to control it. And she helped me to be angry. She did it physically. It involved making a movement with my eyes shut. A violent movement. My eyes were shut. And at one point the teacher grabbed my arm. One arm. And I had to now make the movement against this resistance. And it was like automatic. [laughs] In about thirty seconds I was beside myself with rage. Part of the acting is if you have to show anger, one way of doing it is a memory way. It may be muscle memory that you are remembering. You might remember an emotional memory. You accumulate a lot of these stock, for instance, I have certain things I remember when I'm sad. I can make myself cry, that way. It's extremely useful to know that. You forget what anger feels like to generate it again. And so you finally remember what it feels like and then you can do it.

A second major meaning of the theater is in its socially responsible, accountable nature. Mr. Markowitz still feels himself securely accountable to his peers while engaged in socially valuable activity; now, however, the controlling, justifying peer group has shifted from that of his fellow researchers and the scientific method to the actors in his repertory group and the exercises and method of the theater.

> Now responsibility, I think I've always thought about that. My primary feeling is that it is good for a person to be responsible. I'll give you an example. We recently formed a theater group to be involved in helping to dramatize important things that are going on, like the cutting of the welfare, for instance. And then I suggested that we get in touch with an organization that would serve as a sponsor, although we didn't really need a sponsor, we could have really done it ourselves. But in the back of it was the argument that if we went out simply by ourselves there would be no responsibility to another group and to another group there would be no feeling of self-correction. No way of knowing that what we were doing was right or wrong. I guess that's important to me too. This is a way I have of arriving at positions or conclusions. I will say something that I'm not sure is correct. Then I get some kind of attack, or question from the person I'm speaking to. Which means that whatever position you take, you're subject to modification. Criticism. That has all kinds of interesting implications that I haven't even thought of. [*For example?*] Well, you might interpret that as meaning lack of self-confidence. You might interpret it in just the opposite way, that you feel secure enough of yourself that you can stand criticism and modify your position as it becomes clear to you that your position should be modified. [*How do you interpret it?*] Ah, the second way. [*laughs*]

Given our earlier discussion of Mr. Markowitz, I take this material to reflect continued grandiose fantasies about self (the belief in an absolute morality which can be known and guide one's behavior in all situations) and the presence of idealized people as means of safeguarding an uncertain sense of self. (The latter now are "the people that I really celebrate" and his sense of "responsibility to another group.") These themes continue, then, in Mr. Markowitz's reconstituted sense of who he is.

Mr. Markowitz's perception of having left behind a "corrupt" world of science and becoming a counterculture actor fighting against an "anti-

social" establishment must be seen within this context, in that the idealized nature and reassuring controls of science have been replaced by those
of the theatre. Yet there is continued uncertainty for Mr. Markowitz
about his "true" nature—good or evil—and the role of impulse and affect
in his life:

> This show I'm working on. I'm cast as a kind of fighter type of person,
> someone who has a job to do and just bulls his way through. At one
> point, someone in the studio said, "Boy, you sure scream good." That
> brought me up rather short. I mean is that the kind of person I am? I
> don't know, I get down about that sometimes.

As Mr. Markowitz's comment indicates, there is considerable latent
depression. Hints of an underlying sense of isolation, failure, and despair
are poignantly captured in this excerpt, in which Mr. Markowitz identi-
fies with Icarus, the failed isolated hero whose dreams were unsupported
by his reality:

> I desperately need illumination. I have lots of problems. But thinking
> about them will not, is only one way to solve them. This is an example
> of my life. Auden wrote a poem called "Musée des Beaux Arts." And
> he wrote it about a painting of Brueghel. And the painting was "The
> Fall of Icarus." You're looking down into a bay and the water is beau-
> tiful and blue and there's some people tilling the soil on the side of a
> hill and there's a fishing boat, there's some people fishing there. And
> if you look very carefully you can see the edge, the white end of
> Icarus' leg. He has just fallen down. Nobody sees him. Nobody is pay-
> ing any attention to him at all. One of the most heroic deeds that ever
> occurred, man trying to fly—Ah!—I mean all the symbolism in that,
> and he's failed, nobody, nobody knew he failed.

On the other hand, the sculpted resolution of Mr. Anderson has resulted in a fuller integration of parts of self previously devalued, as well as
some tempering of the perfectionist strivings that underlay the initial
"wished-for" self-definition. For Mr. Anderson, the reconstitution of
meaning and purpose reflects this acceptance and integration of his inner
life. Mr. Anderson now sees himself as the aggressive question asker, able
to draw upon his previously devalued capacity to be "physical," "impulsive," and "natural," in ways not previously possible:

> I get a lot of pleasure of seeing something from a new angle in my
> sculpture that occurs in a certain way. I love to make things appear
> what they are not, or not appear what they are. Because I think that's
> the truth. I think that's what I see around. When you look out the

window, and the appearance of the building and the tree. Is that what that is? Well, we assume that by looking out there, that is the reality. That is real. But what we see is not any more real than what we don't see. That's what my art work is trying to be about. There's a great beauty in that. The limitation is so utterly total, in human perception. It's relieving when I understood that that was so, because the possibilities for what the thing might be become endless.

In all humility, the patterns that I emerge with in my sculpture reveal some inner structures. But it's different than formulating conscious conceptions of what the space is. The configuration that you tend to put in ahead of the sculpture. That is not what art in 1975 in the United States is about. It's on the edge, pushing. I do view sculpture as seriously as that. It has an investigative function which I take very seriously. In a very profound sense. Ultimately it's to break certain patterns. And if I can get a strong enough objectified configuration that is perhaps quite unrecognizable. Initially it has enough power, formally, that is irresistable as an object to be looked at, then something can be learned from it.

I hate it when new students get intimidated by me in my art classes. I always run the critique sessions without saying anything. What I say comes later. I work on ways to give everyone their breathing space. That they don't have to accept what I say without questioning. At the same time I have to be a tough teacher. I want to avoid the feeling that they have really learned how to draw. In six or eight weeks. It's the force of my interest and conviction that may intimidate people.

I think I'm more of an expert as a teacher than I ever was as a lawyer. Sometimes in the classroom situation I'll drive very hard and there's no doubt about the fact that going to art school is as serious as going to medical school. It isn't just relaxation or therapy. It's learning and it's total concentration.

As we have seen, there is considerable conflict present in Mr. Anderson's life. However, this conflict seems accompanied by a sense of self-acceptance, not despair, and, overall, he faces the future with confidence.

We can see that these alternate types of resolutions have led to different types of career changes. We can label Mr. Markowitz's transition as a *defensive career change*, in that it served primarily to defend a threatened sense of self and foreclosed conflict too painful for the ego to bear. The overidealization of the second career and devaluation of the first, accompanying such developments, have already been discussed. In the case of Mr. Anderson, a sculpted resolution involves what we might call an *adaptive career change* in that the transition involves greater access to inner conflict and less distortion of the discrepant experiences of midlife. The career change comes out of an acknowledgment and recognition of "who one is," resulting in a more gratifying, realistic match of self to career. There is less idealization of the second career, or devaluation of the first, and in the case of Mr. Anderson we find a greater sense of sculpture as a less conflicted mastery of a grammar or set of skills.

Summary: The Reconstitution of Self in Sculpted and Foreclosed Resolution

All the participants in this research carried out career changes following the loss of dominant self-definitions at midlife, but the same event has different meanings in the context of foreclosed and sculpted resolutions of this challenge. The different personality and career implications of foreclosed and sculpted resolutions can be summarized as follows:

The Continued Role of Grandiose Fantasies and Idealized Images

Because foreclosed resolutions involve an incomplete psychological differentiation of self and the absence of psychological separation from childhood images of parents, we find personality in such cases still organized around grandiose fantasies and idealized images of others that characterized the young adulthood self-definition. In sculpted resolutions we find greater tempering of perfectionist strivings and separation from idealized images of parents. Thus, in the case studies of Mr. Markowitz and Mr. Anderson, we saw how the former still held on tightly to the ideal image of "godlike persons" to whom he could look for absolute standards of conduct and morality. Mr. Markowitz's post-crisis sense of self was really a recycled version of his pre-crisis grandiose self, both rooted in an identification with his idealized father. In Mr. Anderson's case the grandiose images of his mother and father became less important in the post-crisis self-organization. This is true for other individuals as well. Cases of foreclosure are characterized by continued grandiosity and perfectionist strivings with less separation from ambivalently held parents; a sculpted resolution is characterized by less grandiosity and increased separation from ambivalently experienced parents.

Different Types of Career Change

In foreclosed resolutions the career change came about in response to, but without making full use of, new information about self. That is, these people essentially foreclosed grieving through a career change in order to avoid deeper uncertainty and ambivalence about self. This may be seen as a *defensive career change*, in that the transition avoids and suppresses conflict (much as attempts at "environmental cures," of which we find several in this group), both the conflict aroused by the discrepant experiences and that of the underlying ambivalently held aspects of self. As part of this defensive process we find that the career change is accompanied for such individuals by either a sharp devaluation of the initial career and/or florid overidealization of the second career. Mr. Markowitz and Mr. Prezinski stand as examples of this pattern. Neither person can find any redeeming value in his initial career, and each man discusses his life in the arts unqualified by negative considerations or uncertain thoughts. Most importantly, now the arts are the "ideal" life hoped for in young adulthood. In the case of Mr. Markowitz, there is the fantasy of having achieved a situation of perfect morality and social virtue, and, for Mr. Prezinski, of being the humble, egoless artist of service to all.

Speaking more speculatively, this may be accompanied by repetition of conflicts in relation to work characterizing the initial career and the presence of similar defenses. Thus, foreclosed participants' discussions of the present situation indicate repetition of earlier conflicts in regard to work. Mr. Prezinski at several points worries about feeling "plugged up" and unable to be as productive as he would like in the face of anxieties about the reception his work will receive from the powerful, confident, all-knowing artists he perceives around him.

If we take as our measure of health some sense of the degree to which conflict is accessible to consciousness for rational choice and decision making, then we can label career changes emerging from sculpted resolutions as *adaptive career changes*, since the loss has been acknowledged and used (confronted) rather than avoided. One might speculate that this results in a more "realistic," personally gratifying match of oneself with the work situation, since the reports of participants evidencing more sculpted resolutions indicate such satisfaction and investment in work.

Differential Access to the Past

There are clear differences between individuals evidencing foreclosed and sculpted resolutions in their ability to range freely within their inner experiences. We saw such differences in this chapter, for example, in terms of the degree of defensive distortion of experience, degree of differentiation of key figures, and quality of decision making. It seems to me that our participants' differential access to their past has played a role in the manner in which meaning and purpose is reconstituted at midlife. By "meaning and purpose" I am thinking here of the commitments and investments in the present and future that come out of the person's free access to his individual past history.

In the case of Mr. Anderson, meaning is reconstituted in a sturdier fashion than for Mr. Markowitz, because of the former's ability to hold in mind and tolerate some of the ambivalences and conflicts of midlife. Mr. Anderson has separated ("let go") into the artist role but has maintained his ties to important pieces of the past ("held on"), such as his children, wife, parents, and brother. He is still rooted in his family. This means that he has available an acceptance of who he is and of his inner life, he can acknowledge his intensity, anger, subjectivity, lack of social poise, jealousy of his brother, and conflict around the verbal mode, without cutting himself off from his past. He is in a very different relationship to his past than Mr. Markowitz, who is cut off from his inner life because he has renounced his past: The discrepant experiences of midlife are not accepted as containing valuable information about himself. Mr. Markowitz's anger, rage, and despair remain at the level of unintegrated information. Meaning is built on the rigid projection (the "antisocial" nature of science) or denial (use of drama as a controlling force) of his experience. Thus his own affect and impulse seem adaptively unavailable, and essential experiences within his own life history remain at the fringe of consciousness. Contrast this with Mr. Anderson, for whom the meaning of art lies partly in the sense of being a question asker, one who makes aggressive statements about reality. Here his intensity, lack of social poise, and his overly serious, impulsive, "unrespectable" nature are harnessed. One is reminded of Shaw's comment, quoted by Erikson (1959), to the effect that if one cannot get rid of family skeletons, one might as well make them dance. Mr. Anderson makes the skeletons dance, while Mr. Markowitz still keeps them in the closet.

Individuals evidencing sculpted resolutions of the midlife loss, because of their ability to tolerate the ambivalence of grieving and the ambiguity of delayed resolutions, seem to me to have better access to their past; an access freer of gross distortion and defensive maneuvers. Those men illustrative of foreclosed resolutions seem to me to be more cut off from their life history, ungrounded, without a context. Such people seem unable to bring their impulse and affect to bear adaptively on crucial decisions and experiences perhaps because of their inability to endure the experience of loss and resulting denial of discrepant experience.

Taken as a unit, Chapters 2 through 4 present a view of adulthood in our group of career changers, beginning with the ways the initial careers were intertwined with conflicts around the definition of self in young adulthood and following the evolution of careers, family, and self through to midlife. The next chapter returns to earlier points in developmental history to explore the roots of these conflicts around self-definition in childhood and their impact on the task of identity formation and patterns of career choice in adolescence.

5

Early Development

Separation Crisis in Adolescence and the Idealized Parents of Childhood

THE PRECEDING chapters have developed a perspective on midlife as in part a reexperiencing of crises around separation from idealized parents. This means, most simply, that in our group of career changers some men evidenced at midlife a deepening understanding of the similarities and differences between self and parent. This involved a richer perception of parents as real people different in some respects from their sons. Some of the men seemed more able to feel who they were separately from their parents, integrating valued aspects of the past into the sense of self, yet not "swallowing whole" a childlike perception of parents as omniscient figures, as absolute guides to morality or unreachable standards of success. For these men the decisions and choices of midlife were made with a greater sense of autonomy and responsibility to self and others rather than from values, attitudes, and beliefs resulting from attempts to live up to fantasied standards and images of perfection. For other men in our group the crisis was also one of separation, as idealized, introjected models from the past failed as guides to decision and choice. Yet with these men we find less maturation in the area of differentiation of self and others at midlife.

This chapter explores more of what is involved in the separation crisis of our group at midlife by tracing its developmental roots. A particular goal is to indicate how the unconscious reliance on parents as absolute models helped these men cope with the anxieties of choice in adolescence, an anxiety built upon apparent childhood experiences that led these individuals to question their own subjectivity—their inner world of affect, fantasy, and aggression. Note that this will help us better understand why people shy away from their potentialities. This does not mean the "potential" to have become an artist earlier in life, but rather the everyday interests, passions and plans that form the substrate of a career choice.

The chapter is divided into two large sections, focusing first on adolescence and then childhood. As Erikson (1959) and others have made clear, adolescence is a pivotal time of the life cycle, mediating movement from the narrow family-centered world of childhood to the wider social roles and autonomy of young adulthood. Late adolescence is in particular a time of separation, as the person begins to emerge from a psychological embeddedness in the family origin. During these years the values, attitudes, and ideals of the child gradually shift toward the more autonomous and independent ones of the young adult. I focus, first, on our participants' experience of these adolescent challenges of psychological separation from family of origin and autonomous self-definition. From our participants' reports, I believe this time is essential to understanding both the meaning of their career and marital choices and the subsequent pattern of midlife development. The second section focuses on the origin of these separation conflicts in the child's struggle with ambivalently experienced parents. The press of ambivalent feelings in childhood is analyzed in particular as the initial way in which these men came to understand and experience their own subjectivity.

Adolescence as an Experience of Separation and Loss

Adolescence is particularly interesting in these men's accounts because of recurring reports of overt confusion and difficulty during high school and college. Running throughout these reports are difficulties with three central processes of adolescence:

1. The exploration and testing of self
2. The formation of a strong bond with one's peers
3. Diminution of the psychological role of parents

Each of these processes figures prominently in the central adolescent struggle with self-definition, an experience I want to discuss in terms of separation and loss. Adolescence is a time of separation and loss because it involves a leave-taking from the world of childhood. This process of separation from earlier attitudes, values, and ideas results in a discontinuity in self-organization and a gradual process of reorganization, most clearly seen in the period we have come to identify as the *sturm and drang* of later adolescence.

Let me present a view of the general nature of late adolescence in terms of the ideal developmental gains that occur. In early adolescence the self is generally still dominated by the kinds of idealized parental images and integrations characteristic of childhood. The young adolescent is still strongly involved in his family of origin. By late adolescence, though, processes fostering separation from family and more autonomous self-definition begin to assert themselves. During this period the young person faces the sudden diversity of college and the onset of crucial decision-making situations (Coehlo et al. 1963) which encourage the task of self-definition in the face of a previously undifferentiated world of parental/family values, assumptions, and goals. The freshman year is often the first time that the adolescent has spent an extended period of time away from his family. Dormitory living is something of a "melting pot," as the person is exposed to the clash and excitement of the variety of values, attitudes, and beliefs the different students present. College courses offer a mass of new information about the world and a number of new perspectives about self and the world. A myriad of experiences while in college—both on campus and off, as part of the established curriculum and more informally—offer possibilities for taking new roles, "trying on" different kinds of selves, and thus exploring alternative ways of defining self in the world. As a result, the introspection and self-awareness of the person increases dramatically (Nixon 1961).

Adolescence has often been referred to as a time of crisis. The crisis derives from the sudden ambiguity of late adolescence as the familiar values, desires, and goals of childhood and early adolescence are called into question by the, at times, chaotic diversity and complexity of the adult world looming just over the temporal horizon. The impact of this ambiguity can be seen in the intense self-questioning, introspection, and taking of different roles characteristic of this period. Out of this time of uncertainty and search comes a more differentiated sense of "who I am." Thus a variety of observers (King 1973; White 1966) have described late adolescence in terms of such affective trends as the integration of part identifications into a holistic, satisfying sense of "I," not the domination of "I" by parental introjects; the development of an autonomous set of personal values, not merely the appropriation from outside authority; and of being able to freely choose in terms of personal desire, interest, and capacity, rather than the domination by infantile gratifications and fantasies of omnipotence. These affective developments are paralleled by cognitive growth, described primarily in terms of the decentering of thought processes and social relationships characteristic of formal operational thought, as the person comes to see the relativity of authority and others' viewpoints (Piaget 1962). From this emerges freely made, autonomous choices in young adulthood. This capacity for vocational, sexual, ideological role commitments derives from the sense of inner responsibility and direction that emerges from the crisis of "who am I?" An integrated and confident answer to this question brings with it the capacity for autonomous and gratifying choice.

Difficulty in the integration of experience and testing of self can also occur in adolescence. If unresolved conflict in separation from the world of childhood and early adolescence is too powerful, the crisis of self-definition can be short-circuited or paralyzed. Unresolved conflict around impulse, autonomy, oedipal issues, or sibling rivalry can lead to uncertainty and doubt about oneself. Finding out "who one is" can then be frightening or difficult for the individual—the ambiguity of self-definition only brings with it great anxiety.

Our understanding of the self emergent from late adolescence can be furthered by brief consideration of conceptual advances about narcissism proposed by Kohut (1966, 1971). Adolescence can be conceived as a process of transformation of the self (Wolf et al. 1972). During adolescence a psychic restructuring takes place as the parental introjects of childhood are given up, replaced by identifications with valued characteristics of the parents. From this results the sense of internal standards and ideals characteristic of autonomous self-definition, described in detail by the affective and cognitive developments considered above. However, when the adolescent process of separation goes awry, because of earlier narcissistic injuries, with corresponding low self-esteem and self-doubt, we find compensatory introjection of the parents and resulting problems in self-definition. Here the difficult process of self-definition in college becomes stalled. Instead of the de-idealization of the parents, the "I" is identified with these idealized, grandiose parental introjects and we find a deep narcissistic investment in perfection of the self. For such individuals adolescence is not a time of crisis through which rigid childhood standards and values are transformed into a realistic ego-ideal and definition of self. Rather, we find the continued rigid perfectionistic strivings characteristic of parental introjects. The self emergent from adolescence is in this case a grandiose "wished-for" self (reflecting the strong perfectionist strivings concomitant to the failure to separate from parental introjects), rather than the more realistic sense of self that accompanies fuller testing and separation from childhood images of one's parents. The frightening or devalued inner world cannot be fully explored and the question of "who I am" is sidestepped or avoided and the self organized around grandiose, wished-for qualities, determined by absolute or faulty identification with parents.

The peer group plays an important role in the adolescent transformation of self. College is an environment or "medium" facilitating the process of peer bonding that becomes important in early adolescence. This notion of peer bonding does not mean a blind alliance with a generalized peer group. Close friendships—the "group of two" or a "chum"—can play this role. In college, the challenges of self-definition and separation from family make the presence of peers particularly important. The college peer group serves as a transitional object, helping the individual to separate from parents without feeling completely isolated or vulnerable. As a transitional object, the peer group serves to stabilize and support the individual, allowing him to tolerate the loss of internal psychological structure (i.e., the values, ideals, and beliefs of childhood) that ordinarily leads to the development of workable guiding ideals and realistic ambition. Further, the peer group should foster confrontation with gaps in understanding of the world, exploration and testing of self, and the development of new beliefs and ideals.

College, then, ideally serves as an environment that both challenges the person—confronting him with experiences at variance with his understanding of the world—and offers the opportunity for the establishment of strong bonds with one's peer group to support the self-testing and exploration provoked during this time.

This emphasis on the ambiguity and "psychic restructuring" of late adolescence reveals its nature as a time of discontinuity and loss. What is "lost" is the childhood understanding and assumptions about oneself and the world. There is much to be learned about the world and old assumptions prove inadequate. It is the childhood and early adolescent "self" that faces this demand for change: Formerly meaningful and trusted values, beliefs, and ideals do not work any longer and new ones must be forged. In particular, the idealized parents one knew as a child must be reshaped and integrated into the sense of self.

Late adolescence, then, can be understood as a time of loss, with perhaps a resultant period of grieving similar to that discussed in Chapter 4. As a period of overt discontinuity and change we can expect an ambivalent response over time from the adolescent: attempts to *hold on* rigidly to the established order of assumption and understanding of self in the face of the ambiguity of college alternating with attempts to equally rigidly *let go* of the past. This is the period of testing and exploration of self often observed in college, with an at times bewildering succession of commitments to roles, ideologies, and objects. From this experience of discontinuity and transformation—often carried out within the haven of a college moratorium—comes a reconstituted self linking, to a greater or lesser degree, personal past, present, and future in a harmonious whole. However, the ability to explore and test the self implies a willingness to reopen the question "who am I?" Suppose, though, this question is a difficult or frightening one because it means acknowledging or sorting through—not necessarily consciously—the variety of wishes, desires, and feelings provoked by new situations. Then we may find an inability to confidently or fully explore and test self. In this case, underlying conflicts about one's inner world result in a retreat from, or avoidance of, the discontinuity of adolescence, with its intolerable underlying question of "who am I?" One manner of resolving the discontinuity in such cases would be through a rigid holding on to the understanding and integration of self characteristic of the past. This would involve little separation from grandiose parental images.*

This latter pattern is characteristic of the men in our study. What we find is a retreat from the experience of the discontinuity of college, and the opportunity for autonomous self-definition it represented. The patterns of constricted self-testing and exploration can be traced to: 1) anxiety about, or devaluation of, their inner life and 2) difficulties in the establishment of strong peer relationships. What we find as these individuals struggled to define themselves through adolescence was that they held on tightly to idealized imaged of parents as the basis for self-organization and attempted to let go of their inner world, their subjectivity, by exiling, suppressing, or splitting off difficult parts of self. We find, then, the development of a variety of strategies for coping with ambivalent feelings about self and parents as these individuals faced the adolescent challenge of defining "who I am."

In the following sections I first discuss anxiety about their inner lives during adolescence, then turn to problems in peer relations at this time.

Anxiety Over "What's Inside": Difficulty with Self-Exploration and Role-Testing

I didn't like to have opinions. Like whether I was a Democrat or Republican or whether I was anything. It was just easier to leave it unanswered rather than commit myself to one party or another or whether or not I liked something. In school it was easier not to be the top student because so much was expected of the top student. It was easier to be in the top ten or 15 percent where I didn't stand out as the top student. I was brought up in a Jewish neighborhood, and when I was a kid all the neighbors had children my age and they were so bright, they were so intelligent. Their children were such geniuses. And I didn't want to be treated that way by my parents. I just didn't want to be used. It just looked like I was being used enough by my parents for their own edification, so to speak. I was tall, and I was good looking and everything else like everybody would say, "My

---

*This resolution involves a premature foreclosure of the discontinuity of college. This is implied by Erikson's (1959) notion of "foreclosed identity" in which self-definition in college appears with an exclusionary air, with little evidence of self-exploration or tolerance of the crisis of identity. See also Perry's (1970) work concerning the impact of college on the process of individuation.

God, where did your son come from" My father was average height
and my mother was short. And I just didn't want to be pointed out as
another bright kid.

In college I kind of floated down a little bit because I passed
everything alright. I don't think very much happened during that period. Just seemed to graduate and I went to work. Nothing great happened to me because by that time everything was already set and you
just went along. You eliminated any anxiety-provoking situations. I
was gonna get a job and go to work and just be conventional as much
as possible. Once that decision was made it's very easy to get along.
Not with yourself but the outside world. Nothing rocks the boat. You
just go along and you go to work from nine to five, come home and
have dinner, get dressed and go out to a movie and go here and out
there. You come home and you're in bed by twelve so that you're up
the next morning to go to work again. And in the summer you plan
vacations. The whole thing is just patterns that you fall into and there
is nothing much left to decide on except just insignificant things like,
where you will go on vacation? What movie will you see?

[*When did you make the decision to be like that?*] I guess it must
have been during high school, during my third or fourth year. [*What
was going on then?*] I don't know, just the thought of a lot of the kids
in the neighborhood had gone the wrong way. Several had been sent
to prison or involved in crime in some way. And I just decided to kind
of narrow my sights somehow and not get involved in anything except
just what society considered would be the normal way of life. [*What
had happened to some of the kids?*] Well one kid was involved in major robberies. Go to jail for a couple of years and come out and get involved again and they sent him back to prison for life. The guy next
door was murdered. The guy around the corner killed his mother—
stuffed her in a tub and filled it with concrete and kept her there for I
don't know how long before they found her. I went to high school,
come to think of it, during the World War II period. That period was
just kind of murky. It was just fall into the line like everybody else
who goes to college. Decide on some profession and go ahead and
work at it and develop it and then things stayed pretty steady for
quite a while.

The preceding passage is a representative description of the high
school and college years in our group of men. Note the movement as described in the excerpt for this person away from disturbing, abnormal
parts of himself in college. For this person "everything was set" by the college years and a primary concern was to eliminate any "anxiety-provoking situations." Such situations were those that involved consideration of
his wishes and desires. Choice was frightening and the movement away
from it involved a decision "to be conventional," to fall into patterns so

that "there is nothing much left to decide on." In other words, something was interfering with this adolescent's self-exploration and freedom of choice so that he "decided to narrow my sights" to "what society considered would be a normal way of life." The question of "who I am" was thus answered early—he was "normal," he was "narrow." What made decision and choice in college so difficult? We get a clue to this toward the end of the passage. To narrow sights to the normal means that the person must have at some time had his sights broader, to what he felt was the abnormal. Such abnormal ways of life are suggested by comments about some of the neighborhood kids: violence and aggression, seen in the focus on murder and robbery. Note these themes: "one kid was involved in major robberies," "murder," and "someone killed his mother." The explosive, murderous violence of his neighborhood seems to have frightened this adolescent, and it seems to have had such an effect because he was struggling with anxieties about his own nature as well. It seems likely that this man is telling us here of his own anxieties about "what's inside" himself.

We find here three important themes characteristic of our entire group during college. First, there is the concern with being normal or conventional. What did it mean to these men to be normal? For this person as with others, it meant not to have antisocial or aggressive, angry impulses. Second, there are unanswered questions or anxiety about one's inner world. The focus on normality as a pattern of self-definition has a compensatory quality of defensiveness to it, as if moving away from disturbing, abnormal parts of oneself. This person, for example, does not seem convinced that he really is social or not angry. This is implied by the sense of excluding aspects of himself to be normal—he "narrowed" himself, he "eliminated" situations. A final theme is indicated in the mention of parents, his own and others. At the beginning of the passage note the anger implicit in the comment that he "didn't want to be used. . . . I was being used enough by my parents." Note, too, the probable underlying anger at his own mother indicated by the theme at the end of his passage: A mother was killed by her son, and this was a very disturbing possibility for this man. He "narrowed" himself away from it. We see in this the element of unresolved conflict and separation issues with parents during college. These men were having a difficult time making autonomous choices and exploring and reconciling their own wishes, desires, and sense of self separate from those of their parents. In this case we see anger at feeling "used" by parents. This means this person was still feeling attached in a very direct way to them. The feeling of being "used" in this case implies being "'delegated" or the instrument of others' purposes, rather than one's own.

Mr. Lonzetti and Mr. Markowitz are two men discussed at length in previous chapters who can stand as further examples of the difficulty with the definition and exploration of self in college. In Mr. Lonzetti's case the movement into college is described overtly in terms of loss, and the loss is of the world he knew as a young adolescent, particularly his idealized father-guide:

> . . . the immense size of [state college] and the feelings of loss I had with being injected into it made these feelings [of loss] even worse. . . . I felt like I had been coming to an understanding with my father, and when he died I felt very cheated. I missed him. Not as an example but as a kind of guide or somebody with a lot of experience that I could ask questions of.

This is a very rich paragraph, containing many themes characterizing Mr. Lonzetti's college experience. The loss was of his father as a guide: despite a distant relationship with his son, Mr. Lonzetti's father had played an important role in helping him choose the college he ultimately attended, and he died while Mr. Lonzetti was a freshman. "Feeling injected" is a phrase that carries with it the sense of passivity and external press—as if he were pushed out of his family, somewhat against his will, and thrown into a situation of ambiguity or loss. Mr. Markowitz stands as another example. In adolescence, questions about his own frightening impulse world were not settled and led to considerable anxiety about his real nature—whether he was at heart an evil, impulsive person, or a good, controlled one. At adolescence we find considerable uncertainty and self-questioning:

> I remember in my junior and senior years in college I became friendly with some of the younger professors. One in particular, we were very close. I was continually asking, "Paul, Paul, do you think—should I—am I— should I be a scientist?" I guess I wasn't sure if I was the kind of person who could be a scientist. I used to really pester Paul— questioning about what he thought about me. Did he think I was apt? Was I in the right field? He was most patient with me but after the twentieth time a little annoyance might creep into his mood. One time we were standing in the hall, in school, and about ten feet away I saw a student faint and I said to him, "Look, Paul, that student just fainted." And he whirled around and ran to the student and did what had to be done. As the day wore on I became more and more troubled by my own lack of reaction. Here I was looking as if I were an observer. There was somebody who needed help. Why didn't I do the right thing? What Paul had done is what I thought was the right thing. Without thinking he turned around and went to the person's aid. So I met him later and told him what was bothering me. And he said to me, "Abe, you're not that important." Now that affected me.

That's what I had to be told at that time. I was ready for somebody to tell me. I was so questioning of myself that I was having trouble getting things done. And that's what I had to be told.

Underneath the question about science as a profession lay far deeper concerns about his own nature (captured by such questions as, "if I was the kind of person," and "why didn't I do the right thing?") and the paralysis that resulted, implied in Mr. Markowitz's comment that "I was having trouble getting things done." Thus, childhood questions about the nature of his inner world remained pressing and disturbing questions in adolescence for Mr. Markowitz. Note the reliance on older others, father-surrogates, as sources of reassurance about his true nature.

The inability to mobilize resources and strength to explore the college situation and confront it more fully runs throughout our participants' accounts of the outcome of college. One man described his four years at a prestigious Ivy League school as "a phase one goes through"; another referred to his college years as "a waste."

Our men's continued struggle with the integration of their affective lives gives a context to this difficulty with free exploration of self in the college environment. There are strong uncertainties about self, making the ambiguity and discontinuity of college particularly difficult. There were too many unanswered questions about their own impulses, initiative, affect, and curiosity for these individuals to confidently seek to answer the question, "who am I?" At times the presence of these unanswered questions were verbalized directly by the participants, as in Mr. Markowitz's excerpts above. Similarly, Mr. O'Hara describes himself in adolescence as "hiding from myself. I developed a kind of nice exterior self in high school, generous at times, generally pretty compliant with my teachers, compliant with other people. I avoided fights because of my fear of violence."

More often, the presence of profound inner uncertainties can be seen indirectly in these men's accounts in several ways.

A. First we find a propensity to shame and embarrassment, revealing underlying feelings of inner unworthiness. Mr. Goodson remembers numerous experiences in high school and college of feeling shame and embarrassment in the presence of his peers.

I was really shy in college, no confidence. Once I went out with this girl. I only went out with her once and I was so embarrassed and felt so shy. One of the big things was that I just didn't feel like I had anything interesting to talk about with her. I still have that feeling. Like I don't feel quite like taking the initiative and talking about something that interests me for fear that the person won't find it interesting. I'll feel like I'm a bit of a fool for starting the conversation.

Similarly, Mr. Lonzetti recalls that "socially I just had no confidence at all. I don't know that other people saw that so much, but I felt it." In discussing his "great fear of humiliation—I mean more than most people," Mr. Lonzetti recalls even earlier experiences of being shamed and feeling as if something were wrong with him:

I remember times as early as first grade, of going out at noon and playing baseball with the kids. I must have been self-conscious or something and I wouldn't remember the rules. One time I carried the bat all the way to first base because I forgot to throw it away, and the kids all said that was against the rule and that I couldn't play anymore. And that bothered me a bit. In fact I think that the principal happened to walk by at that time and he told all the kids that they couldn't do that and they allowed me to play. And that didn't help at all.

I remember even when I was in fifth or sixth grade being on a picnic outing, I remember somebody asked me to get down on my hands and knees behind her so that I could push her over. And they did and she fell over and she got up and she started fighting. And I didn't want to fight her at all. And she was really strong. And she essentially beat me up to the point where I started crying. The humiliation that it represented was something that stayed with me a long time. I was very hesitant to even go back to school.

Being an athlete was the thing that you had to do to be somebody in the fifties. Either that or have the black leather jacket and hang out and smoke, skip class. Or you were a scholar or whatever. And I was none of them. I just went to school. Got cut from football. It was traumatic, it was terrible, I was cut all along my life. Little League baseball, I can remember the first time, coming home after I tried out for the team. And I got cut. And I was just crying my ass off. I didn't want to face the world. A big rejection. I remember in junior high school getting into a game late in the fourth quarter and playing guard. I got in the game and I can remember the coach saying, "What the fuck is he doing in there? Get him out of there." Everyone heard. And it just destroyed me.

Note the inner inferiority and uncertainty about self-worth produced by uncertain or negative responses from others. There is an ease to which these men's self-worth is called into question and—to anticipate our argument—this is traceable to childhood uncertainties about the meaning of their affective life and aggression which will be discussed in the next section. In college this meant a particular difficulty exploring and asserting personally valued interests and beliefs, especially those in the artistic or personal realm, that might seem "different" from others. Mr. Goodson commented, for example, that he disliked "taking the initiative," while Mr. Prezinski remembers feelings of being "afraid" to assert his interests in the arts. Another participant put it this way:

> My teacher in college kept urging me to go into English or writing and I just kind of discounted that completely at the time. . . . I felt like it wasn't really a respectable profession for a man to go into.

At times we find descriptions of withdrawal from activities after failures, again as if the person felt not strong enough to defend himself or his products in an interpersonal world. An example, from Mr. Goodson:

> In college I had entered different art exhibitions and got a picture accepted in each one. Then I went to graduate school and there was an exhibition there at the university and I didn't get any pictures accepted. That kind of put a damper on my art work for a long time. Because I felt that there must be something wrong with what I was doing. That I had gone off on either a course that wasn't as favorable to other people or else that I was not in one of the accepted mainstreams of art at the time.

The failure to get into a show is taken as proof by Mr. Goodson of his ineptness as a painter. This person with little belief in his own worth took the rejection as proof that "something was wrong with what I was doing." Regardless of the correctness of Mr. Goodson's judgment about his art, this has meanings also for the process of self-definition and testing of self. Essentially, Mr. Goodson moves away from those aspects of himself. This relationship to his art can thus be seen as expressing a more general difficulty asserting or defending himself. These problems in integrating his artistic interests reflect a general difficulty at that time, rooted in childhood, of valuing his feelings and standing up for his products. We find, for example, similar problems with competition and self-assertion later in relation to science. In this context we can understand Mr. Prezinski's anger at his parents for not having supported more his interest in the arts as a child, and Mr. Goodson's lament at the "narrow image" his parents presented. These were individuals who found it difficult to assert their interests, values, and wishes separately from others. Mr. Goodson, in this vein, comments that he felt "very alone and cut off from people" when working on art in high school, and this feeling made it difficult for him to pursue his interest in the area. Even now, he says, "I feel supported when somebody has a feeling similar to one that I've had. You know I get the feeling I'm not alone in the universe." The propensity to shame and embarrassment, because of profound questions as to his own worth, made self-exploration and the assertion of interests and values difficult.

B. Conversely, we also find a grandiosity of strivings for some men, making deeper uncertainties. Such desires to be the center of attention, the "best," "on top" are exemplified in the following excerpts from two different participants:

I always try to put myself in positions where I don't have to worry about hurting other people. Like being in a leadership role I've always been able to deal a lot easier with people because then I'm recognized as a leader and then they expect me to say certain things. To guide them and to give suggestions and then you do it my way. As a result I've always gone out of my way to rise to the top of situations in organizations or class situations. Always trying to get the best marks, to come up with the right answers all the time. President of my fraternity, president of the church group, you know, get the lead in the play—that sort of thing. I felt then that I was up here above the others and it was easier to deal with me if I felt that the people were at a level below me. And I do that in acting class. I figure out the way for everybody to pay attention. I can remember the very first class that happened. There was an exercise. You could only sing "Happy Birthday" to manifest whatever behavior, whatever feelings that you had just through that song. Before I knew it I had found this high stool and I was on top of this high stool singing this to everybody else and before I knew it everybody was gathered around me singing up to me and I was just sitting there listening to that.

I didn't think I could get into college. We had to take a little test to see if I could get into the college courses in high school and I got in but I didn't expect to. I saw a report once with my IQ on it and I recall looking at it and saying, "Jesus, I got a 100." And I asked somebody what his was because I figured 100 was perfect. I found out it wasn't. I just asked somebody else and his was just higher. And he didn't ask me what I had. I said, "Oh." I just closed it up. I didn't think much of myself all through high school. I didn't think much of myself that much in college. Like there would be times I felt like I was something special. I felt that there were kids that were smarter than me and I wanted to be really sharp and special. And I wasn't. And it seemed like I was associating with these people and yet I felt good because I was part of their group. I had the grades and whatever. But I felt inwardly that I wasn't part of it.

We find in the first excerpt the need to be applauded, to be a leader, to be appreciated. Yet such concerns serve the function of protecting the person against threats to a vulnerable ego and thus mask deeper uncertainties over the meaning of his aggression and of his ability to take care of himself. For this man being "on top" was not accompanied by an inner assurance of strength and self-worth. In the second excerpt note the compensatory need to feel "special" amid profound feelings of inferiority and unworthiness. This excerpt exemplifies the duality of the sense of inferiority-superiority rooted in difficulty in truly valuing and knowing "who one is."

C. For some men there is also an intense envying of the qualities of peers, and compensatory, unsuccessful attempts to "imitate" them. These qualities usually have to do with power, strength, and self-assertion. We can see in this the attempt to locate in other "strong" people qualities about which these men were themselves conflicted:

> I was a science major in college. While I was there I was very friendly with artists. In fact, one of my best friends was an artist. We really got to be very good friends. And then I also happened to know all the other people in the arts program. So I liked being with them and I liked what they were doing. And I thought they were all very talented. And they were all very superior. My feeling was that they were so advanced, far ahead of me in every way, that there was no sense in trying.

> In college I had always been part of a group of four or five guys, but I wasn't quite sure what I was to that group. I was more of a follower—yeah, OK, "you want to go here," "right, yes." As opposed to taking initiative and calling the shots and saying, "What about this?" And being more of a leader than a follower. The guys that I roomed with were all athletes and all on scholarship and all very popular on campus. They were all big names. These guys were all 6'3", 235 to 6'5", 270. Big fuckers. And then there was me. Small in size.

In these cases we find stronger, more assertive persons, representing the other side of the person's ambivalence to self. This represents a locating in the external world desires and interests that the men were unable to integrate in themselves.

D. Then there are the questions about "normalcy" in college, usually in terms of social or sexual adequacy. While their accounts indicate concerns and problems little different from the general population in college during the 1950s and early '60s, we find repeated worrying about being "different" from others in some men's accounts:

> I started to become self-conscious if I went places alone. When I was living in New York, in college, I would avoid places where I knew friends could see. I just fantasized that they would think, "Jesus, he's a loner. What's the matter, maybe he had a fight with somebody, maybe he's really weird or maybe he's gay."

> My first sexual relationship in college. She seduced me one night in her apartment. It was kind of exciting because it was different from

my old self, being shy and not having any sexual experience. [*Was that a relationship that continued?*] Not for very long. I felt kind of insecure in my ability as a lover compared with what I imagined that other men would be like. So when I realized that she was seeing other men I kind of felt that she wouldn't really be satisfied with me any longer. [*What did you imagine other men would be like?*] Well, they'd have more experience and they'd be able to please her more fully. Sort of show her more of an exciting time than I was.

E. We see as well preoccupation with status and prestige, serving an "overdriven" compensatory need for reassurance against a sense of inner unworthiness. For example, getting into fraternities are mentioned by several men as extremely important signs of their social worth. Rejections precipitate intense self-questioning and turmoil:

The idea of being associated with a fraternity got to be a really big deal for me. I look back on it as being incredibly out of proportion. But I was really quite moved by the feeling of being judged or not succeeding in what I wanted to do, which was a nebulous thing. It's so nebulous that I didn't know what to do to promote it.

It was very important to get into a fraternity, for some reason. I didn't get into the one I wanted and was so broken up by it that I actually wept. And refused to go to another one, which was a very good fraternity. My heart was set on this one, for some reason, and it really was a shattering experience. So I refused to be in any of them. I lived for half a year in a rented room.

Difficulties in the Use of the Peer Group

To compound the difficulties of self-exploration in college, the psychological distance between these men and their peer groups made the process of inner exploration and separation from family more difficult, since there were few allies to turn to among the peer group. The roots of these men's peer relations lay in childhood and early adolescence, as other children became part of the characteristic ways in which they learned to cope with their inner life. Distance from the peer group was increased by the fact that inadequacies in social competence made effective use of the peer group problematic. Strong unanswered questions and uncertainties about self made it difficult for these men to be different from their peers, yet problems in social interaction kept them outside the peer group. Defending themselves on the inside (from the frightened or devalued aspects of self) and outside (from their peers), these individuals seem to have had little attention to spare for self-examination.

We see difficulties in peer relations in the following ways.

A. First, we find a psychological orientation toward adults in college, not peers. This runs throughout some of the material already presented. In part this reflects the need for legitimacy and reassurance that things are okay, that they are "normal." In this context, the attention to adults is also indicative of a difficulty separating from the values and beliefs introjected from their parents and relying on themselves for the emergence of valued beliefs and ideals.

Thus, for example, much of Mr. Markowitz's self-questioning in college can be understood as reflective of the failure to live up to intense, rigid standards of behavior, rooted in his struggle with his aggression and impulse. We find him turning to parent-surrogates during adolescence, first in the search for absolute standards of conduct and moral behavior and secondly in the emphasis on pure thought and the powers of the mind. Two figures of importance already discussed were his wrestling coach and a young professor in college. Mr. Markowitz's description of the latter as a role model indicates his search for rational answers to life's questions.

> When I was going to college, I became very much attached to a professor in the biology department. Really brilliant. He put so many ideas into my head. Mostly philosophical ideas that had to do with the philosophy of science. I really truly loved that man. I so looked up to him. He was my model of a scientist. His Ph.D. thesis was just eight pages long and brilliant.

So, too, with Mr. Anderson, who turned to surrogate father figures for guidance and direction during his time of confusion in college:

> Off and on I went through college until my senior year. I began to feel better then because of contact with a history tutor. He was very relaxed and had us write a tutorial in European history. We could choose practically anything you wanted and write a critical essay about it. I was struck how informal it was. I didn't feel the same distance from the teacher as I had.

We also find an emphasis on the desire to please parents, be reassured by them, and of "owing" things to them. Here too we find difficulty in taking responsibility for commitment to one's own beliefs and values. As Mr. Goodson puts it:

> I remember my physics and chemistry teacher in college urging me to accept a science scholarship. I do distinctly remember going there mostly because he urged me to accept it. After I was at college awhile

I remember wanting to drop the scholarship and change my major, but I felt a real obligation to my parents and the people who gave me the scholarship.

Participants report feelings of owing things to their parents and feeling guilty about desires to cross them. These unresolved conflicts made true separation and self-definition more difficult. For some men the death of a father served to intensify their attention to these figures. The sudden loss, given the unresolved conflicts still operative, made it more difficult to acknowledge and express negative feelings and the desire to separate— even if only psychologically—from loved ones. The conjunction of the loss of parent at the time of ambiguity around self-definition represented by college seemed to make the process of clear appraisal of feelings, interests, and desires more difficult. Instead, attributes of the idealized father were internalized. Thus, for example, much of Mr. Lonzetti's college experience centered around a deep sense of inferiority and difficulty integrating aspects of himself into a harmonious, whole sense of self: "It's as though I required a kind of approbation before I felt justified or sanctioned to get on with the other things I basically wanted to do." What were the "other things"? Playfulness, tinkering, self-related interests and desires. Thus the deep feeling of something being wrong with him lingered on for Mr. Lonzetti in college. Part of the reason for a major in engineering was because "it was a challenge in the sense that I couldn't let go of it until I sort of acquitted myself." This sense of having to make up for something wrong—to "acquit" himself—is rooted in Mr. Lonzetti's struggles with his father and his father's having excluded him from the rest of his family. As his earlier comment concerning feeling cheated by his father's death indicates, underneath the intense overt anger and disappointment with father we find Mr. Lonzetti's desire for his father to be available to him. The feeling of guilt and of owing his father something is based partly on his anger and earlier struggle with this man. The attempt to examine his affects and desires in college involved opening up some of the same aggression/rage he had been suppressing since childhood. This would have been hard enough to do, but the death of his father made it even harder. Mr. Lonzetti says he felt like a bastard because of the intense difficulty between them. The word "bastard" is striking in this context because it implied the devaluation of his aggression, not being his father's son, and the affective roots of the project to become more like the idealized image of him. When his father died, during Mr. Lonzetti's freshman year in college, there was little further opportunity to work things through. We then see very likely a strengthening of the internalization of idealized qualities of the father.

B. Difficulties with peer relations also involve an uncertain perception of the peer group. At times our participants seemed to have considerable difficulty deciding whether others were friend or foe, allies or threat. This uncertain mode of relating to peers can be seen in the fraternity concerns described above. Mr. Goodson touches on this uncertainty about his peers as allies or enemies when he describes his worries about his peers' "jealousy" of him:

> Often I feel I should do things for people. Many times friends will ask me to do something for them since they're not able to do it, but I've got a lot of free time, as an artist. I feel like I should. I feel that I'm the one at fault rather than that the person is just dumping their own sort of frustration on me. I find it difficult to resist that if the person is a friend of mine. Because I don't want to lose their friendship by letting this sort of jealousy exist between us. Where they would be jealous of me by just doing my own art work and enjoying myself.

We see also in Mr. Lonzetti's description of his college peers this fluctuation between peers as friends or as judges. His feeling of being judged by admittance to a fraternity was cited earlier, and he continues:

> I think I would have gotten more out of college had I not been defining myself in terms of what groups I was in. And yet I couldn't have done it at the time. [*What was it that stopped you?*] Lack of confidence. And it wasn't confidence about my real interests. It was confidence about being judged by other people and just sort of the need for some sort of a resting place upon which I could do other things that were more of my own free will.

These men indicate a real uncertainty about feeling valued by others, and in themselves valuing their real interests and activities.

C. Beyond these dynamic issues, the participants in this study seemed to lack important social competencies as adolescents that would allow confident bonding with the peer group. Repeatedly we see a lack of knowledge as to how to assert competently and defend self and products, or to regulate effectively interaction with peers:

> All through my high school and college days I kind of went where I wanted and did what I wanted. The problem then was that everybody wanted to tag along with me. I would somehow say just go your own way and leave me alone. Just friends or like in college when you get together with a group of people. What are you doing tonight? Can I come along? And it got to be a big thing rather than just something that I wanted to do with a date or one or two friends. Then once you get there invariably when there are four or five couples one says, "Well I don't really like the place." And then the whole place

begins to get uncomfortable. It just kind of ruins the evening. Whereas if there are only two people to contend with it just doesn't go that way. Chances are that you'll all be together very well and the place will be nice. It's just somehow with larger groups the odds are someone not liking what's going on and expressing it. Then you begin to say, "Well, gee whiz, sorry you don't like it." And then you begin to say, "Well she doesn't like it and we'll go somewhere else." And then the whole thing just gets to be rotten.

Thus, both dynamic issues and the apparent absence of certain social competencies deprived these men of an alliance with their peer group so as to facilitate and support the testing and exploration of self in adolescence.

It is important to note that being cut off from peers also deprives the person of much information about the world, as well as support in the psychological task of separation from families. The person has less information about possibilities because of less interaction and sharing with a source of such information. This helps us understand, for example, Mr. Goodson's feeling of always having been limited and of having based his sense of self so much on his father. Further, we also see the role in these excerpts of the person's need to protect self and the experience of intense inferiority or uncertainty amid the discontinuity of college. What stands out in Mr. Lonzetti's discussion of his shame and humiliation as a child is his psychological isolation from his peer group. Because he was cut off from others and so defensive, he did not have much opportunity for exploration and testing of self among the peer group. His preoccupation at the time of college was achieving security, not giving some of it up in order to truly define himself; the role of his social isolation stands out in limiting his ability to truly define himself. Thus, Mr. Lonzetti's comment, "I've always felt I don't know myself as well as others know themselves." Mr. Prezinski, describing himself in the present, also expresses a feeling of backwardness, as if important developmental experiences were missed, saying he feels as if he were "ten years behind other people" in his development. While on the one hand such comments reflect an idealization of other people and their strength (who does not feel at times as if others have had it better?), they also express the feeling of not having been able to explore fully enough and develop self as much as others in their peer group.

"Holding On" in Adolescence: Separation Issues and the Project to Remake Self

The press of unanswered conflict about self and family moved these individuals away from the confident exploration and testing of self. This meant the lack of freely tested interest and capacity, and essentially a psychological withdrawal from the ambiguity and discontinuity of college. These men coped with the discontinuity by holding on tightly to earlier interpretations of self in the world, at the same time as they tried to separate from them. To be normal meant to define oneself through the tried and true, the idealized attributes of a fantasized father. This attempt to hold on to self-definitions threatened by the ambiguity of college meant a movement away from aspects of their subjectivity and toward a rigid normality, without resolution of the inner conflicts that made the men so concerned about feeling different or odd. What we find instead is the attempt to hold onto the idealized images of parents as the basis for self-definition and to exile, suppress, or split off essential interests, wishes, and desires.

Coming under the anxiety of being defective, of having something wrong with oneself, this pattern of self-organization in adolescence largely reflects a project to remake oneself into the idealized image of parents rooted in childhood. Rather than the integration of disparate aspects of self into a relatively harmonious whole, a personally valued self-definition, we find an attempt to remake onself into something different or better than who one actually is, since who one is, the struggling adolescent feels, is not good enough. This characterization of the late adolescent thrust to remake oneself seems apt because of the compensatory, over-driven push toward normalcy that underlay the process of self-definition. This organization of self was strongly influenced by an attempt to exclude undesirable or devalued aspects of self and to compensate for these feelings of inner unworthiness or inferiority. Thus, in adolescence we find these individuals attempting to let go of these aspects of self by holding on tightly to idealized images of parents. What we find, then, is a very powerful perfectionist wish of undiluted, absolute, unrelenting morality, acceptance, safety. This perfectionist wish expressed the hope of making right, finally, oneself and the world. As Gould (1978) has recently noted, these powerful unconscious fantasies of absolute security or safety can play a key role into adulthood. This is certainly true in our group of career changers, and in this analysis of adolescence we can see the developmental origin of such fantasies.

Let me elaborate the role of perfectionist fantasies during adolescence by focusing on the six men we've discussed in detail in the preceding chapters. In the case of Mr. Markowitz, for example, we find reflected in the two key figures he describes in college—his wrestling coach and his biology professor—a turning away from the ambiguity of college and the organization of self around attributes of his idealized, godlike father. The belief that it is possible to govern behavior by absolute, unimpeachable rules of conduct that are embodied in some individuals was rooted in a perception of the godlike, law-making father forbidding Mr. Markowitz's expression of his aggression or affect. The second major belief—that pure thought is omniscient and can remove one from what Mr. Markowitz called the "muddy," "dirty" everyday world, with its affect and conflicting motivations—was rooted in his need to exile his frightening inner world of affect and impulse. These were salient aspects of the organizing fantasy of adolescence for Mr. Markowitz. In the emphasis on "pure thought" we see Mr. Markowitz's attempt to exile the difficult aspects of his inner world; as we saw in Chapter 2, he was to be the "responsible one," without the strong pull of "irresponsible" emotion, attraction, and desire, nor that of angry, aggressive impulses.

In adolescence Mr. Markowitz was thus in the process of attempting to be like such idealized, brilliant, godlike people. Originating out of deep uncertainty and questions about his own motivations and behavior, these wishes did not represent a flexible, nurturant inner sense of who he wanted to be and who he was. This was rather a rigid, demanding standard allowing no compromise. To become this way would require that Mr. Markowitz remake himself into someone very different than he felt himself to be, eliminating the desire to be irresponsible, playful, or uncontrolled. In this case, then, we can see the perfectionist wish or hope of finding a perfect morality, of being without antisocial or egocentric needs, wishes, or behavior.

Mr. Goodson, too, coped with the ambiguity of self-definition represented by college by holding on tightly to an identification with his father. This idealized image centered on the absence of desires to be dominant or assert oneself, as well as a reassuring sense of being able to give to others and not be dependent or need help/attention/acclaim from others. It was thus a turning away from his desires for help and attention from others, as he turned away from such desires from his father and mother. This idealized image as the basis of self-organization thus centered on two areas of prime difficulty for Mr. Goodson: his desire for attention and to dominate (being egocentric or "selfish") and the feeling of needing help or being dependent (wanting others to "serve" him). Both of these were "unmanly" in terms of an idealized father who was humble, nonaggressive, and unneedy. In other words, these were precisely qualities about which Mr. Goodson was uncertain in himself. This meant that Mr. Goodson's interest in art and the egocentric rewards it brought him, his hedonistic desires, and his dependency needs were—he hoped—left behind in adolescence. Here we see the perfectionist wish of being perfectly self-contained, without need or self-interest in his relation with others.

What we find for Mr. Prezinski is, finally, in college a movement away from the integration of his interests and desires (a more autonomous self-definition) and toward a sense of self as weak and powerless. The essential elements of this idealized image of the father involved the sense of self as without egocentric desires (not being a threat to stronger people) and as devoid of power or strength. The former attribute means that Mr. Prezinski feels he did not have desires to dominate others or to take from them, or have sensual desires. In a sense Mr. Prezinski believed that he did not have wishes or desires—to not reveal himself meant to be safe from the retribution he saw everywhere. The latter attribute means that he felt he did not have the power to oppose people or assert his wishes and desires.

Obviously Mr. Prezinski was far from certain that his inner world was no threat to others or that he would not assert himself in some way that would bring retribution and psychological assault from others. Thus the project to remake himself centered on the banishment of affect and desire and the belief in oneself as nonegocentric, that is without threatening impulse or emotion (e.g., the wish to dominate others). This pattern of self-definition represents a turning away from the opportunity in college to separate from the idealized images of childhood and early adolescence and instead a retreat to them as the very linchpin of self-organization in order to cope with the frightening possibilities or discontinuity of college. This discontinuity had reopened difficult questions for Mr. Prezinski—e.g., am I interested in the arts? do I have wishes to be center stage and assert myself? am I egocentric?—and Mr. Prezinski slammed the door in the face of such anxiety-provoking questions. For Mr. Prezinski the attempt to remake himself centered on leaving behind at adolescence his interest in the egocentric arts and his desires for self-assertion and enjoyment in other areas. The perfectionist wish in this case centered on achieving total safety and the satisfaction of needs without threat from the outer world.

For Mr. Anderson the movement was away from activities unacceptable and very different from the poised, formal activities of his family. He refers at one point in the interviews to an inner dissociation in college, and this is revealing. The earlier devaluing of, and anxiety about, his affective life led to confusion and paralysis, an inability to choose and decide about the future with a sense of pride and assurance, since his inner life was, as he says, useless. What we find is the perfectionist wish to remake oneself into the idealized image of his brother and father: highly verbal and socially poised. The unacknowledged fantasy here seemed to be that it was indeed possible to obtain full acceptance and love from his parents and to defeat his sibling in the contest for these resources. To do so, in the case of Mr. Anderson, meant leaving behind his interests in less verbal activities, those seen as less valued or poised, as well as his unruly inner life that seemed so much at variance with a proper style.

For Mr. O'Hara the perfectionist wish at the core of self centered around achieving the total acceptance and love he had never obtained as a child. In Chapter 2 we briefly discussed Mr. O'Hara's sense of internal division and separation through childhood with his opposing pulls and conflicting motives. In college Mr. O'Hara was unable to integrate and reconcile the different motives, interests, and desires he felt, since these were tightly tied to the terrible rejection he experienced as a child from his father and mother. However, underneath the confusion and uncertainty about who he is and what the future holds we find evidence of ordered fantasies. We find the perfectionist wish or hope of inner reconciliation by obtaining complete outer acceptance. In other words, the fantasy centered on becoming good enough, great enough to be accepted by all. This very centrally involved becoming good enough to be accepted by his father, thus affirming his masculinity. A major aspect of the internalized father was to become great, to be able to justify himself through the magnitude and heroics of his endeavors. To do this, though, meant to remake himself into a person acceptable to others, as he had tried so hard to do as a child for his parents. Mr. O'Hara would be a great intellectual, a great sensitive teacher, a great husband and father. This was a demanding and difficult task, of course, involving great effort and motivated by overdriven needs. And in order to do so Mr. O'Hara had to leave behind in adolescence his desires to be himself, to assert himself separately from the response of the moment, and to not care so deeply for the total acceptance and love of others. The hope was never again to have to experience the internal polarization of divided feelings and wishes and the sense of doubt or rejection about his inner life. Finally, with Mr. Lonzetti the uncertainty of college touched deeply on his feelings of inferiority. What we find is a movement away from this sense of inferiority—identified with his real father, an unambitious extrovert with a drinking problem, who was divorced by his mother—and toward that of superiority— identified with the fantasized father and embodied in a real grandfather present in the home, a hard-working, successful businessman. Thus we have a rejection of the closest parts of the unacceptable father—the socially adept drinking man who was not all Mr. Lonzetti hoped he would be. The idealized grandfather/father figure was above humiliation and criticism. This self-made quality in Mr. Lonzetti's fantasy also implied the absence of others and the ability to do it all himself. Thus the idealized image implied a comparative perspective, of being above his humiliation and criticism, of being ambitious, growth-oriented, superior, self-made, like an ideal father—not a sociable alcoholic like his real father. Since Mr. Lonzetti, however, does not feel truly confident of his worth, he feels the need to remake himself into a person who is indeed superior, not inferior. The perfectionist wish is to achieve a perfect safety and security from the threatening world of others.

"To Become Like Your Work": The Appropriation of an Identity in Young Adulthood

This perspective on our groups' adolescent experience deepens our understanding of the young adulthood career and marital choices initially presented in Chapter 2. These choices now can be seen as a means of appropriating the wished-for self or identity emergent from adolescence. In this group, highly specialized, professional career choices became the vehicle for implementation of the wished-for self. The absence of true self-definition, and separation from childhood conflicts, is captured in the phrase "identity appropriations" used by Goldsmith (1972) to contrast such young adulthood career choices with "identity approximations" or career choices based on adolescent identity achievement. As we've seen from our groups' reports, the notion of remaking oneself implies that a confident self-definition was not obtained in adolescence by the synthesis of disparate experiences, identifications, and interests in a process of inner identity approximations. Since the self was dominated by an idealized, grandiose image, individuals attempted to be this way by appropriating such a self-definition from the outside. The essence of appropriating an identity is an imitation of the desired, the attempt to define self by attribution, by surrounding oneself with the external markers or attributes of desired inner qualities. It is thus a confusion of external appearances with inner attributes. Yet we can understand such a wish when certain qualities seem essential yet lacking in oneself, as these men felt in adolescence. In such situations one solution is to imitate in the hope of being like. And this group attempted to draw the attributes of normalcy around themselves. The idealized role attributes of particular careers became a major means of appropriating this self-definition.

For Mr. Markowitz, for example, the question of true self-definition was not one he could confidently answer, particularly as we assume a large discrepancy between his perception of the godlike figures around him and his own sense of self. What we find is the appropriation of such a definition as a godlike, moral, brilliant person, from the outside through a career (rather than approximate, from the inside) by depending on others and situations to help him be this way. The controls and rigor of methodology and scientific procedure, and the important work of the scientist, were to serve as proof of his own good, controlled, socially responsible nature.

In the case of Mr. Goodson the unarticulated hope was that the autonomous and socially important work of the scientist would be evidence of his own masculinity and unselfish attitude toward others. For Mr. O'Hara, his work as an academic carried with it the hope of being accepted and loved by others in the pure, unconditional manner he had never known as a child, and in the way he did not feel toward himself. Here is the appropriation—Mr. O'Hara did not feel himself accepting of the ways he was, yet hoped to be defined by a career in a way that would provide the acceptance he so desperately wanted. For Mr. Anderson, too, the way of being a lawyer was the way he hoped to be as a person and felt, at an unacknowledged level, that he wasn't: verbally facile, socially poised, and worthy in his own right. For Mr. Prezinski, as he says, the hope was "to become like your work"—that the rationality and relatively unaffective demands of the engineer's life would characterize who he was as a person. As a result, in our summary of Mr. Prezinski's unarticulated hope of young adulthood, he would be rid of the appetites and desires that still provoked so much anxiety in college. And so too, finally, for Mr. Lonzetti—his career attributes would provide the external markers of his superiority and unassailable position over others. It was the failure of these projects by midlife that led to the potential for re-experiencing of separation problems not fully resolved in adolescence.

Childhood: Inner Ambivalences and the Transformation of the Parents

To introduce this section, some comments as to why it was written. In our discussion of the adolescent, young adulthood, and midlife experiences of the men in our group, we have found, repetitively, a link between the expression of aggression, impulse, initiative, and curiosity and the parents and childhood of these men. At midlife we found that the parents figured prominently in our understanding of the dimensions of personality growth; for some individuals parents remained as conflictual figures right through midlife. In adolescence and young adulthood we noted the role for these men of conflicts about their own subjectivity in getting into the adult world, reflected in the initial career choice. There is some evidence that conflicts around identity, self-definition, and separation from parents experienced in adulthood have roots at points much earlier in the life cycle. For example Jacques's (1965) perspective on the crisis of midlife emphasizes its nature as a re-experiencing of childhood trauma around one's aggression and destructive urges toward parents in early childhood. The conflicts discussed at later points in the life cycle, then, may be the residue of earlier struggles in childhood. This section explores these men's childhood memories to learn more about their developing aggression, initiative, and curiosity, and the role played by the parents as these men came to learn of their inner life. To do this I draw particularly on perspectives that emphasize the integration of ambivalent urges and feelings as an important challenge of childhood (Fraiberg 1968).

Certainly, since we are studying a group of men who are now artists we might expect that the question of one's subjectivity—the impulse life, fantasy, and affect that are the roots of the artist's creativity—would be central. Yet in discussing childhood in this group I am interested in the subjectivity we all experience. The general question, then, is: How did these people come to know themselves in childhood? What did they learn about their subjective world—their curiosity and initiative, their affect or feelings, their aggression, and their desire to express self and receive attention from valued others? In the answers to these questions lie some of the origins of the perfectionist strivings and wished-for self of adolescence and adulthood. Note that in Chapter 4 memories of parents and childhood were discussed from the perspective of change and stasis in perception of these key figures and events during adulthood. Now we shall return to these childhood memories to see what light they shed on early development.

This section will be most speculative of all, in that we are discussing a life stage furthest removed from the time of the interviews. We must infer childhood dynamics and conflicts—events cloaked even at the time in defenses and distortions of memory—from a perspective years later, at midlife. Despite this, the coherency and recurrence of themes in the interviews related to issues of 1) difficulties in the childhood experience of impulse and aggression linked to 2) parents as ambivalently held figures leads me to believe that we can see through these memories, albeit darkly, to earlier conflicts and challenges.

The Ambivalence of Impulse in Childhood: The "Strong Mother–Unavailable Father" Pattern

The childhood of these men will be discussed broadly, encompassing the years from birth to puberty in a general analysis. The most general point to note is that we do not find this group describing their childhood in terms of a confident and comfortable learning of their own powers, skills, and abilities. Rather, we find salient memories of the futility of effort, of the accountability of impulse, of the fear of exploration, of feeling as an outcast because of one's initiative and activity, of narcissistic injuries surrounding self-expression, and of the lack of a responsive or supportive family environment. Of particular interest is the manner in which these men as children struggled with ambivalent feelings and desires toward key figures in their life at that time. Problems of coming to terms with powerfully divided, contradictory wishes and desires stand out in the childhood of this group. For all people childhood contains the challenge of coming to terms with a variety of competing motives and feelings. Parents in particular are central figures as they are frustrating agents as well as sources of nurturance and love. Even the most nurturant parent is at times a source of frustration to the developing infant and child, resulting in anger and fantasized aggression. And the child is tied by bonds of love and the realities of his dependency to even the most rejecting parents. All children face the challenge of integrating ambivalent urges toward their parents: both love and hate. The central dilemma involves synthesizing these caring and destructive urges toward figures on whom one is dependent. The wish to aggress brings with it the fear of destroying the loved object, or being destroyed by it. On the other hand, feelings of dependency and love can also be frightening: Does it mean total surrender to the powerful parent? Can one exist independently? Can one love and be separate? The integration of ambivalent urges (to be separate and close, to love and hate, to desire and reject) forms central challenges of childhood.

We find in the childhood memories of the participants in our research evidence of such powerfully ambivalent feelings and wishes toward parents. As examples, consider the descriptions of parents by Mr. Markowitz and Mr. O'Hara. We already considered a description by Mr. Markowitz of his parents; further discussion appears below, followed by an excerpt from Mr. O'Hara.

MR. MARKOWITZ: I was brought up mostly by my mother. I didn't have much contact with my father. Almost anything I did was approved of by my mother. [*How would you describe your relationship with your mother?*] It was almost as if I were her husband. I took care of her. She would come to me for advice and I'd give her advice. I supported her. I went to her concerts, not that it was any great difficulty, because I loved music and she belonged to a very fine chorus in Boston, and I loved their music and the way they sang. But I was the only one in the family that did it. When my father's health was failing towards the end of his life. So he didn't go out in the evenings. But to give you an idea of his sense of responsibility right up to the last when my mother would come home late at night he'd be down the street watching for her, waiting for her. They were entirely unsuited for each other; they married because they were in love. No other reason than that. And my mother's view of him was that he had been ruined by his mother so he was not ready to become an equal partner in marriage.

MR. O'HARA: Another piece of the puzzle which I had given me from childhood, which is always very present to me at my birthday, is that when I was about seven I was very close to my mother. I had come home expecting my father and he wasn't with us. He was supposed to bring presents. So we were all very disappointed. We lived in an isolated place. This was during the winter. The heat, the oil ran out and my father hadn't paid the bill. And his absence was very pronounced. And I really felt a lot of hatred toward him, a lot of disappointment. And I wished he would never come back. And he didn't turn up that night. He wasn't there in the morning. At which point my mother tried to make the most of it. In a way, she was secretly pleased, which I colluded with. And later, in the afternoon, oh, the electricity was out, that was it, because of an ice storm. A person two miles away drove over who had a portable radio from which I heard that my

father had an automobile accident. He broke a hip and was in trac-
tion several months. It was quite a scene, seeing him laid out, totally
immobilized. Well to me I had magically done this. That's another
very important part of the guilt. Also my fear of my father later on as
I was growing up. I felt I had done that to him and that also made me
very frightened of myself. My powers, you know, guilty in terms of
my collusion with my mother.

These excerpts illustrate a number of important themes for our
analysis. In both cases we find what we can think of as a remote or distant
father and a powerful, colorful mother. Further, there is evidence of the
person's divided feelings toward these figures. There is a sense of an alliance with the mother and anger and disappointment with the father. Underneath, though, is a distrust of the mother and a desire for a link to the
father. Thus Mr. Markowitz comments that "my mother's view of [my
father] was not what he was," and his memory paints a portrait of the responsible, excluded father waiting at the window for his wife. Mr.
O'Hara acknowledges what Mr. Markowitz seems to leave unsaid: his uneasiness or guilt over the collusion or alliance with his mother against his
father.

Both these men's childhood memories illustrate a general struggle of
childhood: how to reconcile conflicting impulses, specifically those of aggression and hostility toward loved objects. The manner in which the
child copes with his ambivalent feelings and inner lives is often strongly
influenced by the family setting. A most important dimension of family
setting across all the men in our study is the triadic relationships between
mother, son, and father.

There is a consistent pattern in the memories of family setting among
our participants in that emotion and affectivity is associated with the
mother while control and restraint are associated with the father. While
this is not different from what is reported for most people in our culture
(Guttman 1976), what is striking is the latent meanings surrounding these
sex-role models. When we look carefully at their description, we find that
the affectivity and impulsivity of the mothers is often perceived as colorful
and attractive, yet bordering on the dangerous, out-of-control, intrusive,
or threatening. Note in the following example from Mr. Goodson that the
mother is described as the locus of power and assertion in the family and
as too controlling or assertive:

[*You mentioned conflicts between your mother and father?*] She
would keep urging him to seek raises and promotions. Feeling or saying that he'd really deserved a raise, and she would compare his wage
with other people that he was working with that were getting raises

or who were even starting in at a higher salary level. She didn't like the idea of my father being taken advantage of by other people who were like maybe making a fool of him by making more money than he was, or that he was being taken advantage of was something that came up.

She was sometimes a little more combination of material and goal oriented and looking out for one's own self. Sort of in a jungle type of world. Seeing that as a positive trait for her. Whereas my father would sometimes be naive if you look upon the world as being the jungle.

Consider Mr. Markowitz's discussion of Shakespeare's play *Coriolanus* in Chapter 3 and its relevance to his own life. He uses a theatrical metaphor to give manifest expression to the anxiety I believe he experienced as a child: that the attraction or alliance he felt with his mother, particularly her passion and seductiveness, could lead to terrible consequences for him. He begins that section of the interview discussing his family setting and the relationship he had with mother and father. When discussing his "important ideas about mothers and sons" he shifts away from self to that of *Coriolanus*. A major theme of his subsequent discussion is the powerful force Coriolanus' mother exerts on her son, seducing him away from his proper aims and leading him to his death. An unconscious fear of the destructive or seductive possibilities of their strong, colorful mothers was one all of the men in our group faced in their childhood. Thus the strong mother-son alliance or bonding was, at an unconscious level, probably a source of conflict and anxiety.

When we turn to memories of the father, we find that they have a remote quality, and there is a sense of unavailability to these figures for the child, either because of real absence (due to divorce or separation) or a passive, withdrawn, or aloof stance in the family. The father can be seen as unavailable in at least two ways. First, the father may be physically present but perceived by the son as psychologically unavailable. Mr. Anderson's memory of his father's unavailability is an example, as is the kind of interaction described by Mr. Prezinski:

I felt I could never make real contact with my father. I remember whatever I did was always junk. If I wanted to help my father, working on the carpentry work, and I would just pick up the hammer and hit the nail a couple of times. You know how kids are. I think I must have been a little younger, and you don't have your coordination and all that. But my father would get angry and the minute I'd pick up the hammer he'd say, "Get out of here, you're bending all the nails!" and all this stuff. So like "you're not good, get out of here."

On the other hand, the father may be physically absent and perceived also as psychologically not available for his son. Several individuals from divorced families talk of their search for a father as children, or their hope to find a father in adolescence among their teachers, relatives, or friends' parents.

Taking these memories of mothers and fathers as a whole, I have dubbed the descriptions of parents among members of our study the "strong mother–unavailable father" pattern. This refers to the strong bond (not necessarily pleasurable) between mother and son and the psychologically/physically absent father. This pattern may take many forms: The person may report the mother as overprotective or overconcerned about their welfare (Mr. Lonzetti and Mr. Goodson), or as very accepting and supportive (Mr. Markowitz), or as the most present or available parent (Mr. O'Hara). This does not mean that the person necessarily felt closer to the mother or enjoyed her more than the father; indeed, the opposite is usually true—as mentioned above, these men often indicate considerable distrust, resentment, and uneasiness toward the mother, with a desire for greater contact with the father. The mothers were, however, perceived as more present, colorful, and vital than the more disappointing fathers. Further, the father's unavailability also takes many forms: The father may be physically present but psychologically remote or distant (Mr. Markowitz and Mr. Goodson) and he may be physically absent as well (Mr. O'Hara and Mr. Lonzetti), or he may be perceived as weak and insufficient (Mr. Prezinski).

What is important in this context is the experienced father as reported by the person rather than the real one of childhood. However, there is some indication that this pattern bears a relationship to the actual situation in childhood. We have indirect evidence of the father's psychological unavailability to the son and the existence of a strong mother-son alliance. First, individuals' descriptions indicate that they lacked important interpersonal skills, in particular how to be adaptively assertive as males. Mr. Goodson's account of how he handled problems of self-assertion among his peer group can stand as an example:

> It's very rare that I ever hit anyone as a child. My defense if somebody attacked me would be more to like not fight back in the hope that they would not escalate. I was afraid, I felt that I didn't have the physical ability or the knowledge to fight physically. [*Did you get any help from anyone?*] No, I didn't. [*Sometimes children turn to their parents.*] I'm not sure if I talked to my parents about it or not. I have the feeling that my father probably would have said, "Well, don't fight back. Just ignore that sort of thing." That you're more likely to stay out of trouble by not fighting back. I remember once when I was in ninth grade there was a girl, we had just moved to a new neighbor-

hood, this girl across the block developed a crush on me and she was going with some guy who was about the same age and he got really jealous and came over one time too and sort of was being threatening to me. And I remember there were a lot of neighborhood kids around. And I remember my mother came out and came over. So I had the feeling that she had the feeling of wanting to protect me.

Such reports indicate the unavailability of a father in childhood; had his father been present Mr. Goodson might have learned how to defend himself with others or express himself without worries. As a further example, Mr. Anderson recalls in this connection his father's passivity and his own wish for his father to assert himself more:

Once, as a young boy, we were traveling in the car somewhere. My mother was talking. She was bitching about everything. It's the only time I can ever remember. My father finally turned to her and said something like "be quiet." She shut up immediately.

There is an overall quality in these reports indicating the relative absence of models of what is meant to be masculine and to channel or use affect (particularly aggression) in the service of achieving desired ends.

Secondly, many of the men report difficulties in rearing their own children that indicate not knowing how to be a father. Both Mr. Anderson and Mr. Markowitz, for example, report difficulties taking the father role as warm and nurturant figures for their children. As Mr. Anderson says:

On a Sunday afternoon, the kids want to go out and go to some state park or something like that to show them the river and the park. If I go out there as a parent, and sort of feeling that kind of role, very often my head would be somewhere else. I would disappear from the scene while being there.

Both the lack of masculine interpersonal social skills and difficulty taking the father role can be seen as consequences of the failure to identify with a realistic masculine model, a dynamic figure from whom the young child can learn how to be a personally gratifying man, father, husband, and worker.

Impact of the "Strong Mother–Unavailable Father" Pattern

A major point resulting from this analysis of childhood is that the family setting affected both the person's identification with the father and the attitude toward his inner life of affect and impulse. A developmental situation in which one parent is physically and/or psychologically absent may present several difficulties for the child. First, the strong dependence on one parent means it is harder for the child to step back and objectively perceive the parent. Reality testing of what the parent is really like is thus limited. Secondly, very strong affects, such as anger, may be more difficult to examine without the ally of a same-sexed parent available. Thirdly, there may be problems of sexual identification since there are not two parents available for partial identifications from which a satisfying sex-role identity can be established. Rather, the available parent, or a fantasized image of the unavailable parent, becomes the focus of a total identification in which the parent is introjected or swallowed whole as a model of what it means to be a man. Fourth, an absent, distant parent can be a disappointment to the son and, as such, become the source of narcissistic injury, as the child feels rejected (for his presumed faults) by his sire or takes his sire (with the father's perceived inadequacies) as proof of a faulty male lineage. As noted in this chapter and elsewhere, there is a sense in which the fathers were such a disappointment to the sons, and—in their uncertain masculine modeling—a source of narcissistic injury for them. Finally, the absence of such figures can be experienced as a powerful rejection of them by their fathers and as such may also be the source of narcissistic damage. We find recurrent reports of such disappointment and injury in our participants' accounts.

These considerations point to the possible fantasy consequences of the strong mother–unavailable father pattern and provide a clue as to the manner in which these men coped with powerfully ambivalent feelings toward their parents. The manner of coping with their conflicting feelings of love and hate toward parents involves an idealization or psychological transformation of these figures.

In circumstances where the child is unable to cope with and integrate ambivalent feelings of love and hate toward his parents the frightened child may cope with the presence of these powerful feelings that threaten to overwhelm and destroy the stable, secure world he loves and depends on by—in fantasy—transforming himself (the inner world) and/or transforming his parents (the outer world). Both of these strategies are ways of eliminating half of the powerfully ambivalent feelings. The inner world can be transformed into a less frightening place by eliminating the fearful, aggressive impulses and instead becoming weak, useless, and powerless or only loving and kind. The lion becomes a lamb as the child transforms the frightening, destructive impulses into some form of their opposite. In fantasy, the child can feel as if he is no threat to the loved objects in the outside world. However, we see an impact on the child's self-esteem as his inner life is suppressed and devalued. It is as if the child comes to believe that "my feelings are no good and must be controlled." On the other hand, the child can cope with the threat of his own anger and aggression by transforming the loved objects into powerful figures strong enough to withstand his feelings. In this case the parents become seen as very powerful, strong forces able to control the child.

For some of the men in our study it was primarily the outer world that was transformed, as reflected in their pattern of object relations. For others it was primarily the first alternative, as the child's developing self-esteem and confidence broke first. We find here the basis of two general strategies available for the child to cope with disturbing affects and impulses. In the first case, the frightening inner world is made less threatening, and more controllable, through a process of devaluation of one's inner life; in the second case the frightening inner experiences are located outside oneself. Both strategies have the same result: to split an inner ambivalence, eliminating from consciousness offending feelings and impulses.

These are the patterns that seem to predominate among the men in our study. The salience of the mothers indicates a strong alliance or bonding between the mothers and sons, and the controlled, remote, unavailable fathers became ambiguous figures particularly susceptible to their sons' fantasies as to what the fathers are really like behind their distant, hard-to-decipher surface. And indeed several of the men's descriptions of their parents reflect the sense of mystery and distance: These are figures from whom the person felt cut off. This led to apparent difficulty in our group as the passive, remote fathers became transformed into either idealized, powerful, and judgmental or saintly and nonaffective figures, contributing to childhood difficulty in the integration of impulse and aggression in our sample. A split in both parental images occurred, and the real, remote father and colorful mother became transformed psychologically as the child coped with his ambivalent feelings toward his parents.

For men who appear to have coped with this ambivalence toward their parents by strengthening the outer world (locating aggression and negative feelings outside themselves) a split in the father image occurred with a transformation of the real, remote father into an idealized, powerful, godlike, judgmental figure (forbidding or preventing the son's attraction or alliance with the affective, seductive mother) while affect and feeling came to be seen as feminine qualities, forbidden to males. For these men the inner world of affect and impulse became frightening because it led directly to the dangerously oedipal, crazy, and feminine world of affect and impulse. We find in this the roots of Mr. Markowitz's identification of control and restraint with males and seductiveness with females, Mr. O'Hara's anxiety that his intuition and sense are crazy and not tolerated in our society, and Mr. Goodson's equation of femininity with selfishness and masculinity with humility.

For those who seem to have attempted to disarm the inner world, the split in the father image involved a transformation of the real, remote father into an idealized figure devoid of aggression and impulse, with affect and emotion again perceived as intrusive feminine qualities. In such cases we find clear injuries to their narcissism, as there occurred a devaluation of the offensive parts of self. For these men the inner world of affect and impulse led directly to feelings of inferiority, weakness, and powerlessness. For Mr. Prezinski, anxieties about his inner demons led to profound, reassuring feelings of powerlessness in the face of omnipotent others. For Mr. Anderson, the unruly subjective world came to be experienced as a marker of inferiority. While for Mr. Lonzetti anxieties about being too strong and powerful were coped with by a transformation into feelings of inadequacy and weakness.

To summarize, in order to understand problems in the integration of one's subjectivity into the sense of self we need to look at the child's explanation of the events around him—his constructed understanding of his world within a family as a child. The following discussions of Mr. Markowitz and Mr. O'Hara are examples of this effort. As we consider these two men's attitude as children to their inner life and perception of parents we can find in each case a characteristic thematic statement which expresses the experience of their own subjectivity within a specific family setting.

Mr. Markowitz's Childhood: Feeling Controlled versus Feeling Out-of-Control

In Mr. Markowitz's memories of his childhood we find a struggle with the belief that his aggression and desires are dangerous, with a resulting need to feel controlled, lest things get out of hand.

His father was a small businessman in Boston and worried about being a failure, as there were financial difficulties in providing for his family. For the young Mr. Markowitz there were questions about his father's masculinity, vitality, and strength, as indicated in Chapter 4 by his concerns as to his father's homosexuality.* This excerpt indicates first, the experience of an early, difficult disappointment for Mr. Markowitz with his real father, believing he was not as financially successful, masculine, or responsible as he should have been. Second we get a glimpse of the fact that Mr. Markowitz often took his mother's side in the situation against his father. This mother-son alliance was important. The only child in a Jewish family, with a passive father and an active, colorful mother, Mr. Markowitz formed a close relationship with his mother. There were fantasies of having replaced his father: "It was as if I were her husband . . . a surrogate husband."

Such a situation of an attractive mother and—to the disillusioned son—a weak father poses particular problems for the young child in coming to terms with ambivalent feelings toward his parents: The father is loved, yet hated both as a failure and as an obstacle to his mother. The

*See p. 131.

mother is loved yet feared as a possibly seductive figure casting mysterious lures toward the young Mr. Markowitz. Thus, as Mr. Markowitz becomes a "surrogate husband" one can infer that questions arise, outside conscious awareness, as to the limits of his usurpation of his father's role. Will he take his mother away entirely from his father, who seems unable to maintain his position? Will he destroy his father? There is guilt as well in such fantasies, implicit in Mr. Markowitz's memory of his father "down the street watching for" his wife. In the absence of a father strong enough to set limits for the child, to reassure the developing youngster that his growing impulse life and aggression can be successfully withstood by the parents, such a figure can be created by the child.

To understand this transformation of the father we need to examine Mr. Markowitz's family context. This is a family in which tradition brought with it demands for strong respect for authority and wisdom of age. Mr. Markowitz's recollections of family life as shown in Chapter 4 give the flavor of this atmosphere. For the young Mr. Markowitz, struggling with fantasies of being "the husband" to his mother, needing reassuring limits and restraints from his parents in which to express his aggression and impulse, this family context made it easy for an internal transformation of a passive, stern father into a powerful, jealous, godlike figure whom one had to watch carefully to ascertain deeper intention. This figure can be seen in Mr. Markowitz's description of his father in that chapter. The necessity to "look very closely" and "listen in between the lines" that he speaks of are the intimations of Mr. Markowitz's search for, and construction of, a powerful, vengeful figure behind the weak father he knew. We find in the variety of father-figures or displaced objects of adolescence and young adulthood, the strong, controlling figure—like the Hebrew God, Yahweh, both merciful yet vengeful to those he holds accountable—that Mr. Markowitz fantasized when "reading between the lines." The most powerful embodiment of this image is his wrestling coach in college. However, the primitive childhood father of Mr. Markowitz's unconscious fantasy can still be seen in his discussion of himself at midlife, in terms of the godlike father discussed in Chapter 4.

This unconscious transformation of the weak father into a powerful figure served to reassure the young Mr. Markowitz that he could not really destroy or harm this figure nor pose a serious challenge for his mother. It also served to obtain for Mr. Markowitz, disillusioned perhaps too suddenly with his real father, the attributes of strength and power a young child might want to see in his sire. Certainly from this perspective the necessity of being accountable to a wrathful god seems a small price to pay for the reassuring control and direction he offered.

What we are seeing here are inner ambivalences being played out in terms of parental figures: The variety of aggressive, angry impulses Mr. Markowitz felt toward his father became the fuel for perception of a judgmental, angry father holding him accountable for his actions. Further, attractions to the mother were defended against in a similar manner—they were located in the outside world, in his mother and in woman in general. For Mr. Markowitz females became affective, seductive, irrational, corrupting individuals (with a female lineage to creativity and the arts) while males were controlled, rational, accountable, and nonbiased. Thus the young Mr. Markowitz, struggling with the limits of his desires and impulses, found reassuring restraint and control by the transformation of his parents: his father into a powerful, godlike figure "in control all the time," a figure one had to be careful of not angering, to whom one was accountable. The mother became the origin—rather than the goal—of attraction and desire, the manipulative seducer who embodied the feminine world of affect and emotion. Mr. Markowitz complained bitterly of having "become responsible" at about age 12, and there is the ring of truth to such a statement from a man constantly looking over his shoulder at controlling—possibly vengeful—authorities, and a boy living within a world of godlike figures.

Mr. O'Hara's Childhood: Feeling Divided versus Feeling Whole

Mr. O'Hara's childhood is also characterized by a strong mother-son relationship, with a father truly absent. Mr. O'Hara was the third of three sons, and his parents separated soon after his birth; this, combined with the rural setting of the home in upstate New York, meant that Mr. O'Hara grew up in an isolated family, the "property" of an unstable, intrusive mother, cut off from the rest of the world by the boundaries of their home. Mr. O'Hara's memories of growing up emphasize the "particular fix" his mother had on him:

> My mother had a particular fix on me. I was very obviously identified with the troubles with her husband—he had spurned her after my birth and he had nothing to do with me, apparently, he never touched me until I was seven or eight. Maybe by the time I got to high school we shook hands. A lot of her anger and griefs and grievances were expressed through me. She wanted a daughter, so she rather perversely tried to change over my sex to simply destroy my father, and used to keep my hair in long curls until I was about three.
>
> Because of the surpressed feelings in the family there were a lot of quite violent eruptions, which usually ended up with a scapegoat, beginning usually with my mother's scapegoating and my father coming back with a much bigger arsenal of scapegoating her, and then my trying to deal with my mother and offering myself up as the scapegoat. [In what way?] In her place. My mother would leave and go to her room and bawl and so I would leave and go cry at her door, get her to come back, in the process I would throw away part of myself.

I became my mother's property, and my brothers became my father's. [*How did that come about?*] Well that occurred when they began grade school and I was four. They left and I didn't have his protection any more. I still remember what a terror I felt—I used to crawl up on the roof for hours to see if they were coming. But they made other friends and it was really a very bad two years of my life before I started school. And they moved in one direction and I moved in another. They were very mechanically oriented, colluded with my father. Angry with my mother, angry with me. They formed a sub-group which I was rarely allowed into.

Mr. O'Hara thus became part of a family locked tightly in a struggle between mother and father, with the sons on each of the parent's side. Mr. O'Hara felt tightly bound to his mother, as she spun webs of verbal fantasy about her husband, the children, and herself. Cut off from his father, he early on felt attracted to, and dependent on, this woman, with her frightening imaginative power and affective world:

What was really scary was that I felt my mother had infinite power, that was scary. She still maintains a certain kind of power, that I shouldn't divulge any secrets. She might come back and punish me. That was always the pattern with my mother as a kid, when I'd go to her with my feelings. I'd press my anger towards her. She would lay another story on me to absolve her as the innocent victim.

The only person I could talk to was my mother when growing up. The only one in the family circle, that seemed to know me, from whom I could get empathy, was my mother. You know, I'd go to her.

Mr. O'Hara felt tightly bound to his mother because of his own needs (a feeling expressed in his belief that she was "the only person I could talk to") and her manipulativeness (captured by his description of how "she would lay another story on me").

Further, the hope for a father to provide support and a bulwark against his mother was continually dashed. The father's presence was uncertain, and for Mr. O'Hara he was not a dependable figure. There is, of course, a powerful rejection of Mr. O'Hara by his father, and an early, powerful disappointment in a father who chooses not to participate in the family, or with his son. Thus Mr. O'Hara remembers the lack of physical contact with his father and of feeling excluded, separate from the subgroup formed by his older brother and father. In the face of this frustrated desire, anger and violent wishes against the father were present, as is indicated by the "birthday memory" discussed earlier. In this recollection we see once again the impact of a strong mother-son alliance in the context of a father unavailable to balance this bond. Mr. O'Hara voices his disillusionment or disappointment directly, recalling the hatred he felt for his father for not helping the family (and him, most directly) when they were needy. We get a sense from this memory of the rage Mr. O'Hara felt in the face of his frustrated desire for a father. Such rage was frightening and the fear of doing his father damage is manifest in his comment that "it was quite a scene seeing him laid out . . . to me I had magically done this." The disappointment in his father and fear of his own anger must have been particularly difficult for the young Mr. O'Hara in the face of his desire for a powerful father to counterbalance the sense of being the property of his mother. Mr. O'Hara's father was a banker, and part of his absence from home was due to travel for business purposes. Again we find a transformation of the real father into a powerful, strong father able to withstand a son's aggression:

> The catastrophe was completely repressed in my family. The catastrophe was the split between my mother and father. And the tension that developed and then the family romance that developed to deal with it. Creating an artificial family. A lot of shared lies and mythologies explaining the absence of my father as he was this great man. A real hero figure who could do what he wanted and had absolute power. We had no right, because we were lucky because we had him for a father.

In fantasy a young boy's wish can come true—his father was heroic and powerful, with a good reason to be away so much from the family. Instead of disappointed and hateful, Mr. O'Hara could now feel lucky to have such a father. Further, we find—not surprisingly—the identification of Mr. O'Hara's divided inner life with the actual split between his parents. Mr. O'Hara's intuition and verbal skill became identified with his mother, while his analytic capacities were identified with his remote, distant, controlled father. Instead of an inner integration, for Mr. O'Hara the road to resolving painful inner ambivalences was to heal the outer split between his parents. Now Mr. O'Hara was not the one with magical power, or with guilty desire for, and hatred of, both his mother and father. Rather the mother had "infinite power" and was "seductive" and the fantasized father had "absolute power" and was "a great man." Yet such powerful figures, as in the case of Mr. Markowitz, were two-sided: Their "infinite power" meant the potential for aggression toward him as well as caring. For example, the problem with a fantasized, powerful father—a hero off on long voyages—is that he can return and wreak vengeance for wrongs committed during his absence. Allegiances with, and attraction to, the mother—the collusion reflected in Mr. O'Hara's wish for, and resulting guilt over, his parents' separation—provoked fears of retribution and violence from this powerful, remote figure. A specific memory presents a picture of this anxiety over his father's intentions toward him:

> To give an example of how that split took place and how my father saw me and how my brothers were drawn into this—when I was three, we went to buy a rabbit, so we went to this rabbit farm and the rabbits were in hutches. And my brother and I went out and around and picked out a rabbit. It was a lot of fun and we spent a long time picking the rabbit we wanted. I got to pick out the rabbit, so the man came, pulled the rabbit out of the hutch, held it up by the ears and slit its throat. And I got white as a sheet. My father laughed, my brother laughed. My brother had known all along what it was about, but I hadn't. My father's laugh was very frightening. I mean he laughed at me and I was identified with the rabbit. Nice thing, I thought it was going to be a pet to take home. I didn't know we were going to eat it for Sunday dinner. So it was very scary as far as I was concerned. And I couldn't help but take it as kind of symbolic of his feelings towards me. So frightened. . . .

The perceived malevolence of the father is apparent in this excerpt; Mr. O'Hara himself indicates that the rabbit is only a stand-in for himself. This excerpt also indicates Mr. O'Hara's early sense of rejection and unworthiness. The father's absence and hostility were also the source of considerable feelings of rejection and self-hatred, as Mr. O'Hara seems to have seen himself as the cause of his own misery and that of his family as well: The belief apparently was that the "catastrophe" of his birth was the reason for the difficulty he and his parents experienced. What we find is the hope of, by his own efforts, reuniting his parents and healing the painful sense of separation he felt. Instead of divided loyalties within himself, such ambivalences were located outside, in the powerful figures who could redeem him. By working hard to unite his parents and gain their acceptance and love, Mr. O'Hara hoped to erase his terrible guilt, sense of unworthiness, and divided feelings. Mr. O'Hara would heal his inner split by becoming acceptable to both his divided parents.

What stands out in his memories of childhood is the absence of Mr. O'Hara's own sense of power or aggression. Rather, an internal battle had become located in the outside world, with the real split between his parents. Mr. O'Hara says, "I was very identified with my parent's separateness." His description of his childhood contains the sense of a fundamental split in the world according to the polarity of male-female, mother-father:

> In terms of differentiation of our character, my oldest brother and I carved up the world. He was very possessive: money, objects, proper-

ty, houses, cars, all of those things. His trip was that he fulfills what his wife wants, the needs my mother had for my father, houses, property that kind of stuff. I moved in an opposite direction. I have always had money troubles, shied away from owning property. I tend to be very unpossessive, in relationships. I have always been very cautious about boundaries, not laying my boundaries around another person.

In other words, his brother, in Mr. O'Hara's eyes, became more like his father, while Mr. O'Hara moved closer to his mother. So we can now understand the presence in the interview of a primary organizing tendency around division or differentiation. The splitting of Mr. O'Hara's divided love and hate was a primary way he dealt with the presence of ambivalent feelings toward both parents and the painful narcissistic injuries he experienced from their separation: The power of frightening violence and aggression was located in his father and the power of seductive affect and intuition was located in his mother. By attempting to unite them he could redeem himself.

To summarize, we find in Mr. O'Hara's case a blaming of self for his parents' division or split and their rejections of him. Mr. O'Hara's fantasies centered around the belief that he could heal this split and thus make up for all that was wrong with him and that was the cause of the parents' separation. Mr. O'Hara, further, came to identify his inner life with his parents: his affect life and intuition with his mother and his control and intellect with his father. This projection of an inner struggle into the outer world represented one way for the young child to reconcile his own interests separate from the ambivalently held parents. The attempt then was to heal his own divided pulls, loyalties, and interests by breaching the split between his parents. He was responsible for the parental split, and parts of him were bad, causing the rejections he experienced. He would redeem himself and overcome his inner confusion and sense of being bad or unworthy by becoming acceptable to all. This attempt to make up for inadequacies through his gifts to others would require hard work and great effort. The narcissistic fantasy at the core was that his efforts and work could be acceptable to all. In Mr. O'Hara's world others are bound to respond in an accepting, supportive manner. The underlying hope for Mr. O'Hara was to become without inner conflict or uncertainty, since such conflict was for this child evidence that something was wrong with him.

We have now come full circle in our understanding of the life history of our group of career changers. The analysis began in Chapter 2, with the initial career choice of young adulthood, and the pattern of wished-for self-definition embedded in the decision to pursue a professional career. The evolution of the career and of self-definition was then traced through to midlife. This chapter examined some of the conflicts earlier in the life cycle that led to the kinds of fantasies and wishes built into the career choices of young adulthood. To this point in the book I have, by decision, focused very intensely on the experiences of our one group of men. One recurrent thought for many readers has likely concerned the general issues and findings that emerge from this detailed analysis. The next chapter turns to such general considerations of adult development.

6

General Considerations of Midlife

To THIS POINT the book has presented a single study of career change at midlife, discussed in considerable detail. This chapter presents some of the broader generalizations, and connections to other research on midlife, that emerge from this book. We begin with current understanding of the midlife years as a distinct developmental stage and some problems with this perspective, move on to consideration of the complex intertwining of work and personality in adulthood and the shifting role of work in our society, and then turn to briefer consideration of a number of questions about adult development.

Is Midlife a Distinct Development Stage?

The last several years have seen the appearance of several major reports on adult development (Levinson 1978; Gould 1978; Vaillant 1978).*
A major question still unresolved is whether the midlife years constitute a

---

*See also Neugarten (1968), Block (1971), Maas and Kuypers (1974), and Lowenthal et al. (1975) for discussion of research on major personality changes and transitional points in adulthood. In a more clinical psychohistorical vein, Jacques's classic article (1965) describes midlife as a time of major recognition of one's mortality and a shift in the nature of creative work, Wolfenstein (1966) distinctive stage in adult development, and, if so, what are its characteristic features, dynamics, and tasks.

The most detailed studies of personality development through midlife yet available are the Grant Study of Adult Development (Vaillant and MacArthur 1972; Vaillant 1978) and that of Daniel Levinson and his associates at Yale (Levinson et. al. 1975, 1978). Levinson interviewed a group of forty men (ten executives, ten university biologists, ten novelists, and ten factory workers) at several points during their midlife years. He describes "the mid-life transition" and middle years in terms of such tasks as reappraising the past, modifying the social structure of one's life, and integrating previously unrealized aspects of the self. Levinson and his associates view the years around age 40 as a "developmental crisis" or transition because of the far-reaching impact of these tasks:

> Some men do very little questioning or searching during the midlife transition. Their lives in this period have a great deal of stability and continuity. . . .
>
> Other men in their early forties are aware of going through important changes, and know that the character of their lives will be appreciably different. They attempt to understand the nature of these changes, to come to terms with griefs and losses, and to make use of the possibilities for growing and enriching their lives. For them, however, the process is not a highly painful one. They are in a manageable transition rather than a crisis.
>
> But for the great majority of men—about 80 percent of our subjects—this period evokes tumultuous struggles within the self and with the external world. Their Mid-life Transition is a time of moderate or severe crisis. Every aspect of their lives comes into question, and they are horrified by much that is revealed. They are full of recriminations against themselves and others. They cannot go on as before, but need time to choose a new path or modify the old one. (1978, pp. 198–99)

Reassessing the past, according to Levinson, involves profound changes in familiar perceptions of oneself and the world, while alterations in social structure or definition of one's self also signify a profound struggle with change:

> The life structure itself comes into question and cannot be taken for granted. It becomes important to ask: What have I done with my

---

presents in detail Goya's shift at midlife from being a court painter toward the work that established him as an artist concerned with universal, enduring themes, Shore (1972) offers an insightful probing of the middle years as a "psychological turning point" for Henry VIII, and Mack (1976) discusses how key events in T.E. Lawrence's adolescence and midlife shaped his later behavior.

life? What do I really get from and give to my wife, children, friends, work, community—and self? What is it I truly want for myself and others? What are my central values and how are they reflected in my life? What are my greatest talents and how am I using (or wasting) them? What have I done with my early Dream and what do I want with it now? Can I live in a way that combines my current desires, values, and talents? How satisfactory is my present life structure— how suitable for the self, how viable in the world—and how shall I change it to provide a better basis for the future?

As he attempts to reappraise his life, a man discovers how much it has been based on illusions, and he is faced with the task of de-illusionment. By this expression I mean a reduction of illusions, a recognition that long-held assumptions and beliefs about self and world are not true. (1978, p. 192)

Levinson's notion of "de-illusionment" as a reworking at midlife of cherished expectations and assumptions about self is similar to what I have been describing in Chapters 2 through 4 as the "loss" resulting from experiences discrepant to the definition of self.

The Grant Study has followed over two hundred individuals as they matured from college years through to later adulthood. Reporting findings from questionnaires and interviews with ninety-five of these men Vaillant (1978) offers a view of midlife as a time of inner exploration and personal change:

As adolescence is a period for acknowledging parental flaws and discovering the truth about childhood, so the forties are a time for reassessing and reordering the truth about adolescence and young adulthood.

At age forty—give or take as much as a decade—men leave the compulsive, unreflective busywork of the occupational apprenticeships, and once more become explorers of the world within. (1978, pp. 219–20)

If men in their forties are depressed, it is because they are confronted by instinctual reawakening and because they are more honestly able to acknowledge their own pain. It is not because they fear death. If they are no longer satisfied with their careers, it may be because they wish to be of more service to those around them. If their marriages are sometimes in disarray and their groping toward love seems adolescent, it may be because they are less inhibited than they were in their thirties. . . .

The Grant Study men at forty put aside the preconceptions and the narrow establishment aims of their thirties and began once again to feel gangly and uncertain about themselves. (1978, p. 222)

The research reported by both Levinson and Vaillant is consistent with the model presented in earlier chapters, in that the midlife years are seen as a time of possible innovation, growth, and change in the person's life. Beyond this general statement, we can integrate these disparate studies somewhat further by indicating, as hypotheses, some of the key dynamics and tasks of the midlife years.

First, from our study of individuals who carry out career changes at midlife we have seen that the process of separation from parents and shifts in significant identifications extends well into adulthood. Traditionally adolescence has been seen as the key time for the testing of self, loosening of psychological dependence on parents, and the synthesis of significant identifications into a personally rooted identity. Yet we have seen that the process of separation from idealized parents extended past adolescence and young adulthood and into midlife for the individuals in our research. This is consistent with reports from other studies of midlife. Levinson hinges much of his analysis of the younger adult years around the mentoring relationship at work, seeing the mentor as a transitional figure for the individual, combining elements of authority, parent, and friend. The late thirties brings the termination of this close relationship, as the person outgrows this fathering relationship during the years that Levinson labels "Becoming One's Own Man." It is still unclear, empirically, how many individuals actually have mentors who serve to mediate the process of separation from family and the increasingly autonomous definition of self in adulthood. Gould (1978) and Vaillant focus more directly on the struggle through midlife with the internalized values of parents. In this regard, Vaillant comments that "childhood does not end at twenty-one, and the battle to wean oneself from and to pull even with one's parents continues into middle life" (1978 p. 224).

Secondly, note that for the men in our group there occured shifts in the internal definition of the male sex-role at midlife, and the reassertion of aspects of self left behind at earlier points in the life cycle. A very narrow definition of what it meant to be a male excluded valued interests and talents in adolescence and young adulthood for the individuals in our group. For some, midlife involved the greater integration and acknowledgment of what had earlier been defined as feminine interests. There is evidence from a variety of divergent studies to support a notion of the general course of development past adolescence, particularly for males, as one in which the self in young adulthood organized around activity, achievement, and power is then followed by a period of turmoil and the subsequent richer, fuller reorganization of the self during midlife.

Most of the descriptive and analytic work on the nature of the male life cycle past adolescence is consistent in seeing young adulthood (ages 20 to 30) in terms of activity, strength, and potency. Thus, young adulthood for Levinson et al. (1975, 1978) is the time when the individual forms an "initial life structure" through his career and marital choices. Erikson (1959), in a similar vein, sees the predominant "task" at this time as that of "intimacy"—making and stabilizing satisfying marriage and work choices. In his more recent writings on the adult life cycle Erikson (1976) has drawn on the Hindu sense of this age period as one of active creation or "maintenance of the world." Vaillant and MacArthur (1972) comment on the Grant Study sample: "They tended to sacrifice playing (during the 20's) and worked hard to become specialists." In a more clinical vein, Jacques (1965) claims a predominance of manic defenses in young adulthood, in which activity and denial ward off depression.

By midlife, Guttman (1976) reports evidence of developmental shifts in sex-roles, as males move from their earlier organization of self around "agency" and power to receptivity and nurturance, while the opposite transformation occurs for females. Relying on a Jungian model, Levinson, too, sees the struggle to integrate "feminine" and "masculine" attributes of the self as a central task of what he calls the "midlife transition":

> The effort to attain one's manhood is at its peak in early adulthood. As a young man starts making his way in the adult world, he wants to live in accord with the images, motives and values that are most central to his sense of masculinity, and he tends to neglect or repress the feminine aspects of his self. Any part of the self that he regards as feminine is experienced as dangerous. A young man struggling to sustain his manliness is frightened by feelings and interests that seem womanly. One result of the anxiety is that much of the self cannot be lived out or even experienced in early adulthood. (1978, p. 230)

In this regard, we are fortunate in having chosen for interview study individuals who carry out career changes at midlife into the creative arts. The arts as an "invitation to the subjective" (Geertz 1971) are integrally tied up with the individual's experience of his inner life of affect, imagination, fantasy, and initiative. It was precisely such aspects of their experience in childhood and adolescence that were the source of conflict for the men in our group. Developmental conflicts around their subjectivity led to efforts to exclude aspects of their subjectivity in the self-definition of young adulthood. The manner in which important, conflictual aspects of self returned at midlife and were integrated into the sense of "who I am" is a major theme of this book. These mens' struggles with the meaning of their own aggression and affect is woven into their life histories in clear, consistent ways and is observable in rich detail. From this we obtain a picture of how males cope with and integrate aspects of their own subjectivity at midlife.

As a final general hypothesis about midlife, we can see this time as one of the reassertion of choice and opportunity for reassessment. Few

choices in life—particularly those of career and marriage in young adulthood—allow all aspects of self to emerge: The decision to enter into one
activity means the renunciation of other activities. Midlife often contains
the first returns on the career and marital decisions of young adulthood:
promotions do or do not occur, children are born, parents age. Further,
midlife is, at least for some, the beginning of awareness of aging (Neugarten 1968) and of changes in one's physical capacity and strength. Midlife
is in this context in part a time of learning the limits of ambition and activity as organizers of the self. The work of Gould (1978), Jacques (1965),
Levinson et al. (1975), and Shore (1972) all develop perspectives on the 35
to 50 age range as a time of potential stress related to such factors as the
recognition of one's mortality, the experience of physical limitations or
decline, and numerous, subtle erosions of early dreams in the reality of
midlife, leading to a general questioning of the direction of one's life. And
Levinson et al. discuss the problems for many of their subjects at midlife
resulting from "the experience of disparity between one's life structure
and what [the person] wants for himself" (1975, p. 254). When this disparity is too great, a crisis is generated. There may then be a certain loss
or leave-taking in general necessary at midlife as the individual comes to
terms with the reality of his actual achievements and situation in the face
of the fantasies, wishes, and dreams of young adulthood. There is in this
loss of the old and familiar the opportunity for the new. We do indeed
have a second chance at midlife. Erikson's point that development continues dramatically through adulthood seems substantially correct (Erikson
1963). As Vaillant comments of midlife: "such transitional periods in life
provide a means of seizing one more chance and finding a new solution to
instinctual or interpersonal needs" (1978, p. 222).

Having discussed at length some of our emerging insights into adult
development let me introduce some caveats. First, understanding of these
years is really only beginning, and the emerging picture resembles a mosa-
ic only partially completed. As noted in the first chapter, all our studies of
adult development have suffered to some extent from sample limitations.
This is almost a built-in problem in the study of an area as complex as
adult development, since careful study requires a narrow, carefully defined sample that thus raises questions as to the generality of the results.
Yet the demand for generality often seems premature, since only by carefully studying many different populations can we gradually build up a
rich, valid picture of the complexities of human development. We do not
yet know, for example, for what percentage of the population "midlife
transitions" in Levinson's sense actually occur, or whether issues of career
and marriage become particularly salient in the 35 to 50 age range for
most people.

Further, there are many conceptual issues still unresolved in our understanding of adult development. A major question is that of the age-

linked nature of adult development. Levinson argues that there are a number of age-linked adult development stages, and he takes a very strong position on this question:

> I have set forth a specific age at which each era begins, and another at which it ends. This is not to say, however, that a bell rings at precisely the same point for everyone, demarcating the eras as though they were rounds in a boxing match or classes in a highly regulated school. Life is never that standardized. There is an average or most frequent age for the onset and completion of every era. There is also a range of variation around the average. The variation is contained, however, within fairly narrow limits—probably not more than five or six years. The discovery of age-linked eras is another unexpected finding of our study. This finding goes against the conventional assumption that development does not occur in adulthood, or, if it does, that its pace varies tremendously and has almost no connection to age. On the contrary, it seems to be closely age-linked. (1978, p. 19)

Yet the degree of age-linkage to possible adult development stages is still an open question. The model presented in this book makes little attempt to specify general dates or years in our analysis because development within our group seemed to hinge so much on the nature of individual experiences during midlife and their impact on earlier idiosyncratic expectations and assumptions. Our general model investigates the challenge of discrepancy and loss in life structure, yet it is the intertwining of particular patterns of self-definition with very specific types of vocational and family experience that produce the observed patterns of midlife experience. As a result, I was less impressed with the possibility of locating specific key ages for disillusionment or the experience of loss. So, too, Vaillant argues against a tightly age-linked model of adult development:

> Certainly there is nothing magical about a given year; Elliot Jacques's thirty-seven, Gail Sheehy's "Catch 30," Daniel Levinson's forty-to-forty-two definitions of midlife crisis are as arbitrary as suggesting that adolescent crises occur at sixteen. Certainly, there were many men in the Study who between thirty-five and fifty got divorced, changed jobs, and became depressed. However, divorce, job disenchantment, and depression occur with roughly equal frequency throughout the adult life cycle. If such events occur during the dangerous, exciting ripening of the forties, we can pause and say, "Ah-ha! The midlife crisis, the dirty forties, menopausal depression." But that is to miss the point. Progression in the life cycle necessitates growth and change; but crisis is the exception, not the rule. (1978, p.223)

A problem with a tightly age-linked view of midlife is that it does not take into account some key roles that social factors might play in adult development within a single culture. It is ironic that Daniel Levinson, who is particularly sensitive to sociocultural factors in human development, advances a model that, in some respects, underplays these factors. Let me illustrate this with reference to my own study, because I develop a heavily psychodynamic model in this book and thus am open to a similar criticism. In examining the midlives of these career changers, a number of questions can be asked about the role of sociocultural factors in shaping the course of their adult development. First, note that the career changes in our group occurred during the 1960s, a time when there was considerable social turmoil and questioning of established values. These larger social preoccupations were reflected in many individuals' discussions during the interviews, particularly in terms of the Vietnam War protest, marijuana use, and sexual experimentation going on around them. From this perspective the 1960s were a general time of loosening of constraints, and a period where the powerless or downtrodden struggled mightily to rise up against their oppressors. Thus we find these individuals' developmental struggles with authority and power in their own lives at midlife taking place against a social backdrop of similar content. The 1960s fostered change and innovation in particular ways, perhaps giving shape to individual development different from that of the 1950s or 1970s.

Further, in our analysis of adolescence and young adulthood in this group we saw that there were very strong expectations and assumptions about what a career would bring—almost setting up, inexorably, a crisis at midlife. Yet expectations and assumptions change from one generation to another. Sarason (1977) argues that work has very different meanings for the postwar, atomic-age generation than it did for earlier generations; work for this latter group, Sarason claims, is less tied to an optimistic perspective on the future. If, indeed, organizing assumptions about self and work have changed, then the experience of midlife may, in turn, be different from past generations.

Given such possible different social influences and generational changes across decades within a single culture, it makes one read with pause Levinson's cross-cultural and cross-historical emphasis:

> We energetically offer the following hypothesis: This sequence of eras and periods [of adult development] exists in all societies, throughout the human species, at the present stage in human evolution. The eras and periods are grounded in the nature of man as a biological, psychological and social organism, and in the nature of society as a complex enterprise extending over many generations. They represent the life cycle of the species. Individuals go through the periods in infinitely varied ways, but the periods themselves are universal. These

eras and periods have governed human development for the past five
or ten thousand years—since the beginning of more complex, stable
societies. (1978, p.322)

Attention to the social construction of adult development becomes
particularly important given the increasing interest in midlife among the
public at large. Media portrayal of these years gives an air of determinan-
cy and certainty to the crisis of midlife. Sheehy subtitles her phenomenal-
ly popular book *Passages*, "predictable crises of adult life." If people believe these crises are predictable, then they become expected and people
begin to interpret their experiences in terms of this model. One is not dissatisfied at times with work, or temporarily angry at one's wife, children,
or parents—one is having a "midlife crisis." While it may indeed be true
that midlife crises or problems are characteristics of adult development, a
danger in the increasing popularization of social science research is the
creation of a self-fulfilling prophecy among the population at large.

The Maturation of Work and Personality in Adulthood

A major theme of earlier chapters was that work and personality development are intertwined. First, we noticed that events in the sphere of
work could only be completely understood through an analysis of events
in other domains of the person's life and at different points in the life cycle. There is a delicate interpenetration of career, family, and self across
the life cycle. Secondly, we saw that there was for some individuals a maturation in relation to work that could be understood in terms of psychosocial development. That is, for some individuals at midlife work became
relatively independent of developmental conflict, whereas for others it remained deeply embedded in such conflict. This is one of the differences
between a sculpted and foreclosed resolution of the midlife crisis of loss
and separation, discussed in Chapter 4.

This perspective emphasizes that work and careers are embedded in
life history, and that the nature and meaning of work may shift across the
life cycle. This assertion receives support from other research indicating
that midlife can be a time of dramatic change in the quantity, quality,
and mode of work in the individual's life. Jacques (1965), in his study of
creative artists, notes that midlife is often a time of change in the type of
work of many of these people:

Bach, for example, was mainly an organist until his cantorship at
Leipzig at 38, at which time he began his colossal achievement as a
composer. . . .
    Racine had thirteen years of continuous success culminating in
Phedre at the age of 38; he then produced nothing for some twelve
years. The characteristic work of Goldsmith, Constable and Goya

emerged between the ages of 35 and 38. By the age of 43 Ben Jonson had produced all the plays worthy of his genius, although he lived to be 64. At 33, Gauguin gave up his job in a bank, and by 39 had established himself in his creative career as a painter. Donatello's work after 39 is described by a critic as showing a marked change in style, in which he departed from the statuesque balance of his earlier work and turned to the creation of an almost instantaneous expression of life. (1965, p.502)

Jacques offers a view of a change in the type of work at midlife, from an impulsive, spontaneous outpouring as the mode of working (illustrated by the creativity of Mozart, Byron, or Keats) to a more mature, reflective mode. Similarly, shifts in the productivity of scientists and businessmen at midlife have been noted (Lehman 1953; Pelz and Andrews 1966; Dalton 1977).

Yet our understanding of the complex interweaving of work events and psychological maturation is very limited. Studies of career development generally focus on the maturation of work conceived in terms of professional socialization or the manner in which individuals are shaped by and in turn shape career demands (Hodgson, Levinson and Zaleznik 1965; Schein 1975), or stages of a work or career history (Super 1976), or somewhat static studies of the relationship between personality types and job environments, both pictured as basically unchanging (Holland 1973; Roe 1956; Ginsburg 1972). We know less about the reciprocal impact of events at work and personality development in adulthood.*

In regard to work, our model of "foreclosed" and "sculpted" resolutions of the process of redefinition of self at midlife can be used to advantage, particularly since it can be broadened to encompass and assess either career changes or recommittment to the initial career. In the case of a foreclosed resolution, the threat to self-definition at midlife would result in a defensive outcome—either over- or underidealized recommitment to work (e.g., "apathetic" work where all goals/investment is lost or manic recommitment where magical fantasies flourish) or career change (devaluation of initial career, as in the case of Mr. Markowitz, or perhaps florid overidealization of the second career, as with other men in our group). A more sculpted resolution results in an integrated, adaptive confrontation with discrepant experiences that leads to a realistic commitment to work (with altered, more realistic expectations that produce satisfaction) or a career change (as in the case of Mr. Anderson). Note that recommitment to work or career change can result from either defensive or adaptive processes, depending on the individual case.

*The complex interaction between work and personality has been more successfully studied in adolescence. See, for example, Goldsmith (1972) and Goethals and Klos (1976) and the discussion in Chapters 2 and 6.

The larger generalization about work, adulthood, and careers that emerges from this study is that to evaluate or understand an event at work we must often look beyond the specific event itself to its deeper meaning in the context of the individual's life. There are usually deeper, multiple meanings to a single, simple concrete event such as a career choice or career change. This perspective has significance for current social concerns with the redefinition of work and work opportunities in our society. A number of different observers and researchers have indicated that current conceptions of·work and careers may not be very satisfying among either white- or blue-collar workers (Coles 1971; Sheppard and Herrick 1972; Sarason 1977). In this regard two key questions about work emerge: (1) What are the psychological functions of work for the individual? and (2) Are there other ways of now obtaining the psychological satisfactions that work once gave? For our group of career changers work was conceived in a particular way during early adulthood, and midlife was a time at which a different conception emerged. What we find in terms of our first question is that—both in adolescence and midlife—the career was a means of attempting to autonomously define and to make real in the world a vision of the self. Further, work and careers were the arena for attempting to master disappointments and difficulties in such other areas of life as parenting and marriage. That is, the individuals in this group attempted to overcome, compensate for, or change the frustrations, narcissistic injuries, and despair about self or others rooted in experiences as a father, husband, or son. Given the broad critiques of work and careers among both blue- and white-collar workers that have recently appeared (Wirtz 1975; PHS 1974; Sarason 1977; Sheppard and Herrick 1972), it may be that one's work conceived solely in terms of a career or job no longer offers the possibility of satisfying the twin demands of making real a vision of the self in the future and of mastering disappointments in other life domains. If this is true then our definition of work may change to allow these needs to be met (e.g., the person's work—productive activities that give meaning to his life—may no longer be those by which he earns his living, i.e., his career or job) or other ways of obtaining these satisfactions may develop (e.g., visions of self for men may be rooted not in work and/or careers, but in parenting a new generation, in the creative, passionate use of leisure time, or in political involvement and the struggle for social change.)

Adolescence and Young Adulthood: Work as "Terminal Clarity"?

The adolescent and young adulthood years emerged in this study as particularly important in understanding midlife and the evolution of careers. The role of work as an organizer of the self in adolescence and young adulthood is of particular interest. The importance of postadolescent vocational commitments is often emphasized in discussions of healthy self-definition and identity achievement (Tiedemann and O'Hara

1963; Marcia 1966). However, in our group of career changers we see that clear vocational choices early on masked deeper conflicts that emerged at midlife. In his recent discussion of the adult life cycle, Erikson (1976) discussed this problem; what he calls "terminal clarity" in young adulthood career decisions that—in a defensive, compensatory manner—overdefine the self and thus exclude the potential for continuing growth and development. Discussing the "generativity" crisis in the case of Dr. Borg, the elderly doctor in Bergman's *Wild Strawberries*, Erikson comments:

> For theoretical, as well as clinical, historical, and autobiographic reasons, Identity terms have been emphasized in my writings and have subsequently been widely accepted or rejected on the assumption that in my scheme Identity was the teleological aim and end of growing up. The Identity Crisis is, to say the least, pivotal; but Dr. Borg's case illustrates poignantly what happens when Identity, because of some earlier partial arrests and especially because of a retreat from Intimacy, is overdefined in terms of occupation and civic role and whatever character restriction they may foster. The "achievement" of an over-formulated identity, then may sacrifice too early a measure of Identity Confusion salutory for some playful variability in later choices. (1976, p. 11)

We can see now, however, that such "terminal clarity" plays a key role in the individual's psychic economy. Erikson discusses Borg, for example, in terms of a variety of childhood narcissistic insults and difficulty that underlay the rigid, exclusionary self-definition through medicine. This is similar to the pattern observed in our individuals, whose career choices served as vehicles for the appropriation of a wished-for self-definition.

A general question about work and self that emerges is, Do decisions to enter highly specialized, socially sanctioned professions and occupations (law, medicine, upper levels of business, science, academics) contain for some, at their core, omnipotent and grandiose fantasies, perhaps rooted in earlier narcissistic difficulty? For such individuals we might expect particular difficulty at midlife, as reality chips away at fantasy and ambition encounters limits. Tartakoff (1966), for example, has discussed the "Nobel Prize Complex" in some of her patients, as their professional career choices are expressions of an omnipotent, wished-for self, rooted in developmental narcissistic difficulty. And Sarason (1977), from a more sociological perspective, has recently discussed the heavy burden of fantasy and expectation that work carries for highly educated professionals at the time of career choice, and the resulting intense disappointment often experienced in the later years.

We can also pursue this question from the perspective of work environments: Are particular occupations more attractive by their general nature as vehicles for the expression of grandiose, wished-for selves? Further, are there particular stress points in career development that activate issues of omnipotence and grandiosity? As an example of this kind of analysis, the psychiatric profession has received some discussion from the latter perspective. Sharaf and Levinson (1964) have described some of the stress at entry into psychiatry, among residents, that makes for increased omnipotent strivings, and the manner in which decisions to seek psychoanalytic training can be influenced by such considerations. At the other end of the career ladder, Whellis (1958) discusses the "pain or loss" for experienced analysts confronting the limited curative powers of verbal formulations and insight, with, for some, a "retreat into dogma" serving to preserve—in a foreclosed manner—a sense of value and usefulness in their work. The loss is greatest, Whellis implies, among those for whom the powers of insight and understanding were primary organizers not just of the analytic role, but of the self.

The Dialectic Nature of Adult Development: Progressive and Regressive Movement as Normal Functioning

Our case analyses in Chapter 4 illustrate the foward-and-back manner of reconstitutions of self, indicating the tension between letting go of and holding onto one's parents built into the initial career choices of young adulthood. We saw this in our difficulty labeling individuals as either totally a foreclosed or a sculpted resolution. That is, individuals seem to regress and progress through adulthood. This stands in contrast to a picture of development as an invariant, linear progression of health or pathology. Our ideal types become narrow and confining stereotypes when we attempt to categorize the complexity of the individual. This is true as well of the men in this study in young adulthood, and their psychosocial development at midlife, presented in Chapters 2 and 3. We saw that the initial career choice and life structure united efforts both to separate from one's family origin and to move back into it, and this underlying dialectic was expressed in the discrepant events of midlife as well. Thus we find a picture of the complexity of individual development, not easily labeled as either-or dichotomies; instead, individuals indicate the dialectic nature of their development, with progressive and regressive movement through new stages of development.

This is not often a perspective developed in social research. Vaillant (1978), for example, hinges most of his analysis of adult development on the operation of and outcomes associated with a hierarchy of adaptive ego mechanisms ranging from mature (e.g., sublimation, suppression, anticipation) through neurotic (e.g., intellectualization, repression, reaction formation) to immature (e.g., acting out, hypochondriasis) and psychotic mechanisms (e.g., delusional projection). As sensitive and insightful an observer as Vaillant seems to present a unilinear view of adult development wherein individuals are sorted into categories of those who are characterized either by mature adaptive ego mechanisms or those who utilize immature ones. Similarly, Levinson et al. (1978) offer their concept of "The Dream" in adolescence and young adulthood as a central, organizing force in early adult development. Yet the manner in which visions, goals, and aspirations can be ambivalently held and reflect opposing motives are less emphasized in their analysis.

Coping with Transition and Change through the Life Cycle: What is the Nature of Loss and Grieving?

There is no reason to assume that midlife is alone in posing threats to self-definition and understanding of the world. Most of the life stages described by personality theorists can be seen as posing similar challenges, each in their own stage-specific ways. The late adolescent, for example, suddenly finds himself facing an intrapsychic and interpersonal world altered from the one he knew as a child or early teenager, related to specific physical, psychological, and social changes in his life. Our general model of midlife has taken the form: stable organization of self → threat/alteration of self-definition → process of recovery/reconstruction → reorganized, stable organization of self. This model may prove useful in understanding a variety of stages in life-span human development, as we move toward a view of the life cycle as a series of transitions and change points (Goethals and Klos 1976; Riegel 1975).

The experience of loss and grieving is often conceived in negative terms. However, grieving is also—as the Mitscherlichs (1975) point out—a personality-enriching process that is essential to human growth and development. This is so because grieving is a process of self-reorganization, by which we separate from invalidated or outmoded beliefs, ideals, and identifications. Grieving can be understood as a natural, self-limited process through which we separate from the past in such a way as to more autonomously and completely define ourselves. From grieving comes an acceptance of the "definite change in reality" brought about by the loss of particular persons, places, and beliefs, and the ability to face reality with renewed confidence and imagination. The importance of understanding the process of grieving, for our purposes, is that it provides a perspective on how individuals cope with situations in which the question "Who am I?" is reopened.

Given this, the loss and grieving paradigm may have utility in understanding how self-definition is reconstituted, and thus how individuals change and grow throughout the life cycle. And indeed, the concept of foreclosed identity resolution at adolescence, for example, bears similarity to the notion of foreclosed grieving at midlife: In both cases alterations in self-definition are rigidly resisted in a defensive manner, resulting in a variety of psychosocial difficulties. Our understanding is directed, from this perspective, to understanding what is gained and lost at each transition point in the life cycle. To do this we must be able to describe the particular stage-specific sources of alteration in the sense of self and how such alterations impact on the individual pattern of assumption, expectation, and self-definition with which the person enters the life stage. From this we would then attend to the cognitive and affective attempts to cope with such challenges to self (Coelho et al. 1974; Hamburg 1974) and the self-definition that emerges over time.

The key point is that what we think of as stress and strain and how we understand coping responses to such stress seem importantly linked to the pattern of expectation and assumption with which the individual approaches a particular life situation. What is for one person an advancement or promotion at work, for example, may be for another the loss of valued attributes or roles that defined him in the world.

What Is the Value of a Reflective Attitude toward One's Experience?

The distinction between foreclosed and sculpted resolution of the crisis of midlife in our group hinges on the assumption that the awareness of and willingness to examine contradictory perceptions, desires, and impulses may be an important aspect of healthy development. In Chapter 4 a perspective was developed that examined the degree of awareness or acknowledgment of conflict at midlife, the degree of increased differentiation of self and others, and the quality of decision making. The underlying assumption is that individuals, to greater or lesser degree, develop means of reflecting on and integrating their experiences, so as to learn from them. The term "reflective attitude" refers to assessment and exploration of one's experience (e.g., how did I get where I am? where am I going? what is my role in having shaped events? what is it I want for the future?)

Certainly the question of what value is a reflective attitude remains an open one. Neugarten (1968) spoke of the greater "interiority" of much of her sample during midlife, and many observers of aging have spoken of a greater reassessment and sorting through of one's life in the later years (Costa and Kastenbaum 1967). Vaillant touches on this theme of the value of self-examination when he comments of the Grant Study subjects during the interviews he had with them. "I learned to associate the capacity to talk of one's life frankly with mental health" (1978, p.47).

This emphasis on a reflective or curious attitude toward one's own experience seems linked to the capacity to tolerate ambivalence. Zetzel, awhile ago (1949), wrote of the importance in personal growth of the ability to beaf anxiety. This is an important point. The examination of contradictory perceptions, desires, and impulses requires a capacity to delay, to put off the premature closure of an ambiguous situation so as to better understand it. There are differences in the capacity to bear the pull of ambivalent urges, to delay foreclosing situations so as to arrive at a sculpted resolution. Since we can understand one of the major challenges of the life cycle as developing the ability to resolve experiences of loss and change, this capacity to tolerate ambivalence—the linchpin of sculpted resolutions—seems a crucial personality characteristic, and we need to delineate more carefully the precise ego functions involved in this vague capacity now called "tolerance of ambivalence" or "openness to experience." Further, there are probably developmental precursors in ego function that predispose individuals to precipitate or sculpted resolutions of grieving experiences. Certainly this is implied by Vaillant's (1978) work on the maturation of ego defenses and Loevinger and Wessler's (1970) attention to conformist vs. autonomous ego function (Hauser 1976).

A Final Speculation:
The Reconstitution of Meaning in Adult Development

As a final point, note the importance of the capacity to bear ambivalence in allowing the reemergence of meaning through experiences of loss and transition. As pointed out in the discussion of Mr. Markowitz and Mr. Anderson in Chapter 4, the "reconstitution of meaning" refers to the commitment and investment in the present and future that come out of the person's free access to his individual past history. I have been impressed by the relation between the capacity to tolerate ambivalence and the person's ability to range freely within their inner experiences. This raises the question of a person's access to his past, and the role of this access in maintaining a sense of meaning and purpose in midlife. As we saw in our case discussions, more rigid (foreclosed) resolution at midlife can also be characterized as having let go of the personal past, which may also result in a more brittle, fragile sense of meaning and purpose at midlife. Again we are led to the importance of the capacity to tolerate the ambivalence of transition and change, both holding on and letting go of the past. This seems especially important in terms of a popular view of midlife and adult development that at times locates the roots of difficulty not in the personal past but solely in cultural, social, or historical factors. As Lasch (1979) has observed, some of the emphasis in the popular view of midlife—and the "second career" literature as well—is on what we might call letting go of the past; but unless one is cautioned to hold on adaptively as well, one wonders about the resulting fate of meaning and purpose.

Postscript

The Observer Observed—Comments
from Participants

WHEN an early draft of this book was completed, I asked each of the participants who figured prominently if they were interested in reading the manuscript and commenting on the results of the study. I was particularly interested in the perspectives of these men on the view of adult development and career change resulting from my analysis and use of what they had told me in the interviews. There are special difficulties in trying to do scientific research in psychology while paying attention to the richness and detail of people's lives. In reporting the research on career change, I have tried to respect the individuality of the participants in the research and, at the same time, identify the issues and events that have general significance for groups of men at midlife. I have tried to strike a balance between presenting a theory of adult development and remaining true to the reality of individual lives. Because of these special challenges in understanding and writing about life histories, I wanted to know how much "fit" there was between the picture of adult development that emerges from these pages and these men's own pictures of their lives.

Over three years had passed since the research interviews had taken place; I had had no contact with any of the men since that time. All of the men contacted responded that they were curious about the outcome of the study and were interested in reading the text. Copies of the manuscript were sent to each of these participants. After they had reviewed the manuscript, I met separately with several of the men to discuss their reactions and comments and to answer any questions they had. I will present briefly some of what I learned from my re-interviews with Mr. Markowitz and Mr. Anderson, two of the central case studies in the book. I will at times quote from written comments given to me by both of these men to present some of their current perspectives on their career changes and on the text itself.

Each of the men felt that the book had indeed captured the tone and substance of their experiences, particularly some of the meanings behind the first career choice and the roots of the career change at midlife. Several of Mr. Markowitz's comments had to do with the discussion in the text of his choice of science and the notion of a "wished for self" in young adulthood:

> Your discussion in Chapter 1 of the participants being unprepared for the experiences of midlife is very good and hit home. . . . Good characterization of Mr. Markowitz's move into the adult world in Chapter 2, particularly discussion around wanting his father's respect and the "I know, I know joke."
>
> Second point about the "wished for self" at end of Chapter 2 is excellent—suppressing parts of who one is. Paul Reps' anecdote in footnote—yes! . . . End of second chapter . . . your comment about "personally valued, freely made decisions." How to tell what these are? Don't we have to use arbitrary goals, e.g., pleasure, happiness, ability to function well?
>
> Comment in Chapter 3, "you can resist everything except temptation" meant as a joke. Yet, the summary discussion of Mr. Markowitz in that section and the sense of discrepancy is really put together well . . . End of Chapter 3—good discussion of Mr. Markowitz and the dialectic nature of separation, particularly paragraph having to do with a circle of conflict and "overbearing, uncompromising demands." . . . I feel I have gained more than I have contributed to your study.

Mr. Anderson, too, commented on the description of himself as a young adult in Chapter 2 of the text:

> The understanding of me is amazingly good. Maybe too much emphasis on poise, verbal skills as important to me. The underlying competitive motive *was* to be perfect in order to get love from parents, especially father.

In Chapter 2, strong, idealized expectancies about what a career would bring sets up crisis. Good idea. . . . There seems to be an emphasis on negative aspects of crisis. Is this the fashion? Is this saying what a psychologist wants to hear?

Mr. Markowitz and Mr. Anderson both reported themselves still content with the midlife career choices they had made. Each man was busy in his career—Mr. Markowitz having just finished a theatre role; Mr. Anderson, well-established as a teacher and actively exhibiting his sculpture—and neither of them indicated a desire to return to his first career. They felt the choice made about career at midlife had been the right one. From my discussions with these men I came away struck by a point I made in Chapter 4, that the resolutions described were not final but only part of an ongoing process continuing after the career change. Neither Mr. Anderson nor Mr. Markowitz seemed to be frozen into the picture we had drawn from the interviews several years earlier. Mr. Markowitz writes:

Your comment in Chapter 4 that "the career change may represent only a way station on the road to reconstitution"—Yes, yes! Resolution was not finished. . . . The distinction between premature (foreclosed) resolution and fuller (sculpted) resolution in Chapter 4 is fascinating. Yet, what about economic depression and war? Does some of my resentment come from belief that most psychotherapy aims at allowing the person to function more effectively in *this* world? Thus, I am struck by emphasis on self-knowledge, not enough on self as it exists in an unhealthy, psychologically distorting environment.

Foreclosed and sculpted resolutions perhaps simply 1) them versus me and 2) us. . . . Two polar resolutions and discussion of Mr. Markowitz in midlife of Chapter 4 are generally very good. But I had the feeling that I had changed in my picture of my parents, that as I was more secure, I could see aspects of father and mother that I hadn't seen before. However, discussion is really correct about "implicit perfectionist fantasy" in my view of what I wanted to be as father and husband. . . . By the way, very good on discussion of Mr. Anderson's choice and decisionmaking at midlife in Chapter 4.

Time seems to have healed a number of wounds for Mr. Markowitz. After several years of difficulty in his marriage he told me that his wife and he had reached a deeper understanding and had renewed their commitments to each other; over the course of conversation Mr. Markowitz also described a closer, rewarding relationship with one of his children. Some of his anger at science, his black/white view of the world, and his social isolation seem to have decreased. This is implicit in his wise com-

ment above that one's attitude toward other people distinguishes foreclosed and sculpted resolutions.

In contrast to other participants I re-interviewed, Mr. Markowitz described some lessening of his commitment to a career in the arts. While
still interested in at least some work in the theatre, he now contemplated
work that involved more direct interaction with others; he had just enrolled in a training program that would enable him to become a part-time
emergency medical technician. I came away feeling that the original interviews, despite their having occurred several years after the career
change, found Mr. Markowitz still in a time of turmoil, of guilt and anger
over his midlife experiences, and still early in the process of reconstituting
a life structure. This man still seemed to be growing and changing. Reading the text stimulated some further memories for Mr. Markowitz about
his father; the last memory he mentions below sheds light on an angry
comment Mr. Markowitz made to me during the interviews when pressed
to explore some point; at that time he subtly compared me to a plodding
stamp collector:*

> Discussion of Mr. Markowitz trying to make himself in adolescence
> into someone he is not is very good. Yet, isn't this common in adoles-
> cence? . . . Discussion of the childhood of Mr. Markowitz in Chapter
> 5 is fascinating. I remember thinking of my father as the youngest in
> his family with a strong mother and entirely unprepared for marriage
> and a family.
>
> Essentially correct about transference to parent figure in discus-
> sion of our interviews in Appendix. Use of poetry, stories, etc. to
> avoid direct personal comments about self. Except I did feel free to
> say things like "that's a stupid question, etc." This indicates a certain
> closeness and security with the interviewer. Incidental thought about
> one comment I made to the interviewer, mentioned in the Appendix:
> My father collected stamps.

For Mr. Anderson, too, the process of resolution is not finished; he
told me that he still struggles with perfectionist fantasies, despite considerable achievement in the arts:

> My difficulties with perfection, feeling isolated, *have not ended.*
> Also, the competition, trying to "get good marks," living up to some-
> thing. I think for me the change in career was partly externalizing,
> foreclosing; solving problems which really were inside me. Namely,
> high expectancy for self, sense of failure as father, husband, lawyer.
> The rigid self-definition, resentment, isolation. It was not a solution,

*See Appendix, p.   .

although being an affective person in sculpture is helpful. It is the real, expressive me. The big change is that now I understand better that there was something and what it was and is. . . . Should mention the gradual resurfacing of my own need to reintegrate personal history.

Why career change into the arts? Book treats this in Chapter 1, but I am still unsure why chosen. . . . The arts are not monolithic; sculpture is not like music; pot throwing is not like acting. There are similarities which are too often emphasized; there are many differences, especially social ones. . . . From a distance doing art looks like being free from constraints. A new life style. But there is a lot of uncertainty and hard work in the visual arts. Ten percent inspiration; ninety percent perspiration.

Your emphasis in Chapter 4 on putting off premature closure of grieving is good. Yet, this can become procrastination, as it has with me. I still suffer from low self-confidence.

Mr. Anderson mentioned in our re-interview that he was considering remarriage and told me of a deeper relationship with his children as they grew into their teens and now lived closer to him. As he said to me, "my children are giving me a lot now."

Both Mr. Markowitz and Mr. Anderson expressed good feelings about their participation in the study. From what they told me, I believe that some of this positive reaction lay in the fact that it helped them give order to life experiences—specifically the career change and new life in the arts—that previously had seemed to them idiosyncratic and somewhat unpleasantly singular. From the study they learned that they shared similar experiences with other men. Thus, Mr. Markowitz said, gratefully, that he felt he had gotten more from the study than he had given it.

Methodological Appendix

Notes on the Use of a Free-Associative Interview Methodology in the Study of Life History

THE FREE-ASSOCIATIVE interview utilized in this project is a research methodology with an established history and special advantages and potential in life history research. This specific study is in the tradition of previous explorations of life history using a free-associative methodology (Deutsch and Murphy 1955; Hendin et al. 1969) or similar approaches (Levinson et al. 1977, 1978). In particular, this project owes much to earlier attempts to explicate the psychoanalytic interview situation as a source of data about personality function (Murphy 1965) and the efforts by Hendin (1965, 1966, 1969, 1975) to extend this technique to study of the non-patient.

However, the free-associative interview method remains an extremely difficult beast to lure into the familiar territory of rigorous standardized research. Every interview assumes idiosyncratic features reflecting the special and detailed nature of an individual's life; problems of living, satisfactions, and events that we all experience are talked about in the person's own words and with his own way of telling us about them; topics appear in the interview bracketed by widely varying topics that precede and follow it. Yet the importance of the free-associative interview method resides precisely in this rich detail and adherence to the real texture of the person's life. Further, there are ways of providing some standardization of procedure and data analysis across interviews. A major purpose of this appendix, then, is to present enough detail about this interviewing methodology so as to make it more familiar to the reader.

The free-associative interview methodology includes not only the interviews that are conducted but also what precedes and follows them in the course of the study: how participants are located, introduced to the study, and treated during the interviews, as well as what happens to the interview data after it is collected. So, there are three broad sections to the appendix:

1. The design of the study: how participants were located, how the research was presented to potential participants, the first contact between interviewer and participant, negotiation of meeting times and schedule, and general characteristics of the interview situation itself (how participant and interviewer were seated, where the sessions took place, etc.).

2. The interview process: what free-associative interviewing is and how it was conducted in this research. What kind of topics are covered, what questions are asked, and when probes are utilized.

3. Analysis of the resulting data: how to organize and make sense of the rich, complex life history information resulting from free-associative interviews?

The Design of the Study

Descriptions of the design of this research should most properly begin with mention of how first contact was made with the men who ultimately became participants in this project. The initial task of the study was to locate a significant number of men who had originally established themselves first in professional careers and who had then shifted to a second career in the arts or crafts. Locating such men occupied a considerable portion of the early phases of the project. This was done through descriptive advertisements in a number of professional arts and crafts journals and through mailings to members of several arts and crafts organizations in the Northeast.

Contact began when the person received a letter from the interviewer. A letter describing the research project was then sent to the individuals who responded to our advertisements inquiring of their interest in participation. The gist of the letter was as follows:

With support from the Whiting Foundation and U.S. Department of Labor, I am studying the process of career change, focusing on individuals who have moved from a non-arts profession or occupation into the arts. The goal of this work is to learn as much as possible about the lives of individuals carrying out such changes, thus increasing our knowledge of the process of career change and of adult development.

Specifically, I am trying to locate full-time artists who left their non-arts career (e.g., skilled work, law, medicine, management) between the ages of 35 and 50 to pursue careers as artists. The purpose of this letter is to ask if you're interested in learning more about this study. I am currently interviewing artists who have made the change in careers described. The interviews are arranged entirely at the convenience of the individuals who choose to participate. Funds are available to reimburse you for the interview time and careful precautions are taken to guarantee anonymity and confidentiality of the interview material.

If you have carried out the kind of career change described and wish to learn more about the project, please return the enclosed card. Return of the postcard does not obligate you to participate in the study; and, even if you choose to learn more about the study, you may, of course, decline participation.

For individuals who fit the criteria of the study and were interested in possible participation, there then followed a short initial meeting at the person's home allowing us to meet face-to-face. At this meeting we discussed the purposes of the research and the procedures (e.g., five interview sessions of one and one-half hours each, completed within two weeks). If the person was then willing to participate, an agreement of confidentiality was signed and all five sessions were scheduled. The next time we met was at the person's home or office for the first session. All those who agreed to meet to discuss the research also decided to participate; further, none who began the five-session procedure failed to complete it.

At the first session we would find a comfortable place to sit face-to-face, one that was amenable to the use of a tape recorder. This was a quiet room in the person's home, office, or studio in which we could be assured of privacy and the absence of interruption. By agreement the location of the sessions remained constant throughout the interviews. At the beginning of the first session the person was told:

> I want to learn as much as possible during these sessions about your life. It would be best if you told your own story in your own words. I will have questions at different points but I would like you to feel free to bring up and talk about whatever seems important as we go along.

Sometimes people expected me to have a long list of questions to ask them, and seemed surprised that a social scientist would want to hear their story as they wanted to tell it. My first question in such cases was often, "Where would you like to start?"

The Interview Method

The primary aim of the free-associative method is to elicit the person's own organization of his life history and subjective frame of reference on his experience, past, present, and future.* The goal is to understand the broad life structure of the person, obtaining information about concurrent events, past and present, in a number of different areas of the individual's life. To do this, little restriction is set on what is appropriate to discuss, and the interviewer refrains from overly directive questions or instructions to the individual. The person's relatively free or unrestricted description and elaboration of his life history results in the *associative flow*.

This technique takes the person's spontaneous associations, memories, dreams, and fantasies, as well as responses to structured questions, as essential sources of data. The purpose of free-associative interviewing is to leave the parameters of response open to allow the individual to structure his answers to questions (in content and style) in his own characteristic manner, with the emphasis on understanding the person's own organization and interpretation of his life history.

The attempt is to focus less on answers to specific questions than on the associative flow that characterizes the story of a life as the person tells it. Thus the emphasis is on the sequence of associations, fantasies, and dreams, as well as answers to specific questions, as the data source that will reveal the particular organization of meanings underlying their development, career change, and the work in the arts. Focused questions such as "What led you to change careers?" or "Tell me about your work in painting" are less important than the context of associations—within and across the interviews—in which a particular topic area appears.

The free-associative interview method was the one of choice because this research on midlife career change was an exploratory study in an area

*The label "free-associative interviewing" is something of a misnomer, since the person's talk does not take place in an interpersonal or psychological vacuum. What the person says during an interview is influenced by a number of factors: his initial ideas of what the interviewer wants, the self-presentation and self-defensiveness bound to occur in interviews, the presence of a time limit (on each session and number of sessions), etc. Further, the interviewer's questions or comments will always have some directive impact. And the interviewer often has to elaborate descriptions, clarify statements and pursue areas where information is incomplete or defensively avoided by the individual. However, I use this label to differentiate the interview method developed in this project from semistructured or fully structured techniques in which there is an interview schedule with a specified order of questions. In the former technique the schedule is flexible with wide opportunity for probes and tangents; in the latter there is much less flexibility. However, both these methods differ from free-associative interviewing in that there are standardized questions to be followed in an established sequence and order. In the free-associative method there is no standardized order or framing of questions.

without much previous literature. As a result, this method had the advantage of avoiding problems of built-in data bias and distortion resulting from the use of standardized interview schedules and remaining close to the person's own description of his experience.

Since the manner in which the participant talked about and organized his life history in the interview is an essential part of the data base, it was not possible or desirable to have a completely standardized interview format. Rather, I depended to some extent on my own training and experience as an interviewer and clinician, sensitive to how individuals talk about themselves, free to probe and explore affectively loaded areas of life history as they arose in the course of the interviews.* However, certain general areas of interest to be covered with each person were formulated in advance, with the appearance and phrasing of specific questions related to these areas dependent in large part on how the participant organized his life history in the interviews. The same topic area, therefore, might be covered in session two with one person and in session four with another, resulting in very different types of context of appearance of these life history topics. We can conceive of a number of different domain areas in an individual's life (work, family, friendships, etc.) arrayed against a temporal dimension (past, present, and future). Table A-1 below specifies these different domain or topical areas covered in the interviews, differentiated in terms of past development, present situation, and future perception. Within each of these areas in the table are provided examples of some of the opening orienting questions that the participants were given to respond to.

Beyond these standardized areas of interest, two broad principles guided my questions and comments during the sessions: minimal intervention and attention to affective linkages.

*In general because of the interviewer's salient role in this kind of interview situation he impacts on the obtained data in at least three different ways:

1. What the interviewer sees and hears at the time of the interview. By this I mean what the interviewer selects as important to followup on and respond to, where and how he intervenes with questions and probes, the types of affective links that the interviewer decides are there to be followed. Of importance here are counter-transference elements of the interview situation.

2. What the subject sees and hears in the interview. Who does the individual, at an unconscious level, feel he's talking to? As we pointed out in Chapter 4, the interviewer in this situation is likely to become partly an amalgam of the interviewee's parents and siblings. While this transference relationship becomes an important tool in understanding the process of reconstitution of self at midlife it also means that there is some distortion in the person's discussion of his life history based on these earlier relationships.

3. What the interviewer sees and hears in working with the interview data. In reducing this complex data, what themes does the interviewer attend to? (See discussion of data analysis, p. 226.) What aspects of the interview material emerges for the interviewer as important and which are given less emphasis? Countertransference issues again seem important to note in this context.

TABLE A-1: Life Domain Areas with Illustrative Opening Questions

	Past (Development)	Present (Current)	Future Perception
1. Work:	What led you to choose (e.g., law) as a career? Experiences as child? Adolescent? What was your image of a (lawyer) after college? After professional training?	Tell me how you spend a typical workday. Yesterday, for example, what did you do from the time you got up in the morning through the evening? What do you find most satisfying? Most difficult about your work?	What does the future look like to you at work? Where do you see yourself in ten years?
2. Family of Procreation:	When did you marry? What led you to marry? At the time, what did you think it would be like to be a husband? Father?	What is your relationship with your wife like now? With your children? What do you find most satisfying and difficult about your family?	What does the future look like to you for your family?
3. Family of Origin:	Tell me about your parents. Other relatives? Siblings? Where did you grow up? What was it like?	Are your parents still alive? What is your relationship like with them now? Siblings?	What do you feel lies in the future for your parents? Brother? Sister?
4. Friendships/ Social Relations:	What were your friendships like as a child? In high school? College? Relationships with girls? Dating?	Tell me about your friends. How many close friends do you have? What makes them close friends?	As you look ahead, how do you see your friendships?
5. Recreation/ Leisure:	Hobbies as a child? Sports?	What do you do to relax? How do you spend your weekend?	What kinds of hobbies and leisure time do you see for yourself in the future? Sports? Travel?
6. Health:	What was your health like as a child? Major illnesses? How about the other people in your family?	What's your health like at present? Recent illnesses?	What do you think your health will be like in five years? Ten years?

225

The principle of *minimal intervention* emphasizes the attempt to allow the person's organization of meanings to emerge rather than interfering with the associational flow with overly directive or tangential questions. As Murphy comments, "The associative technique is based on the fact that when the patient is allowed to talk freely without too many interruptions he tells us *more* than he would if he were asked questions" (1965, p. 5).

The principle of attention to *affective linkages* emphasizes the discovery of the linkage or relationship between underlying affective issues and central life events and significant figures that appear in the text. Thus, often I would ask the person to elaborate on or describe further the events or figures surrounded by key affect words that spontaneously appear in the text. The following types of descriptions, for example, would be followed up with questions from me: "The failure to get that promotion was *one of the saddest* times in my life"; "I *didn't like* my boss at all, he really *put me down*"; "I was never before *so enthusiastic* as when I first started painting." These key affective words are clues to the self-relevance of particular figures and experiences in the individual's life. Thus when the person is talking about different domains in his life, the interviewer is listening for, and sensitive to, possible self-relevance of such topics for the participant. At such points, probes or further questions might be asked.

Let's return to a section of interviews already presented in an earlier chapter to illustrate the manner in which the interviewer can probe and explore for key linkages between different domains of life events and their self-relevance and affective meaning for the individual. An important theme in earlier chapters has been the connection of the initial career choices in young adulthood to powerful expectations and fantasies about oneself at that time, which were in turn linked to issues of separation from parents and our men's anxieties about their inner life in adolescence. In other words, a strong link was hypothesized between the different domains of work and family, and a linkage of events in these domains to underlying issues of self-definition. The following passage presents a section of interview material briefly discussed in Chapter 5. In this excerpt I probe for key linkages between these domains of work and family. Without interpretation at this point of the specific content, the excerpt will be used to illustrate how material is produced in the interviews; specifically, how the interviewer listens for the affective meaning of the events and figures discussed by the participant. This material is drawn from the second part of the first interview with this person, and covers approximately fifteen minutes of interview time. There is a break in each interview when the ninety-minute cassette tape (forty-five minutes per side) must be turned over. Since the machine stops with a noise and I must attend to turning the cassette over at this point, there is an interruption for the person. As soon as the machine is ready I turn to the person with an interested demeanor and wait for him to begin again:

Just ask me something and I'll start. I keep thinking about what I'm going to talk about for five days. Just talking on for an hour and a half is like writing an essay. It's all part of my general personality background, not wanting to put something down in terms of commitment. It's easier to say yes or no, or multiple choice rather than sit down and write an essay along a specific topic or question. A yes or no answer is very simple. With an essay you have to express an opinion or feeling and I just don't want to get involved in that commitment. [*Why not?*] It's like when I was younger. I didn't like to have opinions. Like whether I was a Democrat or a Republican or whether I was anything. It was just easier to leave it unanswered rather than commit myself to one party or another or whether or not I liked something. In school it was easier not to be the top student because so much was expected of the top student. It was easier to be in the top 10 or 15 percent where I didn't stand out as the top student. I was brought up in a Jewish neighborhood, and when I was a kid all the neighbors had children my age and they were so bright, they were so intelligent. Their children were such geniuses. And I didn't want to be treated that way by my parents. I just didn't want to be used. It just looked like I was being used enough by my parents for their own edification. I was tall, and I was good looking and everything else, like everybody would say, "My God, where did your son come from?" My father was average height and my mother was short. And I just didn't want to be pointed out as another bright kid.

In college I kind of floated down a little bit because I passed everything alright. I don't think very much happened during that period. Just seemed to graduate and I went to work. Nothing great happened to me because by that time everything was already set and you just went along. You eliminated any anxiety-provoking situations. I was gonna get a job and go to work and just be conventional as much as possible. Once that decision was made it's very easy to get along. Not with yourself but the outside world. Nothing rocks the boat. You just go along and you go to work from nine to five, come home and have dinner, get dressed and go to a movie and go here and out there. You come home and you're in bed by twelve so that you're up the next morning to go to work again. And in the summer you plan vacations. The whole thing is just patterns that you fall into and there is nothing much left to decide on except just insignificant things like, where you will go on vacation? what movie will you see?

[*When did you make the decision to be like that?*] I guess it must have been during high school, my third or fourth year. [*What was going on then?*] I don't know, just the thought of a lot of the kids in the neighborhood had gone the wrong way. Several had been sent to prison or involved in crime in some way. And I just decided to kind of just narrow my sights somehow and not get involved in anything except just what society considered would be the normal way of life. [*What had happened to some of the kids?*] Well, one kid was involved in major robberies. Go to jail for a couple of years and come out and get involved again and they sent him back to prison for life. The guy next door was murdered. The guy around the corner killed his mother—stuffed her in a tub and filled it with concrete and kept her there for I don't know how long before they found her. I went to high school, come to think of it, during the World War II period. That period was just kind of very murky. It was just fall into the line like everybody else who goes to college. Decide on some profession and go ahead and work at it and develop it and then things stayed pretty steady for quite a while.

The person begins by expressing his difficulty with the interview task: "I just keep thinking about what I'm going to talk about for five days." He compares the interview to having to write an essay. Here I ask the person what that feels like. He indicates that an essay implies having to "express an opinion or feeling" and he doesn't want to "commit" himself in that way. This statement has several implications and to learn more I gently confronted the person by asking, "Why not?" This type of probe asks the person to go beyond his initial statement, to expand on it. He links his desire not to commit himself in the interview to feelings he had when younger. We can now summarize several linkages in the following kind of way:

interview situation = essay
essay = not wanting to commit self to feeling/opinion
not wanting to commit self to feeling = how felt when younger

Let me shift to the third person. The interviewer wants to learn more about this desire of the person to not have to commit himself to his feelings when younger. He probes: Where did he have this desire? In what situations? The participant mentions school and not wanting to have to "stand out." This is ambiguous and more detail is asked for: "What would it have meant to stand out?" The person mentions his childhood differences from other academically successful kids, and feelings about his parents, in particular his feeling of "being used" by them "for their own edification." He mentions feeling different from his parents ("I was tall, and I was good looking and . . . everybody would say, 'my God, where did your son come from?' My father was average height and my mother was short."). From this the person turns to high school and college and having tried to remove "anxiety-provoking situations." He discusses the decision "to go to work and just be conventional as much as possible." The person remembers wanting to remove choices from his life, by having everything planned for you: "It's just a pattern you fall into." The interviewer wishes he knew more about this "anxiety" and the associated decision to become "conventional." He asks: "When did you make the decision to be like that?" The person dates his concern back to high school. Now we have the following linkages:

> school = wish not to stand out
> different from other successful, "stand out" kids
> different from parents
> eliminate anxiety = high school/college
> work = be conventional

Again there is a probe, with the interviewer asking the person, "What was going on then?" Here the person remembers "a lot of kids in the neighborhood had gone the wrong way." Examples are prison or crime. He "decided to kind of just narrow my sights and just not get involved in anything except just what society considered would be the normal way of life." The interviewer wonders what is meant by an abnormal way of life and asks about the kids the person was so interested in dissociating himself from. He remembers robberies and murder. One murder was by a boy who killed his mother. Further, this was occurring during the World War II period in New York City, and for this person "that period was kind of murky." Through his young adulthood years things stayed pretty "steady" as the person begins his work career. He remembers his whole life being geared to "working and producing".

Figure A-1 summarizes and restates the major linkages established in this interview excerpt. Whenever possible the major types of affect reported by the person to characterize the linkages are included. These are the "lines of affect" that bind the linkages between life domains and events for this man. Interpretation of the meaning of these observed linkages can be found in sections to follow.

Three methodological caveats should now be introduced. First, linkages between affective, self-relevant dynamics of loss and self-definition and key life events were found in the interviews retrospectively. The interviewer adopted a relatively passive posture during the sessions and probed for linkages in a general fashion. Subsequent analysis of the interview data established the linkages between life domains at midlife and affective issues of loss and recovery of self-definition that were described in earlier chapters. Further, note that there is only one instrument in this study—the free-associative interview procedure—and it is asked to serve a variety of purposes, primarily to reconstruct events that occurred at different, earlier points in historical, life-history time (e.g., young adulthood, midlife, adolescence; Chapters 2,3,4) and to provide a variegated

FIGURE A–1:   A Summary of Interview Linkages between Life Domains across Time and Lines of Affect

---

Interview situation is like an essay (present)
   ↓   Don't like
Commit self to feelings and opinions
   ↓   Felt similar
When younger in school (past-childhood)
   ↓   Didn't like
to stand out
   ↓
So much expected when on top
   ↓
Successful, academic, "Jewish" kids
   ↓   Didn't want
Treated that way by parent
   ↓   Didn't want
"Being used by my parents"
   ↓
Pointed out as another bright kid
   ↓
"I kind of floated down"
   ↓
eliminated anxiety-provoking situations (high school and college)
   ↓
Work meant being conventional, no decision, "fell into pattern" (young adulthood)
   ↓
kids getting into trouble (high school: adolescence)
   ↓
narrowed sights to normal
   ↓
Robberies, murders, boy kills mother, World War II (high school)
   ↓
"things get murky"
   ↓
"steady life in 20s, working and producing"

---

picture of several different dimensions of personality functioning in the present. This latter use of the interview data is the major focus of Chapter 4, on the reconstitution of self at midlife.

Our single instrument is, in addition, asked to perform these services without having been designed beforehand to do so. That is, the study was conceived as an exploratory one, without specific preconceptions of what would be found or the specific elements that would emerge as important. Rather, the theoretical and empirical notions presented in the chapters emerged from the data after it was collected.* As a result, specific sets of questions were not, of course, developed for the interview, or other instruments included that might have allowed more complete investigation of the dimensions that later emerged as important. As a result, the strategy was to explore the important dimensions of our formulations concerning career and personal development at midlife with the actual data available from the interviews rather than from more ideal data— allowing full exploration of all theoretical/empirical questions—that might have been preferable. On the other hand, these deficiencies seem outweighed, or made irrelevant, by the importance of developing and presenting the model and applying it to illustrative case study material, using the data on hand. The presentation in Chapters 1 through 5 is meant, then, as illustrative or exemplary of key issues that have emerged as important in our men's lives and of some of the ways that the interview procedure allows us to study these issues. Much further testing and refinement of the theoretical notions and empirical data presented in this book remains to be carried out.† Further, while this work suffers from all the well-known weaknesses of single-instrument research, it also contains the less-discussed advantages of such research. These include the careful, detailed attention to the full meaning of rich data, the use of all available data, the intensive study and exploration of carefully focused question-asking within the boundaries of a method whose limits become increasingly known through the interviewer's active involvement with the instrument/data (the active involvement and use of the interviewer—in a controlled, supervised fashion—as a research instrument himself) and the absence of a panapoly of convergent instruments providing data, the true

*To be absolutely precise, the loss-grieving model began to emerge at about the midway point of the study. However, further development of the model and empirical dimensions within the interviews did not take place until the interviewing was completed.

†Ongoing research is now exploring different patterns of career, family, and personal development at midlife in a broad sample of men who were intensively studied when they were in college (Osherson 1977, 1979). This research project will allow us to explore the key dimension of growth and adaptation at midlife among men in a variety of occupational and family situations, and to postdict patterns of midlife passage from adolescent data collected when this group of men was in college.

meaning of which is unclear and confusing. In the attempt to stay within the boundaries of this rich, full interview data, which the interviewer confronts with careful attention to his inner responses and the full meaning of complex verbal data, the study can be understood as approaching the interview as a constructed text. This notion of the interview protocol as a text, amenable to detailed reading and analysis, is discussed in the following section.

Analysis of the Data: The Interview as a Constructed Text

Our five-session procedure results in seven and one-half hours of interview time with each participant. Transcribed, this results in over two hundred pages of life history discussion. The key question is how to organize and reduce this material into some meaningful and coherent form. The strategy I have chosen is to treat the interviews as a constructed text. The text constructed is the person's story of his life as told to the interviewer. As such it is amenable to careful analysis, with the effort directed toward a bringing together of key themes in the interviews to allow a deeper understanding of the major figures, events, and experiences described. The manner in which this occurs is not, for me, completely amenable to explanation at this point, since much of the process is integrally tied up with how one learns to listen to and understand people as a clinician. Yet the question of how we make sense of people's lives from interview material of this kind is too important to be sidestepped. So I would like to present three approaches to analysis of data I have used in this project, all centering on close textual reading of the interview material.*

A. The Reconstruction of Affective Linkages between Life Domains across Time.

This approach is concerned with how events and figures from different domains of the person's life are linked together. This amounts to a process of reconstructing the linkages between different aspects of the person's life, slowly understanding the impact of events in one domain on events in other domains. We have already described the free-associative method as attempting to understand how what happens in one domain is related to another, incorporating the temporal dimension. What is linked, from this perspective, is some unique complex of domains across time: work at present to family in past, family in present to family in past, etc. This emerges from our attempt to impose minimal structure and to

*A number of recent approaches to the textual analysis of conversation and discourse may become fruitful sources of understanding for the analysis of free-associative interview data. Especially important is the tradition of hermeneutic analysis exemplified by the work of Paul Ricoeur (1965).

follow the affective threads of the person's talk. The attempt to find the unique organization of different elements in the interview involves the creation, if you will, of life history metaphors. This notion of linkages extends to individual interviews and to all five of the sessions with each person: (1) linkages are found within a single segment of interview material and (2) linkages are established between different parts of the five-session interview sequence for each individual. As an illustration let's return to the long interview passage above. The excerpt presented a sequence of material from one person, in which the interviewer probed for the self-relevant linkages between life domains across time. This excerpt can also stand as an illustration of how it is possible to examine the linkages within a single interview, and between one excerpt and the rest of the person's interview material, to understand life history. First let's focus on the meaning of the content we have described in the long excerpt and summarized in Figure A-1. We begin with the participant's initial difficulty in beginning: "Just ask me something. . . . " The person verbalizes his feeling of having to write an exam, and not liking to have to commit himself to a feeling or opinion. There is more self-revelation in an essay, and one is more responsible for the content, than in a multiple choice exam where the answers are given and the options already formulated. Further, the comparison of the interview to a school essay exam is also interesting because it implies a concern about being graded or evaluated, being marked by the teacher. So at the least we find a concern about exposing himself, revealing himself. There also may be a feeling of being graded or evaluated by others. The person then reveals that this was a feeling he had when younger: of not wanting to "stand out." In this case standing out seemed to have something to do with being seen or evaluated: "so much expected by others." At this point the person goes on to tell us several things. First, he felt different from academically successful students. He introduces an ethnic dimension: "Jewish kids." And he indicates feeling different from, and resentful toward, his parents. The comment, "My God, where did your son come from?" implies that he is not a member of his family only in looks. Further, his comment about not wanting to stand out because "I was being used enough by my parents for their own edification," carries with it some resentment—acknowledged or not— toward his parents. What do we learn from this? The participant indicates that he felt at times like not exposing himself when younger, that he felt different from some kids and from his parents. This is no different from feelings experienced by many children, but how did the person cope with these feelings, and what specific impact did they have on his development? Let's look further. These issues of being different and standing out lead to a comment about eliminating "anxiety-producing situations." Although the person cannot specify which situations were anxiety producing, the associative flow that follows provides a clue. First, though, note that work appears in this context—it is a way of becoming conventional and making himself normal, different from those who are "abnormal." Again the topic of who he is like and who he is different from reappears. The person remembers some high school kids getting in trouble with robberies and murder. He remembers a boy killing his mother, and in light of this person's resentment toward his parents and anxieties about violence such a theme should be noted. Such memories are usually markers of the participant's own inner conflicts at the time, as well as descriptions of actual events that occurred in fact. In this light the mention of World War II has several significant aspects. The person has already mentioned ethnicity and feeling different, with concerns about being conventional and avoiding trouble. He is Italian, and during the war the Italians were the enemy and the aggressors. In this country at that time some Italians felt devalued and the object of ridicule. One wonders of the impact of such an experience on a young Italian boy in this country in high school and with anxieties about his violence and being "different." The participant says that these concerns led to his narrowing his sights, to a particular definition of normality. Added indication of his difficulty with aggression and various impulses at the time is his comment that "things get murky" during the high school and college time. Work and young adulthood reappear as he indicates a "steady life" of "working and producing." Thus work is again linked to being normal and getting away from frightening possibilities within himself.

We can summarize the linkages produced by this material as follows:

1. This person was concerned about not showing aspects of himself when younger, specifically in childhood and adolescence.

2. More specifically, he struggled with strong aggressive and violent fantasies at these times, which led to fears of being abnormal. Some of these fantasies may have had to do with his parents and with his ethnic origins as an Italian.

3. In adolescence the person struggled with the feeling of being different or abnormal, and this uncertainty about self seems related to issues of violence and impulse.

4. Decisions about work in adolescence and young adulthood seem related to this anxiety about being different and reflect in part the desire to be seen as normal and conventional.

These linkages are only the starting point of our investigation and should be seen as hypotheses to now be further explored. As such, we can restate them as questions:

1. Does this man feel he has important parts of himself that he cannot let other people see? Does he have significant problems as-

serting himself? Has this been a significant issue at other points in his life?

2. Does this man feel strongly at times like he is being graded or marked, and has to be a good student, perhaps for his parents? Did he feel this way in childhood and adolescence? Similarly, did he feel at times like he was being pushed to succeed, as the eldest son of an immigrant family?

3. The person displays anxiety about decision making. How is the initial career choice related to his attempt to bind his anxiety?

4. What was the anxiety about in high school and adolescence? Does the person have significant concerns about his own violence and aggression? Is this connected to his feeling different and being an ethnic Italian?

These questions serve as guides to possible linkages between life domains and figures and events that can be further investigated in material from elsewhere in the interview sessions. In other words, we want to look at the linkages between these key figures and events across the interviews in order to refine and elaborate our understanding of their meaning. We would then look at these topics and themes as they are discussed and reworked over the five-session sequence to see how they are interrelated.

B. Learning the Language of the Participant

This approach to the interviews refers to understanding or decoding the personal meaning and significance of key words and phrases in the person's talk. Here we look to the salient images, words, and phrases used by the participant and the manner in which they illuminate figures, events, and choices in his life. People often have characteristic perceptions or ways of describing figures or events, which usually have idiosyncratic meanings and can shed considerable light—once decoded—on the people or experiences they refer to. Many examples of learning the particular meaning of special phrases or words in the interview—and their use in the reconstruction of a specific life history—have appeared in earlier chapters, particularly Chapter 2. As an example, in Chapter 2 we examined Mr. Anderson's mention of wanting to "carve out my own space" in contrast to earlier feelings of being "swallowed up" in describing his initial career choice. A close analysis of when in the interviews these phrases were used, to describe which figures and conflicts, allowed elucidation of Mr. Anderson's conflict around being separate from and close to his older brother and the role this dynamic played in the evolution of his career. The understanding of the meaning of these phrases provided a major clue to the reconstruction of the role of unresolved sibling rivalry and separation issues in Mr. Anderson's involvement in law directly after college.

C. Structural Approaches to the Interview

Variables of interview structure refer to how things are said in the interviews, in contrast to variables in interview content, which refer to what is said. Our first two approaches—the reconstruction of affective linkages and the learning of the person's language—are particularly attentive to the content of the person's talk. I would like now to present two perspectives on interview structure—that of structural dysfunction in the interview "talk" and of the working alliance between interviewer and participant. These perspectives are particularly useful in understanding the reconstruction of self at midlife, that is, the theoretical material presented in Chapter 4.

Let me briefly backtrack in order to explain this notion of structural approaches to the interview material. In examining the interview protocols of our participants we noted that there were characteristic ways of talking about their life history and relating to the interviewer. The importance of this derives from the fact that the interviews are relatively unstructured, interpersonal situations. The situation is unstructured in the sense that although the participant knows the basic purposes of the study, the specific character of his interaction with me and the resources available to him are left ambiguous. The person is told only that I want to learn as much as possible about his life and that it would be best if he told his own story in his own words. Thus, the basic purpose is to create a text, to tell the story of their lives, but such questions as how much of their lives to reveal, in what manner, and what use to make of the interviewer in the process are left up to the participant to answer. What starts out as an interview soon becomes an open-ended invitation to explore one's life with someone else. Individuals respond in a variety of ways to this invitation. A major consequence of the relatively undefined, ambiguous nature of the situation is that the person must resolve for himself how much access to give, and time to devote, to particular topics and subjects in his life history. The degree to which the person is able and willing to explore his experiences is thus open to our inspection. One source of such a picture is observation of the participant's associative flow as he talks about various events and people: Is it a free-flowing exploration with access to experience or is it a constricted, uncertain, defensive description of his life? The associative flow then becomes important as a "stream of consciousness," indicating access to —and integration of—the discrepancies of midlife. That is, by attending to the associative flow of the sessions we can examine points at which the person starts talking, stops, shifts topics, the manner in which he talks, and how he relates to the interviewer at particular points. In particular it has seemed most fruitful to investigate how these men talk about midlife, with its discrepant experiences and loss. We have found that some individuals, consistent with a defensive, nonexplorative stance toward the loss experience at midlife, show greater evidence of constriction and inhibition in the associative flow and in their relationship to the interviewer when discussing midlife than do other participants with apparently greater access to the discrepancies of midlife. In particular we can delineate two dimensions of structural analysis: assessment of the degree of *structural dysfunction* and of the *working alliance* between the participant and the interviewer. The first dimension is concerned with how the interview material hangs together—attending to when and how the person stops and starts talking and the manner in which he talks—when discussing midlife, so as to locate points at which the person brings to an end or radically narrows particular life history discussions or ends altogether the task of story telling. It is such breakage in the "text"— the life story told to the interviewer—that is indicative of constrictions or foreclosure of particular experiences in the individual's life history.

Attention to the working alliance is based on a sense of the interviewer in the free-associative interview both as an ego representative and as a transference object. First, by encouraging free exploration of life history with questions and probes the interviewer at times assumes the status of a well-functioning ego, seeking access to conflict and desire, attempting to synthesize competing demands and conflicting experiences. The person's attitude toward this role of the interviewer as encouraging open-ended investigation and curiosity may bear similarity to his attitude to exploration of the internal world. We thus are interested here in questions and comments from the individual indicative of his attitude to exploration of the discrepancies of midlife: Do such statements reveal a task-oriented, free exploration of the individual's life, or are they indicative of a foreclosed, defensive, overly distanced attitude to the discrepancies of midlife? The former (good working alliance) is indicative of a sculpted resolution of the grieving process, while the latter, limited willingness to focus on such areas (poor working alliance), is indicative of a foreclosed resolution.* Foreclosed, poor access is indicated by such interactions as the following:

I had a difficult time tolerating that kind of pushy woman. [*Why?*] Now that's a stupid question. It ought to be obvious. I mean who likes

*The working alliance should not be confused with simplistic notions of compliance or cooperation. A person may criticize the interviewer, the procedures, or refuse completely to participate without necessarily indicating a foreclosed stance. And, conversely, a ready willingness to participate and give the interviewer everything he wants is not coextensive with a sculpted resolution at midlife. We are interested, rather, in moments in which the intensity (or lack of it) of the individual's response to the novel, ambiguous, or discrepant experience presented by the interviewer's questions and comments reveals whether there is strong conflict present in such areas; at such points the conflict comes alive and is present in the working alliance between the participant and interviewer.

pushy women? I get the feeling I wander off the point when you ask me questions.

[*Where'd you go to college?*] I don't have to tell you, do I? Do you mind?

In both the above cases there is a poor working alliance with the interviewer, reflected in the participants' limited willingness to explore their life history experience. This contrasts with the good working alliance characteristic of participants evidencing more sculpted resolutions. In such cases we find a clear task orientation and a willingness to explore life history, often combined with a vigorous curiosity:

I had a very hard time with my boss at the lab. [*How come?*] Hmm. Good question. I guess I found him far too pushy and demanding. There have been other people like that I've had a hard time with— that's hard to admit but I know you want to learn as much about me as you can.

Furthermore, the person's relationship with the interviewer as a transference object can reveal much about the person's degree of resolution of separation conflicts so important earlier in his life history. In particular we can assess whether the individual reexperiences in the interviews key conflicts in relation to parents and siblings. This is a valuable addition to our content approaches to understanding the degree of differentiation of these figures at midlife for the individual, as discussed in Chapter 4. At moments in the interviews unresolved conflicts with parents or siblings may come alive and reveal themselves in terms of the person's perception of the interviewer. Mr. O'Hara, our potter, provides a striking example of this in the following passage, drawn from the second interview of our five-session sequence.

I'm very sensitive to the context these interviews began with, and your role as undefined. You haven't verbalized it as a particular role. I know something about your project. I'm aware that I'm left trying to fill up this time, according to what I imagine you want to some extent, or what's needed for the project. [*Maybe it would be useful to talk about that. What do you see my role as?*] Well, you're here to take the recording, you occasionally ask questions. Generally you try to make me more concrete, I think. Or to where you want more details. That's not very frequently. Which as a result I don't know where you fit in the process. Because I work more on feeling states, and I guess that's the differences to where you're at. The kinds of questions you ask are not really where I'm at, your mind works differently. I feel I'm being examined. [*Examined?*] Observed, because of the objective stance that you take. That's distressed me, it always does. I would like to have more shared task. [*In what ways do I seem objective?*] You're not sharing any of your feelings and so it leads you to the appearance of being objective. I always feel uncomfortable in that setting. I guess what I'm trying to say is the way the interview is set up—because a large number of unknowns, and the vagueness—how I will react in that kind of setting. Which will be sometimes puzzled, sometimes anxious. I'll do my best to flush you out. [*To flush me out?*] Yeah, in order to get more specific.

The other thing is that this is a criticism I have of most laboratory type settings, in that the setting itself determines a great deal of the patient. Most people who do research about human beings in that setting seem totally unaware that they have set up a setting that is very threatening in many ways. And they're very delighted to find out that the behavior proves Freud's notion of the mass murderer and the primal murder. They seem really unaware that they've set up a setting which can only for the most part introduce that type of behavior. It is a very kind of threatening kind of setting. So you get largely defensive behavior. [*Do you feel that's analogous to what's going on here?*] I feel a little, yeah, because I don't know where you're at. I would like to be more helpful to you in terms of what your task is. In here it's so vague, it's again part of the general response which develops when the person is being examined like a rat so you have a very natural form that your fears take.

Mr. O'Hara's experience of the interview situation is as a very threatening, laboratory-type setting in which he feels "examined like a rat." He feels he must protect himself from an unfeeling, unsympathetic person (the interviewer), desirous of finding out terrible things about him ("Freud's notion of the mass murderer and the primal murder"). In response to the ambiguity and uncertainty of the interview, where there are few restrictions on what is to be discussed, the interviewer becomes an undifferentiated figure for Mr. O'Hara as he relives what sounds like earlier conflicts with his parents about their acceptance of him. Mr. O'Hara feels like a rat and possibly a primal murderer in the interview situation. This bears considerable similarity to the conflicts he experienced as a child concerning his place in his family, discussed in Chapter 5.* Who he is, and his subjectivity, are still very much tied to internalized parental attitudes

---

*Recall that the circumstance of his birth (the "primal event") and his place in his family vis-a-vis his parents and brothers were the source of great conflict for Mr. O'Hara in his childhood.

toward him, revealed in the intense reexperiencing of this conflict in the interview situation. As such, Mr. O'Hara reveals the continued role in his life of his perception of very powerful, possibly rejecting parents, who can do him great harm. He acknowledges this in a later interview session:

> My birthday is a very heavy time. It's a little hard for me to get into my history today. I always get frightened as my birthday approaches and do all kinds of avoidance behavior. It's all bound up with family things. My childhood family. The feelings that my father was badly hurt—he broke his hip. I realize that I was frightened of my birthday because I felt that I had wished or willed my father's accident. I always felt in some way involved with that and it created a lot of distance later on between us. It helped to keep me away from him. A lot of guilt feelings. I managed to break through that and see what was really frightening and that was that I felt my mother willed it. That was pretty scary that she had some infinite power.*

Mr. O'Hara still struggles with the fantasy that his parents have "ultimate power." Mr. O'Hara's struggles with the interviewer in the preceding excerpt indicate the continued operation in behavior of the fantasy described. Mr. O'Hara blames the interviewer and his power for determining his responses in the interview in the same manner as he located such power in his parents as a child, and as he blamed a perceived powerful, distant, unsympathetic university faculty for doing during his midlife years. In both Mr. O'Hara's pre- and post-crisis experiences, then, we find the continued presence of idealized parental figures. The transference relationship in the interview reveals the continuation of this more undifferentiated perception into the present.

For more detailed examples of the analyses of structural variables in the interviews, let's return to two men who were discussed in depth in Chapter 4: Mr. Markowitz and Mr. Anderson. Mr. Markowitz is our biochemist turned actor who was discussed in Chapter 4 as reflective of a more foreclosed resolution of the crisis at midlife, while Mr. Anderson, a

*The presence of transference elements means, of course, that the interpersonal relationship with the interviewer in part shapes the kind of story that the person will tell about his life. That is, he is shaping his story in an unconscious manner by his perception of the interviewer as an ever-changing conglomerate of mother, father, sibling, and other conflictual figures in his life. The impact of this distortion cannot be easily determined and must be kept in mind when interpreting the interview data. We know, for example, by attending to the transference issues, that Mr. O'Hara's life story is in part oriented around a dichotomy between affect and intellect, particularly in relation to his father. Further, he wants to impress the interviewer/father and also get even with him or aggress against him, and both these dialectic factors shape his story.

sculptor trained as a lawyer, was used to illustrate a more sculpted resolution at that time.

First let's focus on Mr. Markowitz. A variety of structural variables in the interview can be used to infer a foreclosed, defensive attitude to the discrepant experiences of midlife. In relation to structural dysfunction, there are a variety of textual devices that close off or restrict exploration for Mr. Markowitz of issues of (1) the role of affect and impulse in his life and (2) the experience of a "personal crisis" at midlife. Table A-2 presents an illustrative section of protocol from Mr. Markowitz. Note the variety of textual devices in the excerpted material that close off or restrict exploration for Mr. Markowitz of issues of his personal crisis at midlife. He moves away from this topic by denying the ability to investigate such areas ("I don't know," "can't correlate"), and by interrupting the story telling with questions and criticisms of the interviewer.

In terms of the working alliance, the person's attitude toward the role of the interviewer as encouraging open-ended investigation and curiosity may bear similarity to his attitude toward the purely internal world. Thus, in his relationship with the interviewer, Mr. Markowitz gives perhaps the most interesting picture of his attitude to his inner life. In the early sessions he retains a tight control over the interaction, filling up the time with a running chronology of his life that fills two interviews. As the interviewer becomes more active, attempting to direct attention to excluded areas of work and family experience, Mr. Markowitz resists, eventually developing a hostile distancing stance. Angry comments and criticism of the interviewer create a struggle, as Mr. Markowitz evidences difficulty in ranging freely over his experience. A variety of questions or comments from Mr. Markowitz serve to distance him from the interviewer, preventing the development of a working alliance around a freely explorative task focus. Some examples:

I was very much interested in personal biographies. Now don't ask me how I got interested in biographies.

You do these creative intuitive leaps if you're doing pure research in any field. I mean the plodding way is not that way. You might as well be an accountant. Or somebody that collects stamps. I hope you don't collect stamps. I mean I just didn't want to offend you.

I feel I wander off the point whenever you ask me a direct question. When you're reviewing these tapes you'll see that.

There is a hostile component to this distancing—captured in the concern with offending the interviewer—that provides a clue to the transference component of the relationship. Mr. Markowitz relates to the inter-

TABLE A–2:   Structure of Associational Flow from Mr. Markowitz, Interview 2 (approx. 10 min.)

INTERVIEW PROTOCOL	COMMENTS
I place a real premium on conversation, arguing. Just like my father. I can't stand it when someone won't argue with me, just says no.	
[*What happens when you can't argue?*]	I's Q: * (probe)
Well, there is a whole area of life besides arguing. When I was 35 or 40, I realized that there were areas in one's own personal life that are not susceptible to some kind of objective verbalization. I was just walking along Fifth Avenue. I swerved into the New York Public Library on 42nd Street, which I did often, and I was walking into the stacks without knowing what the subject was. I put my hand up and drew a book and opened it at random and the first sentence that met my eye was "most important decisions an individual makes are based upon non-rational emotional bases." And I closed the book and walked out. It was like God had spoken to Moses. It meant that all the great pride I took in rational discussion and argument was misplaced. That there were limits.	
Still, I'm proud, I identify with groups. The potentialities of this organ up here [points to head]. A unique species, because of this characteristic.	drifts away from topic with intellectualized discussion
[*Around age 35 things began to change?*]	I's Q: returns to "crisis"
I realized the limitations of that approach, yeah.	
[*What was going on then?*]	I's Q: exploration (probe)
I don't know. Let's see, nothing special, I guess when I was 35 I moved back to New York City. I can't really correlate it with anything. You know, that's really a silly question, I can't answer it. [Five seconds.]	P:*interrupts storytelling with denial of motive, "I don't know," "can't correlate" Criticism of interviewer

Interview Protocol	Comments
Back in New York City I was able to indulge in my playing music, which was a hobby of mine. Music has always been rather important to me. As it is for a lot of physical scientists. And there have been a lot of explanations for that. Are you interested in some of those? The function of music? Why are so many scientists, especially physical scientists, interested in music?	*P*: interrupts storytelling ("are you interested . . .") intellectualized discussion ("functions of music")
[*Music is important to you?*]	*I*'s Q: returns *P* to focus
Sure. Music was important to my kids too. They could play so well, sometimes I would get really jealous. There were days it was hard to go to work and watch them have so much free time. . . . Well, where were we?	*P*: ends discussion with question to *I* and returns to chronological perspective.

*Q = Question
 P = Participant
 I = Interviewer

viewer as if he were a father to whom he was accountable.* He looks to this powerful figure for the right way to behave in the interview; as well, he feels angry at the accountability and control he reads into the interaction which he also feels is constraining:

> I've heard no critical elements in your tone, ever, which is very hard for me to take. I depend on attack on whatever position I take. There is a technique in navigation called "landfall." Early navigators used it. Let's say you're sailing from London to New York. And you're not sure of which way to go. So you point directly towards New York and get to the coastline. There's no New York, you're a little off, which way do you turn? You're not quite sure. Whereas, if you purposely sail to one side, say the sun side, and hit the coast, now you go up the coast and you hit New York. That's called "landfall." I will frequently take a position on one side. I'm not sure what my position is or should be, but I'll take a position which is not very far off from where

*See Chapter 5, pp. 190–192 for discussion of Mr. Markowitz's relationship to his father in childhood.

I truly think it is. And I get brought back to it by criticism. Like going too far, in which case I get criticism again. . . .

That whole parent-godlike syndrome. [*How is the parent godlike?*] Now that's a stupid question. I mean they speak of "God the father." I feel you know the answer but you want to know what my answer is. . . .

In the first passage we see Mr. Markowitz asking for guidance and control when he discusses the importance of "attack" and "criticism" in defining his position. At various points Mr. Markowitz asks for more direction from the interviewer, hoping he will play a father-like role. He says, "The idea of just sitting here and talking is hard. I want some kind of feedback from you." Yet in the second excerpt Mr. Markowitz's hostility and anger at the interviewer/father figure bursts out, as he feels called to account by the interviewer. He has to defend his comment and becomes quite hostile to the potentially critical interviewer in return. In this we see Mr. Markowitz reliving the same child-father interaction he perceived as a child, and which characterized aspects of his midlife struggle in the sciences and at home. Mr. Markowitz is essentially unable to separate from the transference figure in the interview, and, throughout, the interviewer remains a powerful idealized figure against whom he must struggle. This is a transference situation very different from the case of Mr. Anderson, where we shall find greater separation from this idealized interviewer/transference figure.

The point of this brief illustration of the analysis of structural aspects of the interviews with Mr. Markowitz has been to present some picture of how, through a variety of structural maneuvers, he tried to distance himself in the interviews from issues of affect and impulse in his life (the discrepant experiences). A restricted alliance develops that constricts the amount of free exploration that takes place and replicates in the interviews the conflictual relationship he continues to experience with an idealized father. The restricted access to inner experience and life history indicated by these perspectives parallels the defensive stance indicated by the content of the interviews, as discussed in Chapter 4.

Now let's turn to Mr. Anderson, a person who illustrated in Chapter 4 a more sculpted resolution. In terms of interview structure, the sculpted resolution of Mr. Anderson is reflected in both variables of structural dysfunction and the working alliance. Thus, when we attend to how topics of separation, sibling rivalry, and self-definition are handled in the interviews we find evidence of blockage in early sessions. For example:

At the beginning of college, I didn't have much of a sense of what I was doing and what was happening around me. And how I fit into it.

It really was more like dislocation or something like that. I guess that's enough of an explanation. So, where do we go from here? [*What seems important to you?*] Seems important to stop pretty soon. It's a dangerous area.

The competition was to become an expert, you see. Competing with whom? That I couldn't say without spending quite a bit of time.

There were problems about the kids and about me being a good father. Some jealousy on my wife's part of my attention to other women which was really not founded most of the time. I haven't really untangled all that. To try to slop through it here doesn't seem possible. [*Is it hard to talk about it?*] Fairly hard, yes, it seems very personal.

However, by the middle sessions this constriction gives way to greater ability to acknowledge this material, as Mr. Anderson explores some of the source of the dislocation in his uncertainty about self. As we have already seen in Chapter 4, we find discussions of his relationship with brother, wife, and the difficulties of career choice. There is thus, in contrast to Mr. Markowitz, an expansion of focus from earlier to later sessions with less structural evidence of inhibition of access to such material.

The relationship between participant and interviewer bears out the sense of access to conflict and experience. We find a clear sense of both Mr. Anderson and the interviewer working together to construct a text, rather than the more hostile distancing of Mr. Markowitz or the sense of powerlessness of some of the other men. Instead there is a sense of task, and often a vigorous curiosity:

I can sense a lot of the troubles in the marriage, but it's not easy to be very precise. There's still a lot of pain involved in talking about it because it was such a struggle.

I don't know, Sam. Sometimes I think, you know, I wonder about myself. That I'm not always a little uncomfortable. I'm just beginning maybe now to feel that. I get much more comfortable when I accept the kind of tension that I seem to live under and I seem to relax and accept it.

[*Is there a specific time when you first began to feel dissatisified with law?*] No, maybe after a couple of years. But I don't think it was a precise instance. Sometimes I can focus on things for you, although it's a little bit of a distortion because an event doesn't always have that aspect that I know of.

Hmmm. Where to start today? Usually between sessions my head turns over what has been said.

Mr. Anderson's use of the interviewer's first name and his more realistic perception of him as a friendly interviewer trying to learn about his life history is of special note, since Mr. Anderson also struggled with a transference element in the relationship. Mr. Anderson's verbal competitiveness and social rivalry with his brother breaks through into the interview situation at several places, wherein the interviewer is experienced as if he were a poised, verbally facile older brother. At several points Mr. Anderson struggles overtly with his feeling that the conversation of the interview is not good enough and that the interviewer is not really listening to him.

> I'm surprising myself in talking this much about communication. It's not usual to talk this much. This thing isn't usual in the first place. Through the years being mostly a silent fellow, communication was mostly a failure. And I guess I have a lot of determination that it shouldn't be a failure. Conversations. Either there would be some anger or I would realize that the person wasn't really talking to me. It didn't matter who was there—just as long as there were another body. Last time with you, forgetting that this is a contract in ways. There is a reason for this imbalance. I had some tension because I had a hookup in my head that I was using you like I don't want to do to a friend. [*You were using me?*] I forgot that this was a special situation. [*Can you tell me more about the feelings you had last session?*] Well, I knew you wanted to know that and I'm curious too. I felt tired. I thought your questions were out of focus. And I could understand that they were open-ended questions, that you didn't want to suggest answers. And I found them difficult. And in a regular conversation I would insist that somebody focus the question before I would answer it. [*Which means?*] Well, it was too broad. It would entail an answer that was too long and I wouldn't trust the question till I thought it was asked properly. Once asked properly the answers became quite clear. My experience of anything close to this open-ended approach you're using has a purpose. You find out more by my fabrication of what has gone on with me than without interceding, suggesting by your own question. Yet there is a terrific imbalance between me doing all the talking. And I had to remind myself several times that this was a special situation. Even then there's something quite deep that makes me conscious about it. I had to remind myself more than once.

In this context, several of Mr. Anderson's comments in Chapter 4 about good interviewers can be understood as in part subtle put-downs of the interviewer/older brother transference figure. He does this through implicit comparisons of the interviewer to more capable conversationalists. For example, he comments on being "questioned by someone who's thoughtful," and on the "nicely probing" manner of a different interviewer who's "obviously thought about ways to get you to talk about your real likes and dislikes." Both these aspects of competition with the interviewer and defensiveness toward him can be seen in material discussed in Chapter 4 in which Mr. Anderson speaks directly about his brother.* He emphasizes the importance of this passage for him with the comment that "it . . . makes a difference to me in terms of being accurate." He intends to express some caring, positive feelings toward his brother, yet one of his first comments is, "I've given a false impression about my brother. That doesn't make any difference to you." This is a curious remark and a partially hostile one. Neither accuracy nor his tender, caring feeling toward his brother matter to the interviewer, Mr. Anderson implies. Rather, the interviewer wouldn't understand the importance of what he is going to say, nor be sensitive enough to it. It's as if Mr. Anderson is in part seeing the interviewer as just a social clown with no sense of the mysterious. Here we see Mr. Anderson dealing with the interviewer as if he were that bigmouth, socially facile, domineering clown of a brother of his. Mr. Anderson wants to say something important in this passage about his brother but, we can infer, is concerned about how good it will sound or whether he will be put down for saying it. So he asserts what he has to say but in a defensive, competitive fashion. Thus, at the very time Mr. Anderson is speaking about his brother some of his conflict and competitiveness around words and his sibling break through into the interview in relation to the interviewer. This is analogous to Mr. Markowitz's intense criticism of the interviewer at the very point where he is being questioned about his belief that parents are godlike. For both these individuals transference issues come alive in the interview at such points.

The following excerpt presents a similar experience for Mr. Anderson, occurring at the beginning of the interviews, where he again wants to say some important things and becomes bogged down and uncertain.

Telling your own biography is a very difficult thing to be very complete about. So questions from you will help elicit things which hadn't occurred to me. . . .

A very good teacher in high school, making you feel like your comments mattered, whatever they were. It sort of puts one in touch with their own sensations as OK. Things they haven't expressed to anybody before. Private reactions. . . .

I was at an interview for a job that I was interested in. And this guy's questions were very well taken. There didn't seem to be any taboos in what could be asked and what could not be asked. That relates to this. [*Taboos?*] Well, injunctions. Compare that with an in-

*See pp. 139–140.

terview that I also had recently for a job at a high school. You see the rules that are set up there.

In high school I was trapped in the system and I suppose the systemization just wrecks the students. It bothers me. There's a parallel to the law practice. I feel that the system becomes the reality and the structure of the school and they're not willing to question what it is they're there for. At the job interview I said, "You've got to be concerned about it." Have you ever thought about what it was like when you were a kid? Whether that was the right amount of time for a seventeen-year-old. [*Did you think about it as a kid?*] No, as a kid I didn't think about it. I thought about it retrospectively. I was being taught a system where the whole assumption of being a student was the schedule was bang bang bang bang bang bang through the day. And some classes, I'd have been happy if they had been over in fifteen minutes. Some lectures in college, I'd just go to sleep.

And I don't like situations where I feel people are mesmerized by this system that they're in. It grinds along and you don't have to think too much. It's the lack of questioning or real understanding of what's going on. The machine starts to run it because it's already made itself go. [*Can you explain what you mean by a person who's mesmerized?*] I've done that myself. [*You've been mesmerized?*] Yeah. Mesmerized means failing to see as much of the aspects of the situation as possible. The questioning of it and the saying, "Yes I'm going to continue doing that because it seems like a good thing." The questions ought to be asked quite often. About what it is that you're doing and what is happening to other people that are coming in contact with me or the system. I get excited and interested when I think of people who ask the kind of question of themselves and really mean it. Mesmerized means apparently asleep, or hypnotized. I think I was very much asleep in a lot of ways in high school. At the beginning of college, I didn't have much of a sense of what I was doing and what was happening around me. And how I fit into it. It really was more like dislocation or something like that. I guess that's enough of an explanation. So, where do we go from here? [*What seems important to you?*] It seems important to stop pretty soon. It's a dangerous area. I don't want to talk much more.

Mr. Anderson has begun the interviews with a sense of a difficult task—it will be hard to be complete. In particular it will be hard to include (or be complete about) his private feelings and response. He looks to the interviewer for help. He soon discusses very personal feelings and experiences: the feelings of taboo he has known in adolescence, the feelings of dislocation and of being mesmerized, and the importance of questioning such situations. However, when he reveals these very personal concerns and history he draws back from the interviewer and from revealing himself with the comments that "I guess that's enough of an explanation" and "I don't want to talk much more." Yet in our example of transference elements from Mr. Anderson we see a dialectic, forward-and-backward process. For example, in Chapter 4, even at the time Mr. Anderson is unable to see his brother in perspective—as the interviewer and brother merge in the session—he indicates also an ability to tell his brother to back off; that is, he tells off his brother/interviewer with the implicit criticism that it "doesn't make any difference to you," and then says what he wants to say. With this comment he pushes back against his rival. Furthermore, Mr. Anderson indicates an ability to differentiate the interviewer and separate from this idealized figure, an ability not available to Mr. Markowitz. This is implied by the more realistic perception of the interviewer over time described above.

To summarize the examples from Mr. Anderson, Mr. Markowitz, and Mr. O'Hara, in each case the perspective from a structural analysis of the patterns of structural dysfunction in the associative flow and working alliance in the interview situation parallels the kind of midlife resolution identified in Chapter 4 as characteristic of these men.

References

Ansbacher, H. and Ansbacher, R. (1956). *The individual psychology of Alfred Adler: A systematic presentation in selections from his writings.* New York: Harper & Row.

Bayer, A. (1970). Changing careers, five Americans begin again in their middle years. *Life, 68,* 50–57.

Bellow, S. (1964). *Herzog.* New York: Viking.

Block, J. (1971). *Lives through time.* Berkely, Calif.: Bancroft Books.

Blumenthal, I. S. (1959). *Research and the ulcer problem.* Santa Monica: Rand Corporation.

Byrne, Kathleen M. (1974). An analysis of certain personality traits and certain socioeconomic factors associated with adult career change after age thirty-one. *Dissertation Abstracts International, 34* (11-A).

Carr, A. H. (1975). Bereavement as a relative experience. In Schoenberg, B., et al. *Bereavement: Its psychosocial aspect.* New York: Columbia University Press.

Chew, P. (1976). *The inner world of the middle-aged man.* New York: Macmillan.

Coelho, G., Hamburg, D., and Murphey, E. B. (1963). Coping strategies in a new learning environment. *Archives of General Psychiatry, 9,* 433–443.

Coelho, G., Hamburg, D., and Adams, J. (1974). *Coping and adaptation.* New York: Basic Books.

Coles, R. (1971). On the meaning of work. *The Atlantic,* October, 103–104.

Dalton, G. W. et al. (1977). The four stages of professional careers—a new look at performance by professionals. *Organizational Dynamics,* Summer, 19–42.

Erikson, E. (1959). *Identity and the life cycle*. New York: International University Press.

Erikson, E. (1963). *Childhood and society*. New York: Norton.

Erikson, E. (1976). Reflections on Dr. Borg's life cycle. *Daedalus, 105*(2), 1–28.

Figler, H. (1978). *Overcoming executive mid-life stress*. New York: Wiley.

Folger, J. K., Astin, H. S., and Bayer, A. E. (1970). *Human resources and higher education*. New York: Russell Sage.

Fraiberg, S. H. (1959). *The magic years*. New York: Scribner's.

Freeman, R. B. (1971). *The market for college-trained manpower: a study in the economics of career choice*. Cambridge: Harvard University Press.

Freud, S. (1964). Mourning and melancholia. In *The complete psychological works of Sigmund Freud*, Standard Edition, *14*, 243–261.

Fried, M. (1963). Grieving for a lost home. In Duhl, L. (ed.), *The urban condition*. New York: Basic Books.

Ginzburg, E. (1972). Toward a theory of vocational choice: a restatement. *Vocational Guidance Quarterly*, March, 169–175.

Geertz, C. (1971). Deep play: notes on the Balinese cockfight. In *Myth, symbol and culture*. New York: Norton, 1–37.

Glick, I., Weiss, R., and Parkes, C. M. (1974). *The first year of bereavement*. New York: Wiley.

Goethals, G. W. and Klos, D. (1976). *Experiencing youth: first person accounts*. Boston: Little, Brown.

Goldsmith, R. (1972). *The organization of the self: its relationship to vocational commitment and choice*. Unpub. doc. diss., University of Michigan.

Gould, R. (1972). The phases of adult life. *American Journal Psychiatry, 129*(5), 33–43.

Gould, R. (1978). *Transformations*. New York: Simon & Schuster.

Guttman, D. L. (1976). Individual adaptation in the middle years: development issues in the masculine midlife crisis. *Journal of Geriatric Psychiatry, 9*, 41–59.

Hamburg, D. (1974). Coping behavior in life-threatening circumstances. *Psychotherapy and Psychosomatics, 23*, 13–25.

Hauser, S. (1976). Loevinger's mode and measure of ego development: a critical review. *Psychological Bulletin, 83*(5), 928–955.

Heller, J. (1974). *Something happened*. New York: Knopf.

Hendin, H., Gaylin, W., and Carr, A. (1965). *Psychoanalysis and social research: the psychoanalytic study of the non-patient*. New York: Doubleday.

Hendin, H. (1966). *Suicide and Scandinavia: a psychoanalytic study of culture and character*. New York: Doubleday.

Hendin, H. (1969). *Black suicide*. New York: Basic Books.

Hendin, H. (1975). *The age of sensation*. New York: Norton.

Hiestand, D. L. (1971). *Changing careers after thirty-five: new horizons through professional and graduate study*. New York: Columbia University Press.

Hodgson, R. C., Levinson, D. J., and Zaleznik, A. (1965). *Executive role constellation: an analysis of personality and role relations in management*. Boston: Harvard U. Grad. School of Business Admin.

Holland, J. L. (1973). *Making vocational choices: a theory of careers*. Englewood Cliffs, N.J.: Prentice-Hall.

Holland, J. L., Sorenson, A. B., Clark, J. P., Nafziger, D. H., and Blum, Z. D. (1973). Applying an occupational classification to a representative sample of work histories. *Journal of Applied Psychology, 58*, 34–41.

Jacques, E. (1965). Death and the midlife crisis. *International Journal Psychiatry, 46*, 502–513.

Kazan, E. (1967). *The arrangement.* New York: Stein & Day.

King, S. (1973). *Five lives at Harvard: personality change during college.* Cambridge: Harvard University Press.

Kohut, H. (1966). Forms and transformations of narcissism. *Journal American Psychiatric Association, 14,* 243–272.

Kohut, H. (1971). *The analysis of the self.* New York: International University Press.

Krantz, D. (1978). *Radical career change.* New York: The Free Press.

Lasch, C. (1979). *The culture of narcissism: American life in an age of diminishing expectations.* New York: Norton.

Lefkowitz, B. (1979). *Breaktime: living beyond the work ethic in America.* New York: Hawthorne.

Lehman, H. C. (1953). *Age and achievement.* Princeton, N.J.: Princeton University Press.

Levinson, H. (1964a). *Emotional health in a world of work.* New York: McGraw-Hill.

Levinson, H. (1964b). *Executive stress.* New York: Harper & Row.

Levinson, D., et al. (1975). The psychosocial development of men in early adulthood and the midlife transition. In Ricks, D., et al. *Life history research in psychopathology,* vol. 3. Minneapolis: University of Minneapolis Press.

Levinson, D. J. with Darrow, C. N., Klein, E. B., Levinson, M. H., and McKee, B. (1978). *The seasons of a man's life.* New York: Knopf.

Lindemann, E. (1944). Symptomology and management of acute grief. *American Journal of Psychiatry, 101,* 141.

Loevinger, J. and Wessler, R. (1970). *Measuring ego development,* vol. 1. San Francisco: Jossey-Bass.

Lowenthal, M. J., et al. (1975). *Four stages of life.* San Francisco: Jossey-Bass.

Maas, H. and Kuypers, J. A. (1974). *From thirty to seventy.* San Francisco: Jossey-Bass.

Mack, J. (1976). *A prince of our disorder: the life of T.E. Lawrence,* Boston: Little Brown.

Marcia, J. E. (1966). Development and validation of ego-identity status. *Journal Personal and Social Psychology, 3,* 551–558.

Marris, P. (1958). *Widows and their families.* London: Routledge & Kegan Paul.

Marris, P. (1975). *Loss and change.* New York: Doubleday.

Maslow, A. (1962). *Toward a psychology of being.* New York: Van Nostrand.

McMorrow, F. (1974). *Midolescence: the dangerous years.* New York: Quadrangle.

Merton, R. K. (1968). *Social theory and social structure.* New York: Free Press.

Montgomery, M.R. The damndest birds you ever saw. *Boston Sunday Globe,* January 7, 1979.

Neugarten, B. L. (1968). Adult psychology: toward a psychology of the life cycle. In Neugarten, B. L. (ed.), *Middle age and aging.* Chicago: University of Chicago Press.

Nixon, R. E. (1961). Approach to the dynamics of growth in adolescence. *Psychiatry, 24,* 18–31.

Osherson, S. (1977). Adaptation to occupational changes at midlife: a predictive, longitudinal study. Research proposal to the National Institute of Education.

Osherson, S. (1979). Dancing to the music of time: work, self, and family in early midlife. Working Paper No. 1, Career Development Project.

Parkes, C. M. (1972). *Bereavement: Studies of grief in adult life.* New York: International University Press.

Pelz, D. C. and Andrews, F. M. (1966). *Scientists in organizations.* New York: Wiley.

Perry, W. G. (1968). *Forms of intellectual and ethical development in the college years.* Cambridge: Harvard Bureau of Study Counsel.

Perry, W. G. (1970). *Forms of intellectual and ethical development in the college years.* New York: Holt, Rinehart & Winston.

PHS, Vital and Health Statistics—Selected symptoms of psychological distress, ser. 2, no. 37. U.S. Dept. of H.E.W., undated.

Piaget, J. (1962). *The moral judgment of the child.* New York: P. F. Collier.

Pines, R. C. (1968). Disenchantment in later years of marriage. In Neugarten, B. L. (1968).

Pollack, G. (1961). Mourning and adaptation. *International Journal Psychoanalysis, 42,* 341–361.

Porter, E. An explanation. *Harvard Medical Alumni Bulletin,* Spring, 1965, 39(4), 20–25.

Ricoeur, P. (1974). *The conflict of interpretations: essays in hermenuetics.* Evanston: Northwestern University Press.

Riegel, K. (1975). Adult life crises: a dialectic interpretation of development. In *Life-span developmental psychology: normative life crisis.* New York: Academic Press.

Riley, M. and Forier, A. (1968). *Aging and society.* New York: Russell Sage.

Roe, A. (1956). *The psychology of occupations.* New York: Wiley.

Rosenberg, S. and Farrell, M. (1976). Identity and crisis in middle-aged men. *International Journal Aging and Human Development,* 7(2), 153–170.

Sarason, S. B. (1977). *Work, aging, and social change: professionals and the one life-one career imperative.* New York: Free Press.

Schein, E. H. (1975). Career development: theoretical and practical issues for organizations. Paper prepared for Conference on Career Development, International Labor Office, Budapest, Hungary.

Sharaf, M. and Levinson, D. (1964). The quest for omnipotence in professional training. *Psychiatry,* 27(2), 135–149.

Sheehy, G. (1975). *Passages: predictable crises of adult life.* New York: Dutton.

Sheppard, H. L. and Herrick, N. Q. (1972). *Where have all the robots gone? worker dissatisfaction in the 1970's.* New York: Free Press.

Shore, M. (1972). Henry VIII and the crisis of generativity. *Journal Interdisciplinary History,* 2, Spring, 359–390.

Sommers, D. and Eck, A. (1977). Occupational mobility in the American labor force. *Monthly Labor Review,* 100(1), 3–19.

Srole, L., et al. (1962). *Mental health in the metropolis.* New York: McGraw-Hill.

Stevens, W. (1972). *The palm at the end of the mind: selected poems and a play.* New York: Vintage.

Stein, S. P., Holzman, S., Kavasu, T. B., and Charles, E. S. (1978). Mid-adult development and psychopathology. *American Journal of Psychiatry,* 135, 676–681.

Super, D. (1957). *The psychology of careers: an introduction to vocational development.* New York: Harper.

Super, D. (1976). *Career education and the meaning of work.* U.S. Department of HEW.

Tartakoff, H. (1966). The normal personality in our culture and the Nobel Prize complex. In Lowenstein, R., et al. (eds.). *Psychoanalysis: a general psychology.* New York: International University Press.

Tiedemann, D., and O'Hara, R. (1963). *Career development: choice and adjust-*

ment. New York: College Entrance Examination Board.

Trausch, S. (1974). Work: labor of love or lifetime of drudgery? December 1, *Boston Globe*.

Vaillant, G. (1978). *Adaptation to life.* Boston: Little, Brown.

Vaillant, G. and MacArthur, C. C. (1972). Natural history of male psychological health, I. The adult life cycle from 18–50. *Seminars in Psychiatry,* 4(4), 415–427.

Weinstein, F. and Platt, G. (1973). *Psychoanalytic sociology.* Baltimore: Johns Hopkins University Press.

Wheelis, A. (1958). *The quest for identity.* New York: Norton.

White, R. W. (1966). *Lives in progress: a study of the natural growth of personality.* New York: Holt.

Wirtz, W. and National Manpower Institute (1975). *The boundless resource: a prospectus for an educational policy.* Washington, D.C.: New Republic.

Wolf, E., Gedo, J., and Terman, D. (1972). On the adolescent process as a transformation of the self. *Journal of Youth / Adolescence,* 1(3), 257–272.

Wolfstein, M. (1966). Goya's dining room. *Psychoanalytic Quarterly,* 35(1), 47–83.

Zetzel, E. (1949). Anxiety and the capacity to bear it. *International Journal of Psychoanalysis,* 30, 1–12.

Index